Implementing change in nursing

Implementing change in nursing

INGEBORG G. MAUKSCH, R.N., Ph.D., F.A.A.N.

Professor of Nursing, School of Nursing,
Vanderbilt University, Nashville, Tennessee

MICHAEL H. MILLER, Ph.D.

Associate Professor of Nursing, School of Nursing,
Vanderbilt University, Nashville, Tennessee

Illustrated

The C. V. Mosby Company

ST. LOUIS • TORONTO • LONDON   1981

Copyright © 1981 by The C. V. Mosby Company

Printed in the United States of America

The C. V. Mosby Company
11830 Westline Industrial Drive, St. Louis, Missouri 63141

Library of Congress Cataloging in Publication Data

Mauksch, Ingeborg G
   Implementing change in nursing.

   Bibliography: p.
   Includes index.
   1. Nursing—Social aspects. 2. Nursing service
administration. 3. Organizational change. I. Miller,
Michael H., 1942-   joint author. II. Title.
[DNLM: 1. Philosophy, Nursing. 2. Social change—
Nursing texts. WY86 M449i]
RT86.5.M38   610.73′06′99   80-16576
ISBN 0-8016-3476-8

GW/M/M 9 8 7 6 5 4 3 2 1   03/A/329

To
Larry and Valerie
who taught me the meaning and joys of change
and to
Cindy, Heidi, and Julie
who make everyday special

PREFACE

As researchers and teachers in nursing, we believe that nurses increasingly wish to control their own destiny. In order to do this, however, much change will need to take place. There will have to be changes in the society and changes in the health care delivery system. Nurses also will need to change personally and professionally. It is imperative to change the organizational structures that contain the settings in which nurses practice.

In this book we deal with change in nursing. How does change occur, particularly planned change? Understanding constitutes a basic prerequisite to participation in the change process. Change requires knowledge, skills, and understanding; it demands appreciation of the worth of others, an ability to relate effectively to individuals and to groups, and, above all, the determination to succeed.

What is the change process like? This question forms the basis of this book. We have attempted to show how values and beliefs shape attitudes toward change and how the change agent prepares and plans to be ready for the implementation of change. The reader's judgment will tell us if we have succeeded in describing and discussing change in nursing.

Ingeborg G. Mauksch
Michael H. Miller

CONTENTS

Chapter 1

INTRODUCTION

We both believed deeply that this book needed to be written. Interestingly enough, we did not exchange these thoughts until recently. One of us, a sociologist, had been studying nursing for a considerable time. Professionalism presents significant issues to the sociologist; the fact that nursing offers some unusual dimensions as contrasted to the usual conceptualization of a profession made the study of nursing both interesting and venturesome. However, the realization that the most significant observations to be made about nursing today are the rather drastic and monumental changes that this occupation has undergone was the real starting point of the book. The other member of the team, a nurse, believes that since change in the society is significant as it relates to nursing, it deserves understanding and investigation. Thus, the collaborative effort was a result of an exchange of ideas that persuaded us that a sociologist and a nurse could take a candid and a profitable look at past and future changes in the nursing profession.

Nursing and sociology have many things in common; most significantly, both are people oriented. As a result, nursing has adopted sociological theories and conceptualizations as frameworks within which to meet the needs of patients and clients. The nurse's approach to patient care also involves sociological methodologies, particularly research methodologies. The sociologist, on the other hand, has found nurses and nursing willing subjects for research; thus a great deal is known about nursing and its body of knowledge that, in turn, has resulted in further attention to this occupation.

The justification for this book is the utilitarian and theoretical values its readers should derive from it. We believe that nurses are constantly faced with change. Change is difficult for everyone. It is certainly difficult for nurses who, adhering to the normative behavior of women in our society, have not been particularly change oriented. The occupation is faced

1

with present-day realities; however, the stress in nursing education and in its practice certainly remains unresolved. Not implementing change for change's sake, but to create change that will improve things is imperative. Many nurses agree that change is necessary because the delivery of health care, specifically nursing care, does indeed need to be improved.

By approaching the topic of change on two levels, it is our hope that the varied needs of nurses will be met. By presenting theories of change and their applicability to implementing change, it is our hope that we will assist nurse researchers and nurse leaders, as well as practicing nurses, to institute change. On the other hand, by offering case studies of attempted change—successful or unsuccessful—we also expect to assist the nurse–change agents of tomorrow in their change-oriented endeavors. It is our hope that we will assist the nurse who has not devoted time and energy to the study or the reading of research related to change but rather has proceeded to implement change on an intuitive basis. This type of nurse includes those who practice in hospitals and a variety of other settings. It certainly is significant that the study of change is included in nursing curricula and that nurses are considered patient advocates in a time when the patient's role is changing: his interests are becoming increasingly more prominent in the health care delivery system. All these factors lead one to expect an attitude favorable to change; thus we believe that a book describing the many aspects of change is both timely and warranted.

CHANGES IN NURSING

Nursing is the occupation in our society that has undergone more change since its official founding than any other occupation.[1] One is at a loss to know where to begin the description of all the changes this occupation has undergone. We chose to reflect on it by means of the perspective of autonomy and accountability. What was nursing like 100 years ago when it first became a profession? The nurse was indeed the physician's assistant. It was her job to assist him "in his important work" (Presidential address, 1907:799). The nurse initiated few interventions on her own. She principally implemented the physician's orders and directions. She was also responsible for providing a comfortable and safe environment for the patient. In the hospital, she was cook, maid, janitor, plumber, flower arranger, window washer, as well as patient care provider; this last designation probably took less than half her time on duty. Today, 100 years later, nursing has developed a modest yet respectable body of knowl-

---

1. The first three professional schools of nursing—Massachusetts General, Bellevue, and New Haven Hospital—opened their doors in 1873.

edge through research. It is in the process of developing a varied, extensive literature. Most significantly, nursing is on the way to becoming an autonomous, accountable occupation. Many nurses are attaining professional status as they perform research or because their interactions with their patients are initiated by them, based on their own observations, and directed by their own competence.

Furthermore, to understand many of the changes in nursing practice, one must look at the technical and scientific changes, which are enormous. These changes range from drugs and surgical interventions to computerized monitoring of vital signs and the use of lasers and cryotherapy. But it is not sufficient to only look at changes in the management of illness. Computerization of health records, electronic relays of information of immediate relevance, and the role of public media in information transmittal are additional components bringing about change in the nature and delivery of health care. Nurses are part of all these changes. They act not only as providers of care in the context of all these innovations, but they also contribute ideas and innovative approaches geared toward survival, coping, and the necessary tempering of the winds of change so that the society may be served better.

As observers of professional practice in our society, we have noted that the changes in nursing, as well as changes in other professions, are brought about because of: (1) societal demands, (2) interprofessional expectations and demands, (3) intraprofessional decisions, and (4) an overall climate of change in our society. The last reason is particularly true in relation to the status and behavior of women, which are bound to have serious and lasting effects on a traditionally female occupation such as nursing. Thus, in understanding the changes that have already taken place and in observing changes that are in the process of taking place, the student of change in nursing is afforded an opportunity to view change from two perspectives: (1) going along with inevitable change imposed or brought about by forces beyond one's control or even the profession as a whole and (2) changes that may be brought about as a planned undertaking.

THE NURSE AS CHANGE AGENT

Traditionally, women, and thus nurses, have been considered followers rather than leaders regarding major changes in the society. Furthermore, efforts for basic changes that women have undertaken, notably the suffrage movement preceding the passage of the 18th amendment, proved to be so difficult, so divisive, and so energy draining that after the accomplishment of the goal, women withdrew again into inactivity.

Today's nurses may find it necessary to make difficult decisions: whether to continue following rather than initiating change and thereby forfeiting any possibilities of being a change agent or to engage in substantial personal change that can result in her effective leadership and implementation of change. More and more nurses seem to follow the latter course. There may be many reasons for this, but we believe that the primary one is that nurses have become increasingly more aware of their responsibilities to the public they serve. In so doing, the need for change to improve services to the public is paramount, and nurses are responding to this need in larger numbers and in an ever-increasing variety of efforts.

To account for the significant willingness of nurses to engage in basic changes, one need only realize that nursing has indeed acquired a set of behaviors that must be considered part of a new role. It represents the greatest single change an occupation can demonstrate. Once the physician's assistant, the nurse has now become "an action nurse" (Mauksch and Rogers, 1975). Nurses are aware of their own potential as a result of becoming initiators of interventions, which are both implemented and evaluated by them. Furthermore, this role has also acquired a sense of accountability, which has long been a coveted component of the nursing profession.

For a considerable time, some nurses have advocated the abandoning of the medical model of health care delivery, that is, the approach through the systems of the human organism. They favor new approaches, such as an approach according to systems or the maintenance of the integrity of basic functions (Levine, 1967). It has been difficult for the nursing profession to pursue this as extensively as desirable because secondary care settings are organized in the former manner. Nevertheless, there are many indications that nurses have made some breakthrough and true change has taken place. Examples of this are the integrated curricula in baccalaureate programs, the development of clinical nurse specialists, and the development of new fields, such as ostomy clinical nurse specialist. Lastly, it must be pointed out that nursing's capacity for change may well be measured in terms of its wide distribution of activity as well as the variety of settings in which nursing takes place. Thus the opportunity for change is compounded geometrically as a result of the stimulation, encouragement, and demand for change. Nursing's response to change is more and more predictable in accordance with needed and/or desired change. In fact, nurses may well be on the way to recognizing that change must be added to the two other traditionally proverbial certainties: death and taxes.

The change agent is an individual who influences how, when, and where alterations in social systems occur. In the case of planned change, the change agent is the modus operandi through which change occurs. Unplanned change, on the other hand, occurs without the aid of an officially designated change agent, that is, authorities, such as the head nurse and hospital director, do not give the role of altering the system to anyone. The system changes through the efforts of one or more change agents who typically work in opposition to the authorities and to the status quo.

A change agent is a person (or a team) in a system (for example, hospital, public health department, hospital ward, family nurse practitioner clinic, school, class, or family) whose role is to assist members of the system in making alterations in themselves or in the system. The change agent may be a professional from outside the system (that is, consultant, therapist, or researcher) or someone within the system who acts in some official capacity as a change agent (that is, director of continuing education, clinical specialist, or head nurse.) The change agent may also be a layperson. In this case, the change agent is usually a person within the system who works, usually part-time, to influence change from within.

There are formal and informal change agents. The formal category includes those persons whose roles dictate that they assist in changing or guiding the social system of which they are a part. For instance, the hospital director of continuing education fits this designation. Registered nurses can be both formal and informal change agents depending on their role. On the system level, head nurses or nurse clinicians are strongly encouraged to act as change agents for the staff and patients on their units. In this capacity, they direct most of the energy at changing the behavior of their staff to maximize patient care. Staff nurses, on the other hand, are expected to direct their efforts as change agents toward their patients. Their role requires that they work to change people's behaviors, attitudes, and values toward health. They also try to educate people about self-care procedures, signs of illness, and the like.

Informally, nurses may be change agents in their interactions with colleagues and with other staff members. They may, for instance, actively work to change people's attitudes about various political and social issues. They may solicit for a voluntary agency (for example, Red Cross, United Way, Salvation Army, Humane Society), and they may attempt to organize the staff for membership in a union. There are almost unlimited ways in which a nurse may informally work as a change agent. Because of role restrictions and status differentials, it is most difficult for a nurse (or almost anyone for that matter) to assume a formal change agent role. The head nurse, for example, might feel seriously threatened if a staff nurse attempted to get other staff nurses to change from team nursing to primary nursing care without her concurrence and leadership. In addition, formal change agent status carries authority; informal change agents can only operate through persuasion. Therefore, the informal change agent may have difficulty getting the nurses on the unit to switch from team to primary care nursing because she cannot convince them of its value. The head nurse needs only to inform her staff of the ensuing change. They will have to try out the new system of care delivery whether they are convinced of its value or not. (They may resign or attempt to change units.) What the staff then does with the new delivery system depends on the head nurse's authority and ability to communicate with her staff. The point is that the informal and formal change agents operate on different premises: persuasion in the formal case and authority in the latter.

The goal of the change agent is to successfully enact some alteration in a social system. To accomplish this, the change agent first must carefully examine and analyze the system of events under study. Then from data gathered, the change agent can develop strategy for intervention and ultimate change. To accomplish this goal, the change agent must develop a perspective on the events or components of the system to determine their true relationship to one another. The change agent must learn how they previously related to one another as well as how they presently relate. This process of examination should provide the change agent with invaluable data for ultimately implementing a change. The following example provides insights regarding the usefulness of this procedure.

Ms. Krantz was recently hired as the new director of a city's department of public health nursing. She was selected because she professed to have many exciting ideas for changing the major thrust of the department. Many of the nurses employed by the department were somewhat apprehensive about Ms. Krantz because they feared a major upheaval in the department as a result of the changes she might make. After Ms. Krantz had been director for 2 months and no changes had been enacted, these nurses were becoming even more concerned. Finally, at a staff meeting, Ms. Krantz was questioned about the changes she was going to make. She told the staff that no major alterations need be expected for at least 6 months. She stated that she honestly did not know how this particular system (public health nursing department) functioned, and until she had sufficient time to ascertain where the department had been, where it presently was, and how nurses in the department related to one another, it would be impossible for her to initiate changes with high prospects for implementation and success.

HOW NURSES CAN PARTICIPATE IN CHANGE

One thing is certain: there is no agreed on standard or a proven set of requirements to be a change agent or a supporter of change. Nurses can assist in change by supporting, participating, or implementing. They can also initiate change. They can engage in joint ventures for planned change, and they can be the evaluators of completed change. The variety of roles within the process of change are multiple. They all are available to today's nurse. It is hoped that they all will be viewed as potential opportunities for tomorrow and that nurses will increasingly participate in change, adopting the change role most suitable at the time.

Education for change occurs on the day we are born. There is no set curriculum that prepares a person for change. What is crucial is attitude, appreciation, and acknowledgment that one can learn about change and engage in it effectively by being deliberately aware and prepared. This book will assist the nurse to do just that. It is written for all nurses, regardless of their clinical specialization, nature of their educational background, or future career plans within nursing. What is required of the reader who is to benefit from this book is a conscious desire to learn about change and an ability to appreciate that change must start with oneself before it can indeed become part of the overall picture for professional action.

WHAT THIS BOOK WILL OFFER

This book is organized into eight chapters. Chapter 2 deals with the nature of change, some theories of change as they are known as of this writing, and the process of change within organizations. Chapters 3 and 4 are devoted to nurses' roles in change: how nurses can become change agents, what implementations of change agentry have been recognized, and how change can be determined in terms of its implications as well as in terms of its planned or unplanned nature. Chapter 5 concentrates on strategies and tactics in the deliberate implementation of change. Examples will be used throughout these chapters to illustrate how change can or cannot be implemented. They will point toward the do's and don't's of change agentry. Chapter 6 is devoted to the overall issue of implementation and includes many examples illustrating positive and negative approaches. It also shows how different methods of implementation result in varied outcomes. Chapter 7 describes ways in which nurses can attempt to make a successful change permanent. Chapter 8 describes a variety of evaluative efforts that are helpful in realistically determining the effects of change.

A sincere effort has been made throughout the book to cover as many bases within nursing as is feasible. If a setting, specialty, or nursing role has been omitted it was not intentional. The purpose of the book is to reach the widest range of nurses and nursing practice. Above all, this book is intended to describe change as the human and inevitable process we perceive it to be.

Chapter 2

WHAT IS CHANGE?

Change is the process by which alterations occur in the function and structure of society. By definition, change impacts on all behavior patterns. The diffusion or spread of an idea, process, or behavior pattern through a population (that is, an exchange of one idea, process, or behavior for another) may occur quickly or take a considerable time. For instance, it has taken approximately 12 years for the profession of nursing to accept, accommodate, and implement the new role of the nurse practitioner as first conceptualized by Silver and Ford (1967). Conversely, it has taken considerably less time for nursing to utilize modern technology.

In this chapter, we will discuss the process of change. Specifically, we will examine the two major categories of social change: planned and unplanned. We then will examine some subsets of these two categories including predictable and unpredictable change and intended and unintended change. The consequences of change will also be discussed. Finally, we will present two of the major theories used to explain social change: conflict and systems theory.

In nursing, change accounts for (1) the dramatic growth of the nurse population (from less than 300 RNs per 100,000 population in 1960 to more than 400 RNs per 100,000 population in 1978), (2) the variation in the role of the nurse today compared with the role of the nurse 100 years ago, or even 10 years ago (from traditional role to new role), and (3) the development of new nurse behavior patterns (strikes, independent practice, obtaining earned doctoral degrees, accountable practice, and the like).

The basic premise of this book is that change is omnipresent. Change is conceptualized as a pervasive process occurring, to a large or a small degree, at all times and in all places even when social conditions and human values appear stagnant, even resistant to change. Change, in other words, is ubiquitous but it does not always occur in obvious, manifest ways. For example, in a nursing unit in which the supervisory staff wants "conditions to remain the same," changes can be observed, nevertheless, in patient care practices, nurse patient interaction, and the like.

Ms. Ramsey, a head nurse for 25 years in a surgical unit, prides herself on her professionalism. Her experiences have shown her that the best nursing is that which has been "tried and trusted." It is reasonably fair to say that Ms. Ramsey's main goal is to run her unit as it has been run since she took over some 25 years ago. Ms. Ramsey is not against change; to the contrary, she maintains a positive orientation as long as the change coincides with her perspective. She is, however, unmistakenly change resistant. By and large, Ms. Ramsey tries to maintain the status quo by controlling the independence (action and decision making) of her staff nurses. She vigorously denounces any nurse who does not consult with her about every aspect of patient care. In spite of this atmosphere, changes do take place on Ms. Ramsey's unit, and they occur with regularity. Ms. Ramsey places the blame for these changes on the constant influx of new RNs who are hired to counteract the high turnover rate of nurses on her unit. (The rate on this surgical unit is not, incidentally, higher than that for the rest of the hospital.) With each incoming group of new nurses, the "way things are done" and "amount of independent action taken by the nurses" change. Regardless of Ms. Ramsey's efforts to "control" her unit, the nurses rely on the skills and techniques they were taught in nursing school. When confronted by their "deviation," most nurses either profess innocence, say they had no other choice because of Ms. Ramsey's absence, or imply that their methods are more up-to-date than those promoted by Ms. Ramsey. But they introduce change, and Ms. Ramsey has to cope with it.

People's attitudes and behavior may change before change occurs in the larger social system (for example, hospitals, churches, government). For instance, in 1968, the American Nurses' Association (ANA) relaxed its no-strike policy of 18 years. However, beginning in 1965 and extending into the early 1970s, nurses actively engaged in work stoppage actions. From 1965 through 1968, nurses engaged in these actions without the formal approval of the ANA. Thus there was a substantial lag between the time nurses first initiated work stoppage action on a large scale and the ANA-approved nurse work stoppage action as a legitimate mechanism by which nurses could gain their professional ends. Furthermore, it was not until nurses clearly indicated their intention to "fight" for higher wages that their wages actually began to catch up with the rest of the American economy (Miller, 1977).

No longer is it a debate of whether or not change will occur. Instead, attention is directed at diagnosing the speed, direction, and impact of change and how it might be controlled. People generally accept the idea that change will occur regardless of their own vested interests. Everyone agrees that change is inevitable. Now, people concentrate on making change work to their advantage or they establish warning systems to herald change so that they will not be surprised by its occurrence. Some change is not labeled as such. Continuing education, for instance, is a form of social change even if people do not acknowledge it. Yet, if effective, continued education is accepted as an addition to an individual's or an organization's life.

THEORIES FOR IMPLEMENTING CHANGE

Of the numerous theories of social change, some are more effective in accounting for change in organizations and others for explaining change in individuals. We will first discuss some of the theories that are useful in understanding and implementing change in organizations; then we will examine various theories associated with change in individuals.

Organizational change theories

Conflict theory. Most frequently, people are not aware of social changes as they occur, let alone after they have occurred. However, occasionally changes occur without people being cognizant of them until they have actually transpired. How frequently do people complain about the enactment of laws with which they are unfamiliar? Surely, not everyone was aware of the abortion legislation while it was being prepared. Likewise, how many nurses were unaware of the Professional Standards Review Organization (PSRO) legislation before it became law? Is it entirely unusual for nurses to find that changes have occurred in their work settings without their knowledge of the pending alterations? According to Olsen (1978), this is not the norm. He contends that "most social changes are preceded by conflicting forces seeking to prevent change." Obviously, conflict is not a necessary and sufficient condition for change, but there is considerable evidence that conflict promotes change. Olsen's point is that most change occurring in a hospital, public health center, school of nursing, or other organization is usually the result of conflict within the organization; it follows logically that these changes are resisted by opposing forces within the organization. Forces outside an organization can also be the source of conflict that results in changes being initiated within the organization. In other words, a group within an organization comes into conflict with another group or the entire organization. The conflict may occur over such issues as working conditions, salaries, quality of care, hiring practices, and so forth. The group in conflict attempts to alter or change the situation so that the conflict (defined, perhaps, as frustration, insecurity, or the like) will be reduced or eliminated.

In essence, when nurses go on strike, they are attempting to eliminate a conflicting situation in their work environment. Whatever the basis of the strike or work stoppage action, the efforts of the nurses necessarily engender conflict and strife with the administration of the hospital, nursing home, or public health agency. Administration typically tries to prevent the nurses (or other group) from initiating the change because of great concern with control, fiscal responsibility, profits, budgetary restraints, and the like. Not infrequently, one group in an organization will oppose the change initiated by another group because of vested interests in the status quo. Thus the efforts to change things by the group that is dissatisfied with the way things are (the status quo) may result in replacing the controlling group (that is, revolution) or in still another group replacing the group that is displaced (for example, change of administration).

As previously mentioned, conflict does not always result in social change. Change is only one of several possible outcomes of conflict. For example, conflict between the nurses in one unit in a hospital and their supervisor or the hospital administrator may result in firing of nurses (perhaps for insubordination), in a compromise between the nurses and the administration that effectively maintains the status quo rather than altering the situation, or in some temporary change that is allowed to lapse back into the original status quo before the conflict arose. The point is that conflict effects social change only when there is "some kind of relatively permanent and extensive alteration in the organization as a result of this conflict" (Olsen, 1978:330).

There are several reasons why a proposed or attempted change in an organization's structure or composition may engender conflict. First, all organizations have people who have a vested interest in the status quo. Physicians, for instance, are opposed to most changes in health care delivery regulations that would allow for less skilled workers to provide services heretofore provided exclusively by them. Thus, physicians have a personal (or vested) interest in conditions remaining the same to protect themselves from loss of income, prestige, power, and/or status.

Second, just because one group is dissatisfied with a condition or several conditions in an organization does not necessarily mean that the changes they might propose will be in the best interests of the entire organization. In fact, their proposed changes may have profound discrepancies and weaknesses that could, in extremes, result in the demise of the organization itself. The wage demands of hospital workers may be so great that if hospital administration capitulates, the hospital may go bankrupt.

Third, differences in values and attitudes between groups within organizations are also the basis for conflict over potential and actual change. For example, some nurses prefer team nursing while others believe primary care nursing results in the patient receiving optimal nursing care. Nurses who adhere to the primary care nursing model, but are employed in a facility using a team nursing approach, may come into conflict with nurses who prefer team nursing when they attempt to alter the way nursing is delivered.

Fourth, a group that wants to change some aspect of its organization may generate conflict from other members of the organization who are so settled in their ways that they do not want anything altered. The issue in this case is not specifically vested interests but inertia. People recognize that there may be better and more efficient ways of doing things, but they also recognize that any change will force them to alter behavior, use different forms, increase their accountability, and the like. In other words, any organizational change is viewed as destructive rather than as beneficial.

In summary, the conflict theory of social change contends that at the basis of most organizational change is some form of conflict (that is, alienation, dissatisfaction, frustration) experienced by members of the organization. These members, in an effort to resolve or eliminate this conflict, work to change circumstances within the organization. However, their efforts to change behavior, conditions, or circumstances usually put them into conflict with other groups who do not experience similar conflicts. Furthermore, these other groups may have reasons to resist the proposed change.

Systems theory. This theory has recently received considerable attention in the social sciences as a means for exploring social change. It contends that "society is a series of interdependent units or systems whose very existence depends on the nature of various societal relationships" (Thompson, Miller, and Bigler, 1975:6). The usefulness of this theory lies in its ability to show that "in society and in all subsystems therein, everything is related in some way to everything else" (Thompson, Miller, and Bigler, 1975:7).

Each social system is part of a larger social system (or suprasystem); in turn, social systems can have components or smaller systems within them that are referred to as subsystems. For instance, health care is a system. A hospital within the health care "system" is also a system—a sub-

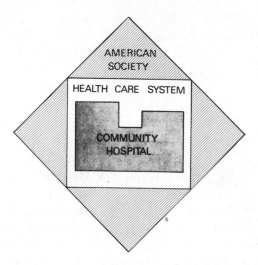

Fig. 1. The health care system is a subsystem of American society. The hospital is a subsystem of the health care system. (From Thompson, L. F., Miller, M. H., and Bigler, H. F.: Sociology: nurses and their patients in modern society, ed. 9, St. Louis, 1975, The C. V. Mosby Co.)

system of the health care system. American society represents, at the same time, a suprasystem of both the health care system and the hospital (Fig. 1).

All systems, large and small, are more or less similar. They are orderly arrangements of components that are interrelated, interdependent, and semiautonomous. For instance, health philosophy functions as a controlling doctrine in binding together doctors, registered nurses, licensed practical nurses, laboratory technicians, medical social workers, pharmacists, patients, visitors, ward arrangements, and the like (Fig. 2).

Systems theory, unlike some other theories of human behavior, allows the student to obtain a comprehensive understanding of the interdependence of all the components of society. In other words, systems have a kind of reciprocal interrelationship of their components or parts: a change or alteration in one part of the system will result in a change or alteration in some other part of the system.

As we indicated, health care can be conceptualized as a system. It is well known that a patient's hospital experience is directly and indirectly influenced by many divergent factors. For instance, the educational system greatly determines the extent of a patient's health care information and his level of trust and satisfaction in his providers. The economic sys-

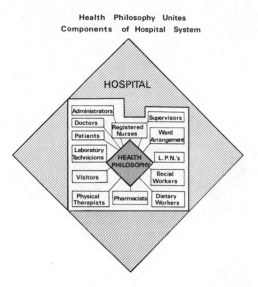

Fig. 2. Doctors, staff nurses, supervisors, licensed practical nurses, laboratory technicians, medical social workers, pharmacists, orderlies, patients, visitors, ward arrangements, and the like are interrelated as a function of health philosophy. (From Thompson, L. F., Miller, M. H., and Bigler, H. F.: Sociology: nurses and their patients in modern society, ed. 9, St. Louis, 1975, The C. V. Mosby Co.)

tem establishes the services the patient will receive and how much his hospitalization will cost (Thompson, Miller, and Bigler, 1975:8). Obviously, technology, the political system, and the community also have a great effect on the patient. The point, however, is that unless nurses, for example, realize the interdependence of these relationships, they will have difficulty providing optimal health care (Fig. 3).

Systems theory explains social change through its conceptualization of equilibrium. According to Homans (1950:303-304), "the state of the elements that enter the system and of the mutual relationships between them is such that any change in one of the elements will be followed by changes in the other elements tending to reduce the amount of that change." Systems, whether defined as society, health care delivery system, hospital, school of nursing, group of friends, or family, are seen as either in or seeking to attain equilibrium between their various components. According to Parsons (1964:84), a system seeks stability (or relative stability) in equilibrium "when the relation between its structure and the processes which go on within it and between its environment are such as to maintain those properties and relations." Furthermore, there are other processes and forces that work to produce system change.

The hospital is an example of a very highly integrated system in which

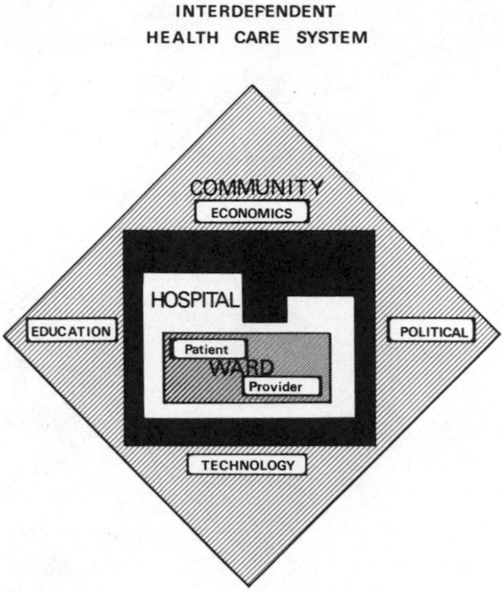

INTERDEFENDENT
HEALTH CARE SYSTEM

Fig. 3. The health care system is influenced by a variety of factors. (From Thompson, L. F., Miller, M. H., and Bigler, H. F.: Sociology: nurses and their patients in modern society, ed. 9, St. Louis, 1975, The C. V. Mosby Co.)

a wide variety of materials and people are gathered together to help people attain their optimal level of health. But should anything happen to any component, employee (for example, nurses, physicians, dieticians, pharmacists, and the like), or equipment (for example, x-ray machinery, surgical theatres, and kitchen and laundry equipment), the entire hospital will be affected. Sunny Hospital, a voluntary, nonprofit hospital, is 55 years old. It has adequately served its community and has had 94% occupancy. Recently, two other hospitals in the community completed new physical plants that included the most modern equipment sought by physicians. Many of the physicians who had routinely admitted their patients to Sunny Hospital decided to send their patients to the new hospitals because they offered better facilities. Sunny Hospital found itself in a situation in which it had to make changes to accomodate this situation. Sunny Hospital had several options:

1. To initiate a campaign to increase its capitalization to either purchase more equipment and renovate the hospital or build a replacement facility
2. To lay off staff and/or reduce staff wages to meet the decreased patient census
3. To make concessions to the "protesting" physicians so that they might resume utilizing the hospital's facilities
4. To close

The ambiguity of this situation, whether Sunny Hospital would remain open or have to close, had a dramatic impact on the hospital's employees both at work and outside their jobs. It became obvious to supervisors that the performance and function of the workers declined sharply, especially as far as efficiency was concerned. Workers became tardy, including those who had never been late before. There were increased reports of family disagreements and disputes. Employees became increasingly tense and in some cases were judged as distraught, particularly the older employees in the unskilled and semiskilled occupations. The situation at Sunny Hospital remained unstable until the decision was announced that the hospital would undergo an extensive renovation program including the purchase of new equipment. Thus once the system was stabilized, the subsystems, too, returned to normalcy.

Changes in the suprasystem of which a hospital is a component are crucial because forces far removed from the hospital can influence it in various ways, including its financial viability. Congress' decision to pass Medicaid, Medicare, and PSRO legislation, and more recently, Health Review Agency (HRA) legislation has profoundly influenced operating procedures in many hospitals. No longer can a hospital decide unilaterally to purchase a computed axial tomography (CAT) scanner. Hospitals must now apply to their regional HRA for assessment of "need." This same policy applies to hospitals that want to expand or renovate their facilities. Before Sunny Hospital could undertake its major renovation, the HRA had to give its approval. Approval of need is separate from Sunny Hospital's ability to *pay* for the program. The critical criterion is whether the community needed an improved Sunny Hospital. It should be noted that there are appeal mechanisms for a hospital or other health institution denied HRA approval.

This example illustrates how a change in one part of a system (physicians' use of a hospital) forced changes in other sectors of the same system (the hospital's survival, employee morale, efficiency, and effectiveness) and even influenced other systems with which it came into contact (families of employees). It also shows how the system attempted to re-establish equilibrium by making adjustments in its composition-configuration. Finally, this illustration noted how a suprasystem (government) influenced the subsystem. Systems theory, unlike conflict theory, does not conceptualize some type of conflict as necessarily the initial cause of the social change.

Individual change theories

Attitudinal change. On the individual level, change can take place in people's attitudes and behavior. Clearly, there is a close relationship between the two. Nurse supervisors attempt to alter their staffs' efficiency; nurses tell their patients about the benefits of following a particular health regimen. In other words, if people change their attitudes it is likely that they will alter their behavior. The link between attitude change and behavior change is not perfect, however; accordingly, it cannot be expected that a change in attitudes *will* always result in a change in behavior. For instance, changing a person's attitudes toward health does not mean that he will stop smoking, use less salt, or give up alcohol. The point is "while attitudes predispose behavior, their expression also relates to the individual's social situation. The mere fact that you like something does not mean you will act on that attitude in every circumstance. Much depends on what is appropriate or approved in a particular instance" (Hollander, 1976: 171).

Inversely, people's behavior is not necessarily consistent with their attitudes. People may observe the 55-mile-per-hour speed limit without liking it. Likewise, while nurses may help patients with bed pans, it should not be concluded that they like the task or that they have changed their previously negative attitude toward doing it.

Several factors have been related to people changing their attitudes and, in turn, their behavior patterns. Included are new information and a change in a person's social situation. New information is capable of modifying cognitive structure, for example, attitude change, if it clearly conflicts with other information. The likelihood of an individual undergoing an attitude change increases with the magnitude of dissonance, that is, lack of harmony or agreement, between the new and the old information (Hollander, 1976:171).

Social situations are important to attitudinal change because they are either conducive or antagonistic to their occurrence. For instance, according to Miller (1977), the higher the proportion of "inbred" faculty in a school of nursing, the greater the possibility that new ideas will be squelched by people's dependence on the tried and trusted. Conversely, other social situations encourage innovation as a necessity (that is, disaster relief, work as an emergency room nurse, and the like).

Not all new information has the potential to change attitudes; only new information that is both obvious to the individual and in conflict with pre-existing knowledge has this potential. Nurses may change their attitudes about abortions on demand when they discuss the relevant issues with someone who provides them with a new insight and perspective. If nurses advocate abortion on demand, for instance, a member of a right-to-life organization would need to provide sufficiently persuasive new information to influence them to reassess their position. The basis of this change is "perceived inconsistency among significant attitudes" (Hollander, 1976:171), which is very likely to produce both instability and change.

Various theories have been proposed that account for attitude change. Herder's *balance theory* (1958) shows similarities to systems theory as it indicates that "there is always movement toward a balanced state" because imbalance produces stress and tension (Hollander, 1976:171). As a result, there is pressure for resolution of attitudinal differences. In practical terms, this means that a nurse, who is apprehensive about the advantages of collective bargaining, discovers that another nurse believes that collective bargaining is beneficial to nursing; they are likely to resolve this dissonance to share similar attitudes.

The *theory of congruity* by Osgood and Tannenbaum (1955), which advances the analytical thrust of Herder's theory, explains how people resolve attitude dissonance. They use a degree of "balance" as a measure of the importance a person places on an attitude. Thus, an individual ranks his attitudes from high to low against the attitudes of other individuals whom he also ranks. From this perspective, then, nurses who place a high value on abortion on demand will alter their attitude if other nurses whom they highly respect disapprove of abortion. If the nurses only slightly or moderately respect these other nurses, their attitude toward abortion probably will change slightly, if at all. They may only feel some ambivalence toward their own attitude.

Social situation perspective. The social situation perspective asserts that people "may react differently to different situations, as a function of how they perceive them" (Hollander and Hunt, 1976:379). However, situations have a certain uniformity and order that impose constraints on the individual regardless of his particular disposition. In this orientation then, one finds that social situations may act to cause certain attitudinal and behavioral changes. Conformity to group is one of these changes, because in social situations conformity is but an outgrowth of a group process. Although group process frequently acts to stifle individuality, expression of individual, independent views can evolve if, as Hollander and Hunt (1976) point out, the impediments to free expression are reduced. In any event, this is not easily accomplished because groups have a tendency to influence their members to live up to specified social expectations. Two points are relevant here: (1) for society to manage, there must be a certain degree of conformity, and (2) it presently is possible for an individual to be independent in American society. According to Hollander (1976:59), independence is defined as "choosing when to conform and when to nonconform. Conformity need not undercut individuality." He believes there is a place for both conformity and independence, "What matters most is that the individual have a free choice" (1976:459).

The social situation perspective is relevant to nursing in several ways.

For example, there is evidence that the nursing social situation is of such a nature that it tends to reward conformity while penalizing independence. It is only recently that nurses in primary care roles have had an opportunity to find practice settings where independence is valued. The well-known doctor-nurse game also illustrates how the hospital, as an established social system, compelled nurses to follow certain prescribed role behaviors even if they did not like the role (Stein, 1968).

Solidifying attitudes. Individuals are open to changing their attitudes prior to making a choice between alternatives. But once they have chosen, their attitudes become firm in their minds and they will defend them vigorously. Hollander (1976:181) refers to this effect as *postdecisional dissonance reduction.* In other words, individuals must eliminate conflict concerning the validity of their choice. Therefore, they defend their decision because it is cognitively inconsistent to believe that they could have made an incorrect decision. Nurses and other health care providers frequently engage in postdecisional dissonance reduction. For instance, the nurse who must decide whether to call a patient's physician is in this category. Prior to making a decision, the nurse carefully weighs all the data: patient's vital signs, physician's notes, supervisor's judgment, physician's attitude toward being called, and so forth. However, after making the decision to call the physician, the nurse will vigorously defend the decision against possible rebuke by the physician. In fact, the nurse is very likely to justify the decision on the grounds that there was no other alternative.

PLANNED AND UNPLANNED CHANGE

Planned change refers to changes that are proposed to improve living, working, or recreational conditions. According to Bennis, Benne, and Chin (1976), all people do not necessarily want the stated benefits of planned change. Many have difficulty foreseeing the outcome of the proposed change. For example, a hospital's administration decided to change its policy from admitting patients to specialty areas such as urology or surgery to admitting them to any open bed in the hospital regardless of their illness classification, that is, surgical, urology, medical, and so forth, to conserve economic resources. The nursing staff was apprised of the planned change and informed that this change would increase occupancy bed rates and that nursing service personnel would receive higher wages and better fringe benefits. The nursing staff was also told that patients would be moved to their respective clinical area when a bed became vacant. Thus a surgical patient might be admitted to a medical unit, but as soon as a surgical bed was available, the patient would be moved. The nursing staff did not approve of this change. It saw this planned change in policy as another administrative ploy to (1) increase nurse work loads and (2) reduce the quality of nursing care.

In this example, we have the classical struggle between the planners who perceive a change to be an improvement and the implementors of the planned change who view it as pernicious.[1] Any planned change raises the philosophical question: Progress for whom? In this case, the organization and the employees were at odds over the benefits of the planned change. If the hospital administration could have convinced the nursing staff that the change would be beneficial, the staff would have favored the change. If employees do not cooperate in implementing the change, it may fail—not only because it is inappropriate or ineffective, but because the employees subvert it. For example, when open admission was introduced in the example just cited, the morale of the nursing staff dropped as did the efficiency of the nursing care. Since nurses were required to care for patients with a variety of illnesses, they showed reluctance to familiarize themselves with the types of care required by patients with different clinical characteristics. The situation deteriorated until the hospital administration guaranteed the nursing staff that more nurses would be hired to ensure the present agreed on nurse/bed ratio. The nursing staff believed this commitment by the hospital ensured that optimal care could be provided, and accordingly, it supported the new open admissions policy.

The change agent is especially valuable in effecting planned change. Bennis, Benne, and Chin (1967:12) contend that "the outcome of any planned change-attempt hinges . . . to a great extent on the relationship" between the change agent and the recipient of the change. The change recipients must trust the change agent. Without trust, the recipients will not believe what the change agent says about the kind and extent of the importance of the proposed change. Clear communication between the change agent and the recipients will enhance trust and thereby facilitate change implementation.

It is also extremely important for the change agent to understand the problems of the change recipients, especially in regard to the forces opposing the planned change in their lives. In one situation, these were evident when a hospital's administration wanted to alter its working hours for nurses. It was decided to move from the traditional 8-hour, 5-day workweek to a 12-hour, 7-day workweek, followed by a week off duty. Initially, the nurses adamantly opposed this change because they contended

---

1. Bennis, Benne, and Chin (1966) note that conflict based on discrepant and dissimilar perspectives is not uncommon when planned changes are involved.

that it would disrupt their families. Who, they asked, would take care of their children after school? The staff assigned to implement this change, in collaboration with staff nurses, created new policies and facilities designed to allow for an efficient transition to the new 84-hour workweek. A free nursery was established at the hospital for children of the staff. School-age children were encouraged to come to the center after school. The result of the change was general acceptance. Very few of the nurses resigned.

Unplanned change refers to change that occurs even though it was not wanted. Since the unplanned change was not desired by authorities (for example, head nurse, director of nursing, and the like) and therefore, not anticipated or planned for, its outcomes are unpredictable, unintended, and nondeliberate. Unplanned change need not, however, be negative. Sometimes through change (in the behavioral sciences, we refer to this as *serendipity*) an unplanned change may actually result in a situation that is better than that which it replaced. Affected staff (and other groups too) do not know in advance about unplanned change. Sometimes people find out about an unplanned change while it is occurring or even after it has been completed.

For example, an inner-city hospital decided to expand its operation by building a satellite hospital in a distant suburb. The hospital's board of directors theorized that this change was necessary to provide care to the city's expanding population. The satellite hospital was completed in 1978. Unfortunately, the gasoline shortage of 1979 radically affected the nursing staff who worked at the satellite hospital. Since the suburb in which the hospital was located had, like other suburbs in the area, a woefully inadequate mass transit system, most of the nurses employed in the hospital drove to work. With the shortage of gas, many of them believed that the hospital should either transfer them back to the inner-city hospital, which was nearer their homes, or compensate them for the increased cost of commuting. The hospital, which prided itself on careful planning, did not anticipate the drastic increase in the cost of gasoline. Not only were the staff members adversely affected, but so too were patients who had to drive to the facility. The hospital wanted to compensate its staff but patient utilization, especially in the clinics, was declining and therefore the hospital's income was down. Since the hospital could not provide the staff with financial compensation for travel to work, which was suddenly a major expense, many of the nurses resigned and found positions in hospitals closer to their homes. As a result of the loss of many staff members and a decline in patient utilization, the hospital's board decided to close the hospital except the emergency room and one medical unit.

This example shows how an unplanned change, that is, a scarcity and increase in the cost of gasoline, can force consequences on an organization and its employees that are unexpected, unintended, and negative.

PROCESS OF CHANGE
Direction of change

Few people value change for the sake of change itself. The ultimate value of change depends on the degree to which it fulfills its purpose.

Change occurs within systems as well as between systems. In both situations, the course or movement of change will vary according to the circumstances. Change within systems may be either vertical or horizontal; it may be initiated at the top, bottom, or middle of the hierarchy; and it may move up or down the hierarchy or within a single grouping. Change may originate with a hospital's housekeeping staff or with another group in the hospital such as physicians, nurses, or technicians. An example of horizontal change is a family unit attempting to get one of its members to alter his behavior or nursing services attempting to replace team nursing with primary care nursing.

Change between systems also has a point of origin and a goal. In this situation, one system attempts to impose changes on another, for example, the government on the health care system, one department on another. The second system may either acquiesce or resist the change. Whether change occurs within or between systems, there is a definite bidirectional flow that can be anticipated and measured.

The direction, course, or movement of change is determined by the origin or sources of the change, the goal(s) of the change, and the means employed for implementing it. For example, nurses at Westward Hospital, who, like other nurses are in the middle of the hospital's status hierarchy, conducted a successful strike. As a result of the nurses' success, the advocated policies, benefits, and procedures (for example, increased wages, improved working conditions, better shift rotations, increased benefits, and replacement of LPNs and nurse's aides with RNs) were implemented. The strike also resulted in major changes among the hospital administration as well as among lower level employees. Westward's administration, first of all, had to recognize nurses as a new power source in the hospital. Second, costs had to be controlled elsewhere in the hospital to generate funds necessary to meet the financial package won by the nurses. Third, hospital administration had to work intensively with the LPNs and the nurse's aides to work out alternative employment possibilities.

As a result of the success of the strike by the registered nurses at Westward Hospital, other hospital employees decided to change their strategy for gaining increased wages, security, insurance, and other benefits and threatened to strike unless their demands were also met by the administration. Furthermore, employees who had been thinking about taking LPN training began to reconsider their decision since the future of that occupation appeared bleak. Following the lead of Westward Hospital nurses, nurses in other hospitals began to use work stoppage action as a means for achieving better conditions of practice.

The above illustration shows how a change initiated by a single group within a large social system can generate major repercussions throughout the components of the system and in adjacent systems. It also illustrates that change moves in a specific direction as determined by the source of change, its goals, and the manner in which it is implemented.

Levels of social change

Change can be conceptualized as occurring on two levels: macroscopic and microscopic. In the former case, it affects the entire social system (or a very large part thereof). In the latter case, change has only a minor effect on the system (Fig. 4). It may, however, affect various components of the system in a dramatic way. Medicaid and Medicare are examples of macroscopic social changes introduced into a social system. Designed to facilitate greater access to health care for the indigent (Medicaid) and the aged (Medicare), these health care payment plans have had a major effect on the health care delivery system in the United States as well as on other aspects of the larger society. The political and economic impact of these programs has been major. The cost of health care increased dramatically after the introduction of these programs; the government, in an effort to control the inflationary spiral of medical costs, became more active in cost control of the health care system. It altered Medicare and Medicaid to reduce the number of eligible persons and to eliminate provider and patient abuse; new regulatory programs (Regional Med-

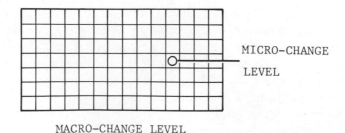

MACRO−CHANGE LEVEL

Fig. 4. Macro- and Microscopic change levels.

ical Program [RMP] and Health Systems Agency [HSA]) and new delivery models (Health Maintenance Organization [HMO] and national health insurance) were also introduced by the government to contain costs while increasing accessibility to care.

National health insurance promises macrolevel changes in the health care system. Changes can be anticipated in areas such as: (1) role of government, (2) role and status of health care providers, (3) location of health care resources—regionalization, (4) taxation, (5) medical, dental, nursing, and other health education enrollment, and (6) relationship between providers and patients—access to care.

The following changes affect the health care system on the microlevel: (1) introduction of the role of the nurse practitioner, (2) government provision of capitation funds to schools of nursing during the 1970s, and (3) New York State's decision to require future RNs to have baccalaureate degrees if they wish to practice nursing as professional nurses. The following example illustrates the "minor" impact of microlevel change. This example should be familiar to many nurses.

Jeanie Durham and Peggy Landers are RNs who graduated from diploma nursing programs. They have been employed at City Hospital for 3 years. The state nurses' association in conjunction with City Hospital offered an assertiveness training course at the hospital that the two nurses were encouraged to take. The assistant director of nursing told them that it would be excellent training for their future roles as head nurse or supervisor. The two nurses thoroughly enjoyed the course and found it extremely beneficial. Almost immediately, they began to be more assertive in their relationships with supervisors, fellow nurses, physicians, and other co-workers. Their observed change in attitude and behavior created serious strife on their unit. One major difficulty arose because Peggy refused to play the "doctor-nurse game." She believed that it was totally inappropriate for her to condone a physician's mistakes with levity, especially when he did not reciprocate. Both nurses frequently confronted administration because of its ambiguity or indecisiveness. Some of the nurses' assertiveness began to rub off on other RNs who in turn refused to continue the traditional passive role. Within 3 months after Jeanie and Peggy had completed their course, the hospital made a concerted effort to fire them. Obviously, the changes introduced into this unit by Jeanie and Peggy were not significant enough to affect the entire hospital. Possibly, macrolevel changes might occur at City Hospital if these two nurses were permitted to continue to influence others. But they were not. Also, needless to say, the assertiveness training course was discontinued at City Hospital.

The above example illustrates an important aspect of change. It shows that while change is ubiquitous, people do not always anticipate the consequences from the introduction of a change. Manifest (or obvious) and latent (or unexpected) change consequences will be discussed in depth in a later chapter.

CONSEQUENCES OF CHANGE

In planning for any social change, attention must be given to ascertaining the consequences of change. Too frequently, people involved in initiating or in implementing change do not consider the possibility of unexpected or unintended consequences of their planning. In other words, they do not ask, "What can go wrong?" From the example of assertiveness training, it is clear that the administration did not envision that the RNs newly acquired assertiveness would be "detrimental" to the functioning of their hospital. They did not even conceive that there would be any so-called "side-effects." Planners, too, frequently fail to foresee "what might go wrong." They focus on the success of the change; it is incongruous for change agents and social planners to be anything but optimistic about the results of the change. After all, change agents must be positive toward their own efforts to improve conditions. Why else introduce the change? Sometimes they allow their enthusiasm for their projects to supersede thorough assessment.

Conversely, change agents are not always at fault when their planning goes awry. Even "experts" using sophisticated simulation computer models to evaluate the impact of contemplated changes are not free from an occasional unintended (and unwanted) outcome. Who predicted the high inflationary spiral caused by Medicare and Medicaid? Who can accurately predict the impact of the new nursing role on the nursing profession, the health care delivery system, or the quality of health care given in this country? Although one cannot expect to have all these answers, it does not mean that one should not attempt change, or that one should not predict the outcomes of it. Nurses also need to try harder to develop better methods for predicting the impact of social change on them. This generates a need to devise contingency plans to meet some of the *most* unwanted outcomes of change. If organized nursing does not do this, it will continue to find itself excluded from participation in national health insurance planning to the same extent that it has been denied active participation in PSROs (Miller, 1975) and many other occurrences that affect them profoundly.

The outcomes of change fall into two categories depending on whether the outcome is predictable or unpredictable, intended or unintended, deliberate or nondeliberate, or anticipated or unanticipated as shown in the following:

Planned change	*Unplanned change*
Predictable	Unpredictable
Intended	Unintended
Deliberate	Nondeliberate
Anticipated	Unanticipated

Planned change is an attempt to increase the predictable, intended, deliberate, and/or anticipated; with unplanned change, on the other hand, opportunity for unpredictable, unintended, nondeliberate, and unanticipated change is increased.

Predictable and unpredictable consequences

The consequences of change have been categorized as both predictable and unpredictable. This means that the consequences of some change can be foreseen, while they cannot be anticipated for other change. Obviously, the more predictable change is, the more readily people can cope with its effects. According to Toffler (1970), there will be more instances of change that will not be predictable. He develops the thesis that people may be co-opted by industrialization to the extent that their ability to make decisions concerning their very existence will be markedly curtailed. Toffler does not perceive this condition as being inevitable; he believes people can and should forestall the time when they will not be prepared to adapt to a very dynamic, constantly changing environment.

Unpredictable change is generally viewed with apprehension. It is disconcerting and disquieting for people to be unable to anticipate the consequence of change. Environmental conditions (for example, drought, tornadoes, floods), death, or sudden illness are examples of unpredictable change. Doubtless no one could have predicted that during the period when Drs. Henry Silver and Loretta Ford trained the first pediatric nurse practitioners that their prototype would become what we now know as the nurse practitioner movement, which in turn would virtually change the profession of nursing. Wise organizations and people, however, try their best to cope with the unpredictability of change by imagining as many different consequences as possible and by developing contingency plans for these possible consequences of change. For example, in response to a strike threat by employees, a hospital may develop several plans of action: (1) no new patients will be admitted, (2) vacation and leave time of administrative staff will be eliminated, and (3) a public arbitrator, acceptable to both employees and administration, will be sought. Individuals also develop contingency plans, even though they do not always realize that they are doing it. For example, graduating registered nurses may wish to work for local county health departments, but since they cannot predict whether or not they will be hired by one, they also interview at hospitals in the same locale. They may also consider attending graduate school if they can't get a job.

Individuals have considerably more difficulty than organizations in developing contingency plans for a changing situation in which they cannot fully anticipate the short- or long-term consequences. The development of contingency plans—actions that can deal with all or most consequences of social change—requires great creativity. The change agent must not only be imaginative enough to anticipate all or most of the possible outcomes of a change, but must also be able to enact the appropriate plan to cope with the change. For example, registered nurses who graduate from nursing school with the intention of obtaining a job with the local health department may plan other alternative actions if they do not obtain the positions they want. However, whether or not they can plan to go to graduate school as an alternative depends on (1) having sufficient resources (or access to sufficient resources) to finance schooling and (2) meeting entrance requirements. Large organizations, on the other hand, generally set aside resources for unanticipated or unintended consequences of change. A major resource in this effort is the high-speed computer that can devise plans for dealing with many unexpected outcomes.

Intended and unintended consequences

The health care system has long struggled with both intended and unintended consequences of change. While behavioral scientists deal with social change, health care administrators and providers are concerned with a wide variety of change. This change may be externally suggested or enforced, or it may arise from needs determined within the system. Analysis of these changes, regardless of their causality, yields a wide range of consequences. For example, pathology and disease are major causes of abnormal physiological changes in people. Drug therapy is a means for correcting tissue and body alterations. But drug-initiated therapy is not without varying consequences. In fact, drug therapy usually results in several dimensions of "change" outcomes.

The American Hospital Formulary provided information regarding the intended outcomes (expected results) and unintended outcomes (side-effects) of all drugs dispensed in the United States. Unintended side-effects can be divided into expected and unexpected side-effects since some side-effects are anticipated and others are not. Research has shown that a given drug may produce certain unintended side-effects even when administered under ideal conditions. Infrequently, but occurring nevertheless, the same drug may produce unintended and unexpected side-effects that are totally unpredictable.

Drug researchers have been successful in developing compounds that will achieve specific, desired results. However, their efforts also produce compounds that can cause one or more unintended and generally unwanted effects. For instance, thalidomide was successfully developed as a sedative and hypnotic. Unfortunately, the drug also caused severe birth defects when taken by pregnant women. Although the intended effects of the drug are desirable, the side-effects are so catastrophic that the Federal Drug Administration does not permit it to be sold in the United States. Clearly, the intended consequences of drugs, like social changes, may be outweighed by the unintended negative side-effects.

Another example may further help to explain the above point. According to the American Hospital Formulary, buclizine (Bucladin) is an effective drug in combatting vertigo, car sickness, and related conditions. However, patients using this drug may experience a variety of side-effects ranging from dryness of the mouth to fatigue. Given the possible side-effects of this drug, it may be inappropriate to prescribe it for persons whose life-styles could be seriously, even dangerously affected, such as singers, pilots, and truck drivers.

It should be understood that the so-called side-effects of a social change may in time dissipate like the side-effects of some drugs. For people taking buclizine (Bucladin), for example, it is not uncommon for the "side-effects" of fatigue and dryness of the mouth to disappear after several weeks of taking the drug. Likewise, new policies at a hospital may meet with disapproval resulting in some nurses' resignations. After some period of adjustment, the nurse turnover may decline as the job expectations of nurses become consistent with the new policies.

In the previous example of how assertiveness training for the two RNs affected the interpersonal relations in City Hospital, it was pointed out that administration planners do not always anticipate all consequences of a planned change. This example also showed that although the hospital administration intended to upgrade the decision making and responsibilities of RNs, the actual outcome of the new training did not materialize to the hospital's satisfaction, at least not sufficiently to overcome what the hospital perceived as detrimental consequences. Thus, change was perceived by the hospital administration as more negative than positive. The assertiveness training was discontinued before its actual, long-term consequences could be realized. This example also points out that change that is viewed as desirable by some is viewed exactly the opposite by others in the same setting.

Deliberate and nondeliberate consequences

Change can be divided into two major categories, based on who sets the goals for the change (Bennis, 1966). In the first category, goals are mutually set by all groups interested in the change. For example, the hospital management and nursing staff, after discussing the situation at their institution, jointly decide on the changes necessary to maintain the quality of care while still controlling costs. The second category includes goals designed to impose a change by one individual or group on another group without determining its concurrence with the change. For instance, the director of the public health center, a physician, may direct the public health nurses employed there to spend less time with each client to increase their patient loads. In this case, the physician may or may not gain the nurses' approval for this change. Since the physician occupies a much more powerful organizational position than the public health nurses, they are forced to comply. Obviously, they may engage in some work stoppage action to forestall this change. The director of the center may also attempt to persuade the nurses to conform to the change goal. Even if the director is successful in getting the nurses to see their clients for a shorter time, this is still an instance of nonmutual goal setting because the director established the goal without consulting the nurses.

Bennis (1966) has further divided change goal setting into two categories: deliberate and nondeliberate. Deliberate change occurs after the prospective goal has been studied and assessed in advance. The group of individuals wishing to initiate the change wants to obtain optimal results and thus acts deliberately throughout the process. Nondeliberate change takes place by chance or without much forethought. There are some very interesting differences between these types of change. They may fall into the mutual goal setting category or the nonmutual goal setting classification. Again, according to Bennis (1966), one type of deliberate change in which all parties involved have had input is planned change. Examples of a planned change are (1) the nursing staff and the director of nursing jointly decide to initiate a campaign to reduce iatrogenic infection by 50%, (2) faculty, prompted by students, put students on committees that will plan a new curriculum, and (3) the head nurse brings together the staff to plan for the reorganization of the unit.

Socialization is the process through which individuals learn about the culture and the values of their society. Socialization change is an example of nondeliberate change. It occurs when all individuals involved agree (more or less) on the need for change, but the change occurs more or less without planning. Some families, for example, do not plan how they are going to raise their children. They may have ideas, but they do not consult a master plan. They may recall how their parents raised them; they may decide to act similarly or differently, but essentially, they will respond to situations as they arise.

There is, however, the process of anticipatory socialization that fits more into the deliberate than the nondeliberate change category. The teenage boy or girl who does volunteer work in a hospital or nursing home, works summers in a clinic, or reads books about nursing and/or medicine is involved in the process of preparing for the time when actual training for a career in nursing or some other health care profession occurs. Anticipatory socialization also permits the novitiate the opportunity to obtain some understanding of a prospective life change and its real versus perceived benefits and liabilities. One might say that through anticipatory socialization, prospective nursing students learn whether they can or want to "swim" before they jump into the pool.

SUMMARY

In this chapter we have analyzed the process of change. We pointed out that change occurs on two levels: macroscopic and microscopic. On the macroscopic level, change affects the entire social system, such as the health care delivery system, while on the microscopic level, it only affects a small component of the larger system, that is, an individual, family, or hospital. We noted that change has direction; it may be vertical or horizontal and may be initiated from the top, middle, or bottom of the status hierarchy. We also discussed planned and unplanned change.

Most of our attention was directed toward planned change because it is in this area that nurses can have an influence in their own lives and careers. We stated that planned change is desired at least by the group with authority; unplanned change occurs even though it is not wanted. Usually planned change has positive outcomes or consequences because of the planning that went into its creation. Unplanned change, on the other hand, may have either negative or positive outcomes. Since this type of change is not anticipated, intended, or deliberate, the likelihood of it having negative outcomes is high.

We also discussed conflict and systems theory. While there are other theories of social change, these were selected because of their relevance to nurses. It was concluded, however, that systems theory probably offers nurses and nursing the best vehicle for understanding social change. Finally, we addressed the issue of individual change. We contend that the social situation perspective, developed by Hollander and Hunt (1976) is most useful in explaining individual change in nursing.

Chapter 3

CAN NURSES IMPLEMENT CHANGE?

Can nurses implement change? Because nursing has undergone such fundamental changes in its structure, educational objectives, and practice, one would assume that change has become part of its existence. Thus one would propose that nurses can implement change because change indeed is inherent in the practice of nursing. Nevertheless, one must be aware of the great resistance to change that is prevalent in the profession. There may be a number of reasons for this, not the least of which perhaps is that many nurses who "work" principally to earn a living do so with the least amount of effort and the least jeopardy to their position. Thus, embracing change or even entertaining the possibility of introducing change would be counterproductive to their basic purpose—not rocking the boat. The unsuitability of this attitude toward fulfilling a nursing role is being increasingly pointed out by all concerned—other nurses, other health professionals, and the public.

In this chapter we discuss how nurses can implement change. We show that there are two categories of nurse–change agents: spontaneous and planned. The labels used in this chapter (spontaneous category: rebel, advocate, catalyst, and educator; and planned category: implementor and supporter) differ from those used elsewhere (Havelock and Havelock, 1973 and Merton, 1956); however, we believe our designations are more descriptive of the nurse–change agent's activities than those descriptions used elsewhere.

THE ROLE OF THE NURSE AS CHANGE AGENT

As nurses who have graduated recently become practicing nurses, they not only bring new ideas, but also significantly different attitudes; they want to do the best for the patient, even if it means rocking the boat.

Hopefully, institutions are beginning to notice this change in attitude. Protecting the status quo of the institution to avoid any possible legal or other difficulties is becoming secondary to the imperative of providing adequate humane and socially acceptable care to consumers. This requires a variety of responses on the part of the administrations of institutions as well as on those who implement the policies of the administration.

Nurses are involved in administrative activities, particularly through the position of head nurse and through that of the traditional supervisor (who is rapidly fading from the scene). The head nurse faces a true dilemma and will have to make a decision soon in terms of which direction to take regarding patient care, patient advocacy, and bending institutional services to meet patient needs. It appears that the latter choice is taken by increasing the number of head nurses, because they recognize their true professional commitment. It will take time, education, support, and reinforcement on the part of those who would like to see this happen to provide the climate needed to make it a reality and to overcome the resistance to it. Settings outside the institution, such as community health clinics or group practices, are infinitely more change oriented, even frequently demanding it.

Thus the most future-oriented persons in the traditional hospital setting will have more obstacles to overcome if they reject the status quo. To put it another way, one needs to be realistic about the fact that the nature of the setting in which change is to take place constitutes a significant determinant regarding the possibility of the success of the planned or expected change. Most institutions in our society represent arrogance or resistance to change. This is true of religion, education, and health care delivery systems. This realization should be helpful to would-be change agents because it will help them to decide if their setting will tolerate change. Then they can determine if they need to work for immediate change or if they can tolerate resistance and conflict for a period before change can be accepted.

In addition to determining the nature of the setting in which one wishes to act as a change agent, one also needs to look at the characteristics or qualifications that are logically a part of the personality of the change agent. The key characteristics of the change agent are the following:

1. The ability to take risks. This means to develop the ability to calculate potential risks surrounding the implementation of the change and then to decide whether or not these risks are indeed worth taking. Traditionally, nurses are not risk takers. They are more likely to seek, even demand, security. No change can be im-

plemented without some risk taking. Thus, the issue of risk taking plays a major role in the planning of change and needs to be of prime significance in the deliberative effort preceding the planning and implementing of change.

2. A commitment to the efficacy of the change. Change for change's sake is meaningless and understandably leads to negative attitudes on the part of those affected by the change. The change agent must develop a true commitment to investigating the worth, value, effectiveness, and necessity of the change before proposing it. Once this has been done, the change will have a chance for acceptance and success.

3. Three areas of competence: (1) knowledge of nursing that combines research findings and basic science information, (2) practice competence, and (3) interpersonal relationships and communication skills. The ability to demonstrate these qualities will make nurses credible change agents in the eyes of their peers.

Change is meaningful only if its full implications are understood by all concerned. To achieve this, the change agent must present the change meaningfully, foresee potential pitfalls, and evaluate the effects of change. A change is serious business. Only if it is recognized as such will it be given the appropriate attention and significance to see it through effectively.

The goals of a change must be in an obvious and deliberate congruence with the goals of the setting in which it is to take place. A change that is aimless and does not coincide with the institution's goals is not a meaningful undertaking. The goals of a change must be defined in terms of a number of perimeters, to be discussed later, all of which must be the armamentarium of the change agent. They will characterize her behavior, and her presentation of self as a change agent.

A *nurse–change agent* is a nurse who influences target population[1] (that is, nurses, patients, LPNs, aides, administrators, and the like) decisions to adopt[2] new ideas, products, or programs (referred to as innovations) in a direction believed beneficial (that is, good or desirable) by a change agency (for example, hospital, nursing unit, public health department, clinic, American Nurses' Association, state nurses' association, nurse special interest group, government, corporations, and so forth). (This definition was adopted from Rogers, 1972:194.) Several components of this role require clarification:

1. *Influence.* Nurse–change agents attempt to influence a target popu-

---

1. When the target population is a single person, it is frequently referred to as a client.
2. The nurse–change agent may influence a target population to reject an innovation if it is not deemed beneficial.

lation's attitudes and behaviors through personal interaction. They are successful in this endeavor if their actions result in the target population (1) becoming aware of the innovation, (2) being persuaded of the value of the innovation, (3) actually adopting the innovation, and (4) continuing to use or hold the innovation after its initial adoption (Rogers, 1972:195).

2. *Direction believed beneficial.* An old fable refers to a monkey and a fish who were both caught in a sudden flood. The monkey quickly climbed a tree to safety. From his safe perch, he could see that the fish was having difficulty fighting the current. The monkey, feeling sympathy for the fish, reached down into the water and rescued the fish; but, to his great surprise, the fish was not appreciative of the aid (Adams, 1960). What is beneficial to one group may not be beneficial to another. It is important for the nurse–change agent to work closely with the target population and to attempt to make the objectives of the change program and the needs of the target population as congruent as possible. The more congruence between the target population's needs and the nurse–change agent's objectives or goals, the greater the likelihood that the nurse–change agent/ target population relationship will remain "intact" (Rogers, 1972: 195). Success of the change program is also related to the target population having some impact on the development of the change program's objectives: the greater the vested interests (that is, beneficial) in the change, the more likely people are to adopt the change.

3. *Change agency.* The nurse–change agent may be employed by any number of organizations ranging from the American Nurses' Association and the Teamsters to the government (federal, state or local), nurse practitioner clinic, or hospital. Any organization can be a change agency in the sense that it wants to change the attitude or behavior of some target population.

FUNCTIONS OF THE NURSE–CHANGE AGENT

The importance of nurse–change agents to the change process itself is that they can help to accelerate change. Change occurs without change agents, but "spontaneous change is simply not rapid enough" to meet the needs of organizations (Rogers, 1972:195). Therefore, through promotional endeavors, the nurse–change agent can speed up the process of adoption of innovations.

The nurse–change agent, like other change agents, has seven functions in the change process (Rogers, 1972:196-197). These include: (1) developing a need for change within the target population, (2) establishing a change relationship with the target population, (3) diagnosing the problem the change will correct, (4) identifying alternative courses of action for the target population and then creating the desire to change it, (5) translating desire to change into action so that the target population actually makes changes, (6) stabilizing the change and attempting to prevent discontinuance, and (7) achieving a terminal relationship with the target population.

Developing a need for change

Although the target population may recognize that a problem exists and something has to be changed to rectify it, the target population may be unable, through inertia or lack of knowledge, to eliminate the problem. As was the case of the monkey assisting the fish, persons may scratch other persons "where they do not itch" (Rogers, 1972:166). That is, the nurse–change agent may think there is a need for a change when the reality of the situation is that the target population does not define the situation as problematic. If the nurse–change agent does implore a target population to change something, "where they don't itch," the chance of change discontinuance following initial adoption is very high (Rogers, 1972:196). First and foremost among the responsibilities of the nurse–change agent is the identification of the target population's needs or making the target population think that it needs to change.

Establishing a change relationship

After the nurse–change agent has succeeded in making the target population cognizant of a need for a change, she "must foster a belief . . . (that she) is competent, trustworthy, and empathetic with (the target population's) position (Rogers, 1972:196). This task is not easy because of people's general mistrust of a change agent's motivation (that is, does she have a vested interest in their changing the status quo?). The nurse–change agent must attempt to develop rapport (and thereby trust) with the target population through extensive personal interaction. Target population knowledge and understanding of nurse–change agents, especially their role in the change process, will facilitate their acceptance in the role.

Diagnosing the problem

Nurse–change agents must analyze the target population's problem to tell it why present conditions and behavior will not allow for elimination of the problem. In this endeavor, they diagnose the problem from the perspective of the target population; only in this way will they be able to empathize with the target population and fully comprehend its problems (Rogers, 1972:196).

Examining goals and alternative courses of action

The nurse–change agent must present to the target population the various alternative behavior and/or actions that it can take to reach its goals (and thereby eliminate its problem). The target population may expect the nurse–change agent to dictate which alternative it should follow. However, it is the responsibility of the nurse–change agent to assist the target population in developing its own decision-making apparatus.

Translating intent into action

The nurse–change agent seeks to get the target population to both change and continue with the innovation after its initial introduction. The trial stage is important for continuance because if the target population experience during this time is positive as a result of the efforts of the nurse –change agent, the group is likely to continue to use the innovation.

Stabilizing change and attempting to prevent discontinuance

Target populations try to get confirmation that they made the correct innovation decision. The nurse–change agent can reinforce the target population in this need by providing it with supportive "messages to those clients who have adopted innovations" (Rogers, 1972:197). Reinforcement of the innovative decision will increase the likelihood that the target population will continue to use the innovation.

Achieving a terminal relationship

Nurse–change agents should attempt to put themselves "out of business by enabling . . . (their) clients to be their *own* change agents" (Rogers, 1972:197). In other words, nurse–change agents must shift the target population's reliance from themselves to reliance on itself.

In the capacity as a change agent, the nurse hopes to modify the target population. One method of indirect modification is alteration of the target population's physical and/or social environment. The target population's physical environment refers to aspects of its physical milieu such as the size or parameters of a hospital unit, parking facilities, location of the clinic, and construction of the public health facility. Aspects of the social environment of the target population include unionization of nurses, development of credit union among the hospital's staff, and development of a representative council of nurses to make suggestions to the administration.

Whereas nurse–change agents may attempt to modify the physical and social environment of the target population, most frequently they will attempt to modify the target population itself. Efforts in this endeavor include working to increase the target population's knowledge about an innovation (that is, education) and changing its beliefs and attitudes in such a manner that it will adopt a specified innovation (Rogers, 1972:198). For example, a nurse at the Easy Rest Senior Citizen's Center attempted to get members to participate in a health fair. In her efforts to persuade the members of the center that the health fair would be beneficial to them and the personal costs minimal (there was no financial cost), she found it was necessary to educate them about the health fair (for example, types of services offered, availability of follow-up, assurance of confidentiality) and to alter some of their negative beliefs and attitudes about health screening. In other words, the nurse's efforts as a change agent included both education and attitude and belief altering. If the senior citizens using the center did not change their attitudes and beliefs about the benefits and liabilities of health screening programs, the education efforts of the nurse–change agent would have been for naught.

TYPES OF NURSE–CHANGE AGENTS

Our analysis of the contemporary nurse–change agent population reveals two major categories with different types in each as shown in the following list:

Spontaneous	*Planned*
Rebel	Implementor
Advocate	Supporter
Catalyst	
Educator	

The categories are (1) spontaneous and (2) planned. Within the spontaneous category we have identified four types: rebel, advocate, catalyst and educator; in the planned category, there are two types of nurse–change agents: the implementor and the supporter.

Each of these nurse–change agent types is considered to be an ideal type; that is, a mutually exlusive classification that ostensibly is pure in its composition. Thus, a rebel nurse–change agent is said to be an individual who has characteristics exclusively those of the rebel type nurse–change agent. The reality of the situation is that these classifications are not mutually exclusive. Nurse–change agents who are classified as rebels have mostly rebel type characteristics; they probably also have characteristics of the catalyst, advocator, and/or educator nurse–change agent. We use the format of the ideal typology because it is useful in allowing the reader to better understand the differences between types of nurse–change agents. Again, we must caution the reader from thinking that in the "real world" of social change, these types of nurse–change agents are pure. Each nurse–change agent has at least some characteristics of other types of change agents besides the type that is predominant.

One of the primary reasons that nurse–change agents are not pure types is that the typical nurse–change agent engages in change activities only on a part-time basis. The spontaneous category includes nurse–change agents who voluntarily work to change behavior, conditions, or attitudes; the planned category, on the other hand, is composed of individuals who are selected or appointed to fill the nurse–change agent role. In both categories, nurse–change agents spend most of their time working with patients, colleagues, staff, community, and so forth. They are, first and foremost, staff nurses, nurse administrators, public health nurses, nurse practitioners, or nurse clinicians. Even most nurses who are employed by the American Nurses' Association or state nurses' associations cannot be considered full-time change agents because, in addition to initiating change programs (that is, to increase membership, resolve contractual differences between nurses and employers, and educate nurses about new procedures and techniques), they also have a predominance of nonchange-oriented responsibilities. There are probably more full-time nurse–change agents employed by professional nursing organizations than by other organizations. Some organizations (for example, hospitals, clinics, public health departments, nursing homes, and the like) usually do not think they have enough change activity to warrant a full-time nurse –change agent. In addition, they have used part-time nurse–change agents successfully in the past and see no reason to change that policy.

As mentioned above, the difference between the two categories of nurse–change agents, spontaneous and planned, is that the former volunteer for the job while the latter are appointed. Spontaneous nurse–change agents are usually members of the target population toward which the change is directed. They might also belong to another population. In either case, the spontaneous nurse–change agents have become aware of the problem, condition, or inequity, and its existence has caused them to want to help "change things for the better." The planned nurse–change agents are nurses who were selected or appointed by their supervisors to implement a nurse change program. Unlike the spontaneous types, they generally do not have a strong personal feeling about whether or not change should occur. If their employers think the change program is beneficial, so do they.

Spontaneous nurse–change agents

The rebel. The rebel nurse–change agent is an individual who not only rejects the goals and norms of the unit or organization (for example, employer) but also attempts to develop new or modified goals with new means for attaining them.[3] Rebels are opposed to the status quo because they do not believe that it serves people's needs and interests. They are not officially designated by their employers as change agents; usually they emerge from the staff and tend to work against the establishment (that is, organization). The rebel is always on the lookout for causes to champion.

The target population soon tires of the rebel's efforts to change everything or to question the motives of the administration whenever it wants to initiate a change program. Rebels are most highly supported when a problem has become so difficult or a condition has degenerated so extensively that they are considered to be the group's last resort.

Cindy is a rebel nurse–change agent. For several years, she has been on the faculty of a prestigious school of nursing that her colleagues describe as tumultuous. Throughout this period she fought, sometimes successfully, but usually unsuccessfully, against most of the standard policies and procedures of the school. She was always quick to argue that these policies and procedures were significantly more beneficial to the school and the university than they were to the faculty or students. Cindy attempted to organize the faculty. For instance, she tried to get them to (1) join the American Association of University Professors and the University's Women's Center, (2) protest inequities in salary levels between the school of nursing and other schools in the university where salaries were higher, and (3) challenge the traditional 6 year AAUP up-and-out policy for tenure. Cindy also championed many unpopular student causes. Whenever students had faculty or administrative problems, they could count on Cindy for advice, support, and action.

Faculty members recall only one time when Cindy was a popular nurse–change agent. During one deanship, all departments within the school of nursing were eliminated. Many faculty members were displeased with the change because they believed that it put too much power in the hands of the dean and took it away from department chairpersons. Faculty members turned to Cindy for leadership in an attempt to reverse the dean's efforts to substitute a grid system of programs and divisions for departments. Cindy was not successful in her endeavor to reestablish the department structure, but she did gain increased admiration from her colleagues.

All rebel nurse–change agents are not as aggressive as Cindy. Usually this type of nurse–change agent is very much an activist who thoroughly

---

3. The rebel seems to fit Merton's (1956:140) notion of rebellion, which is a mode of individual adaption to anomie or normlessness.

enjoys initiating (or preventing) change. It is several years now since Cindy went through her "rebellious" or "activist" state. Since then she has "mellowed out" considerably and has been appointed dean of a well-respected eastern school of nursing.

The advocate. This type of nurse–change agent emerges usually from the staff as an unofficial change agent after perceiving the presence of a gross "disequilibrium of power" (Havelock and Havelock, 1973:12). Unlike the rebel nurse–change agent, the advocate is not a constant thorn under the supervisor's or administration's skin. The advocate does not find fault with the status quo, but only feels a need to change a situation or condition when it becomes morally untenable personally to allow it to continue.

The advocate nurse–change agent supports only certain causes (the rebel seems to patronize all causes). Generally, this individual carefully examines the problem situation before deciding to work for a change. Unlike the rebel, advocates work hard to maintain and protect their legitimacy and effectiveness. They like the "call to duty," and they know that the next time there is a problem on the unit or in the organization that requires resolution, the target population will not call on them for help if they have not been helpful before.

Ken is an advocate nurse–change agent. He is well thought of by his colleagues on the urology unit at University Hospital. He is both analytical and moral. He rarely gets into disputes with his supervisor or colleagues. He does, however, occasionally write letters to the editors of the city's two major newspapers and to the editor of the hospital's newsletter. During the 2 years Ken has been at University Hospital, he has been an advocate twice.

On one occasion, the decision of the hospital's administration not to accept all indigent emergency cases caused Ken to become a change agent. The administration decided to set a quota of cases it would accept, with all others being sent to other metropolitan hospitals. Ken believed that the decision of the hospital was completely irresponsible and unethical. "Some people might die between hospitals," he said. Ken immediately started circulating a petition among the nursing staff stating their astonishment at the hospital's lack of moral turpitude. He organized a group of nurses who went to discuss the situation with the hospital's administrator. The hospital's administrator was quite dumbfounded over the concern that his decision had generated. He told the group that he and the board of directors believed that the hospital's staff would support the decision because of the economic implications for salaries. Ken and the other spokespersons quickly indicated that they believed there must be some other ways to save money besides turning emergency cases away from the hospital. The administrator said he would examine the situation further and report back to the group. After a week, the administrator announced that the hospital would no longer turn away patients. Ken felt very good about his effort.

Nurses may be advocate nurse–change agents many times or only a few times during their nursing careers. This type of nurse–change agent will generally be very apathetic toward social change except when conditions or situations arise that are so problematic that resolution can only occur through effecting social change. Examples of conditions that have resulted in the emergence of advocate nurse–change agents are (1) the announced closing of a community hospital, (2) a state board of nurses' decision to take away the license of a registered nurse who practiced nurse-midwifery, (3) unequitable salary increases for nurses, and (4) the refusal of a hospital administration to honor its agreement to a specified nurse/bed ratio.

The catalyst. Most nurses, like people in general, do not welcome change even when it is the only solution to their problem. They prefer the status quo and the security it brings. However, nurses who become catalyst nurse–change agents are similar to other members of their group (that is, unit, department, and so forth) except that they become extremely dissatisfied with the status quo and decide to try and change it. Interestingly, catalysts do not advertise that they have answers to the existing problems. If anything they inform their peers that they are no better at solving problems than anyone else. They feel, nonetheless, compelled to raise their voices in protest of the situation or condition. By voicing their dissatisfaction with the situation, they activate the problem-solving process. In other words, they get the change process started by legitimating (in a sense) the need for change. Their declarations of dissatisfaction also help to make other people realize that there is a general dissatisfaction with the status quo.

Sara and Lois are catalyst nurse–change agents. Both women are reserved and passive. They have been nurses for 10 and 12 years, respectively. Each nurse is known for her rationality, maturity, and ability to influence people. Sara has acted as a catalyst nurse–change agent six times; Lois, nine times. In this capacity, each has had considerable success.

Lois works the 11 P.M. to 7 A.M. shift. She became very disturbed with the hospital when it totally eliminated all staff food services after 8:00 P.M. Although 400 staff members were in the hospital between 8 P.M. and 7 A.M., the hospital believed that it was not efficient to keep the staff cafeteria open. Many staff personnel were displeased with the closing of the cafeteria for two reasons: (1) no one consulted them about the change, and (2) there were no optional sources for food in the area. Since the hospital is short staffed at night, one person on each unit would get food for everyone.

Lois became very personally annoyed with the situation because she did not like bringing food to work. She thoroughly enjoyed a "lunch break" and believed that it improved her morale and patience. Besides her house was in chaos when she got ready to leave for work. Her children had to be put to bed and preparations made for the next day. Lois decided to see if the situation could be changed. First, she wrote a letter to the director of the hospital and the director of nursing service indicating her concern with the lack of food service. She sent a copy of the letter to the executive director of the state nurses' association and put carbon copies on all the bulletin boards throughout the hospital. She also suggested to other staff members that they express their dissatisfaction to the hospital director. Finally, Lois wrote a letter to the district nurses' association newsletter informing its readers of the hospital's lack of consideration for its staff.

Lois' efforts resulted in a huge response from staff members who were equally apalled by the hospital's lack of sensitivity to their needs. The executive director of the state nurses' association wrote the director of the hospital that this change might jeopardize the present night wage differential that had been agreed on when the cafeteria was open. Within 2 weeks after the cafeteria was closed, it was reopened. The director of the hospital stated in the hospital's newsletter that he did not realize the importance of the cafeteria being open. He said that a small staff would always be available to provide for the staff's food needs.

Sara was very interested in the quality of the care that nurses gave to their patients. She believed very strongly that a specified nurse/bed ratio had to be maintained for quality to remain high. Sara's hospital was in the midst of a building campaign, and the hospital was trying to save money wherever it could. One area in which the savings seemed to be most obvious was the replacement of new staff nurses for those who resigned or were fired. The hospital had agreed to a 1 to 5 bed ratio; during the building campaign, the ratio increased to 1 to 7 or 1 to 8 on many units.

At a staff meeting, Sara asked the hospital's director about the administration's pledge to maintain the 1 to 5 ratio. The administrator said that the hospital intended to uphold its agreement but at present could not find any replacement nurses. The room was very quiet. Sara then suggested that the hospital should close some of its beds to restore the 1 to 5 ratio. The administrator looked at Sara in disbelief. He told her that the hospital had the same per bed expense whether the beds were full or empty and it was his job to keep them full. No one said anything more at the meeting about the nurse/bed ratio, but everyone was thinking about it. Many staff members had discussed the situation in small groups, but it was not until Sara had broached the subject in the large meeting that everyone realized how concerned everyone else was.

No one knows exactly what happened after that meeting. According to various reports, the director of nursing told the director of the hospital that she would resign and organize a strike among the staff if the nurse/bed ratio was not honored. Shortly, thereafter, the hospital began a very energetic recruitment effort, which included an increase in base pay, and closed down several beds until more nurses were hired.

The educator. Educator nurse–change agents tend to be more active in initiating individual change than social change. Their target populations are, then, referred to as clients. Educator nurse–change agents are teachers. They emerge from the group to assist individuals in changing their behavior and attitudes. The educator works with colleagues and patients who have problems and are searching for a solution. They are well respected by their associates. They are unlikely to come forth in a large group setting and make their ideas known; instead, they work behind the scene with one or two individuals whom they have identified as needing help or who have approached them for aid.

Most nurses have various amounts of the educator type characteristics. They use patient education as a normal component of their nursing. But the real educator nurse–change agents go out of their way to help others, besides patients, to solve their problems through change.

Oretha is a public health nurse. She is also an educator nurse–change agent. She has been a change agent many times during the 3 years she has been in public health nursing. Prior to public health nursing, she worked in a hospital and for the Red Cross. Oretha is quick to acknowledge that she likes helping people. She says that it is her responsibility to direct people in the right direction (she does not use the word change). To be able to help people, Oretha reads vociferously any material that she thinks can be of use in her work.

Recently, Oretha visited a women client who was suffering from a prolonged illness. She finds great pleasure in helping this type of patient because they have so very little; she tries to make them as comfortable, productive, and happy as possible. The patient had a niece who lived with her. Patient complained to Oretha that her 15-year-old niece was mentally retarded, and she was having sexual relations with a friend. The woman said she could not stop her niece from going out because of her condition, and she was concerned that her niece would get pregnant. The women went on to say, "If she gets pregnant, she will not be able to care for the baby."

Oretha told the woman about the various family planning agencies in the city. The woman thanked her for the information, but she said she could not convince her niece to use a birth control device. She asked Oretha what she should do. Oretha told her that she would talk to her niece. In the evening, Oretha returned to the woman's home to see the niece. The girl was very defensive because she suspected that her aunt had convinced Oretha to talk with her. Oretha discussed the situation with the girl and tried to make her understand what would happen if she did become pregnant. She asked the girl why she wanted to get pregnant in the first place. She told her that if she became pregnant and had a baby, her condition (mental retardation) was likely to cause her child to have trouble adjusting to life. Oretha suggested that after the girl was older and had married that she and her husband could adopt a child.

The girl seemed very interested in what Oretha said to her, especially after she realized that Oretha was both sincere and knowledgeable. She asked Oretha about her work and her family. Then she asked where could she get a birth control device. Oretha told her that she could take her to the family planning clinic. The next morning Oretha took the girl to the family planning clinic where she was provided with a birth control device.

Planned nurse–change agents

The second classification of nurse–change agent is the planned type: implementor and supporter. These types of nurse–change agents do not spontaneously become change agents, but do so because they are selected for the role. The planned nurse–change agent does not spontaneously come forth to lead a change program but is appointed or designated by one group (for example, hospital director, director of the public health department, head nurse, nurse supervisor, American Nurses' Association, or the government) to develop a change program in another group. For example, the director of nursing at Rural Hospital appointed an assistant director of nursing to change the high turnover rate among the staff.

Generally, the planned nurse–change agent is better able to carry a change program through to a successful conclusion than the spontaneous nurse–change agent. There are several reasons for this: (1) the planned nurse–change agent is usually supported by the powers that be (that is, the administration), while the spontaneous type is usually working in opposition to the administration; (2) the planned type usually has had some training and experience as a change agent, while the spontaneous type is likely to have had only experience; and (3) the planned type usually will have resources (for example, funds, consultants, assistants) at their disposal while the spontaneous type will not. Throughout the change process, the planned type remains under the control and supervision of the employer.

The implementor. Implementor nurse–change agents lack the passion and dedication of the spontaneous nurse–change agent. Their investment in the program is usually more economical than emotional.[4] They try to implement the change program because it is part of their job. The actual selection of the implementor nurse–change agent may be political. For instance, an organization may appoint a minority nurse to direct a program to recruit more minority nurses. Implementor nurse–change agents are selected to direct the change program specifically because of their managerial and leadership qualities. Their employers are confident that they can easily establish rapport with the target population and gain its trust and confidence.

Marsha, an assistant director of nursing, is frequently appointed by the director of nursing to direct important change programs. Marsha is a registered nurse, with one master's degree in medical-surgical nursing and another in business administration. (Her goal is to become a director of nursing.) Her business administration program included several courses on the change process, which helps her considerably when she has to plan a change program.

Most recently, Marsha was directed to teach the staff about patient rights. She found this to be a very challenging task because many of the older RNs do not believe in the concept of patient rights; most younger nurses, on the other hand, had received some prior information about patient rights in their nursing program. The procedure Marsha followed in this program was first to inform the nurses in small groups why they had to know about patient rights. She explained to them that the hospital had recently developed a patient's bill of rights manual, but before patients could use it, the nurses had to understand the information contained within it. "Without a doubt," she said, "patients will ask you questions about our patient's bill of rights, and you will be expected to answer the questions." In this way, Marsha attempted to develop a need for the nurses to

---

4. Hornstein et al. (1971:265) write that some change agents are affiliated while others are not. Those who are not emotionally involved with the change do not have the same disposition toward making the necessary changes as those who are personally involved. "Sometimes [the uninvolved] are disinterested and even opposed to any alteration in the status quo." At the same time, the unaffiliated change agent is free to ask questions that might otherwise not be asked.

learn about their hospital's patient's bill of rights. She also mentioned about American Hospital Association pressures on member hospitals to inform patients of their rights.

Marsha explained to the nurses that the patient's bill of rights would actually be beneficial to the nursing staff because now the patients would know what their rights and responsibilities were. She gave all the nurses a copy of the bill of rights and told them that they would have an opportunity the following day to discuss it and ask questions about it.

The following day Marsha discussed the patient's bill of rights with the staff and answered all their questions. She told them that each unit would receive a supply of the manuals, which were to be given to all new patients. Marsha told the nurses that she would meet again with them after the patient's bill of rights had been in use for a month. She also told the nurses that she was always available if they needed her.

After the patient's bill of rights had been in use for a month, Marsha met again with the nurses on each unit. She answered questions and discussed their problems. Then, to prevent discontinuance and at the same time to terminate her relationship with the change program, she appointed one or two nurses on each unit who would act as consultants to the other nurses. One year after the patient's bill of rights was introduced, it is still being used in the hospital. From a survey Marsha administered to a sample of patients, it was clear that the nurses were explaining to them the various aspects of the patient's bill of rights.

The supporter. The supporter nurse–change agent is, at the same time, the most common type of nurse–change agent and an atypical type of change agent. Supporters, for example, do not work alone; they do not feel competent enough to propose a change to a group. But once a change program has been initiated and organized by a nurse–change agent, the supporter as the name implies, will assist the nurse–change agent in implementing the change program. It is necessary, however, for the supporter to receive adequate supervision and encouragement.

Supporter nurse–change agents play the important role of emissary between the change team and the target population. In this capacity, they assist the nurse–change agent in informing and interpreting the proposed change to the target population.

Supporters do not become implementor nurse–change agents because they lack the confidence that they can organize and lead a change program. Nonetheless, when they are given adequate supervision, they can be of great help in implementing a change program.

Janie is a staff nurse at Southern Hospital. She has a baccalaureate degree in nursing and is well respected by her peers; most of whom define her as slightly passive. Janie is a supporter nurse–change agent quite frequently. Most recently, she assumed this role when the hospital altered the procedure for bringing patients their meals.

A nurse proposed a change to the director of nursing service to eliminate this problem. She suggested that two nurses on each unit assume responsibility to see that patients were ready for their meals before the trays were brought to the patients. The director of nursing was enthusiastic about the suggestion. She contacted the dietary department and informed them that before food trays were taken to a unit, someone on the unit had to notify the department that the patients were ready to eat. She then requested the assistance of a select group of staff nurses, including Janie, to help in making the new system work.

Janie was delighted to help in implementing the new program on her unit. As a supporter nurse–change agent, she was given instructions by the director of nursing concerning her duties. She contacted two nurses on each unit, one on the 7 to 3 shift and the other on the 3 to 11 shift. These individuals were to contact the dietary department when all their patients were prepared to eat their meals. Janie also identified a substitute person on each shift in case one of the primary people was absent. Janie then met with the staff on each unit and explained the new program to them. She asked them if they had any questions and told them that they were to contact her if they had any problems or suggestions. Because of the effort of the many supporter nurse–change agents like Janie, the new program was successfully implemented.

Planned nurse–change agents are involved in all aspects of planned change. The change process is planned because the nurse–change agent is expected to develop a plan of action for implementing the change. Spontaneous nurse–change agents may also plan their change program but usually it is not planned to the same extent as is that of the implementor.

The degree of initiative for change is represented in the typology of change agent. As we discuss all components of change and the place it occupies in nursing, it will become readily apparent that there is room for and a need for each of these types of change agents. The big issue, of course, is to determine how one best utilizes one's talents to exemplify or execute one of these change agent roles. In the course of time, many nurses find that they move through each of these different change agent types; for example, many start as rebels and end up as catalysts, advocates, or educators.

SUMMARY

In this chapter we have asked whether nurses can implement change. The answer is a resounding yes. Not only can nurses implement change, but they already spearhead change programs under many circumstances. We showed that there are a variety of types of nurse–change agents. They fall into two categories: spontaneous and planned. Four types of nurse–change agents are in the spontaneous category: rebel, advocate, catalyst, and educator. Planned nurse–change agents include the implementor and the supporter.

Chapter 4

RECOGNIZING THE IMPLICATIONS OF CHANGE

Nurses and other health care providers learn quickly that change, whether the result of individual or group behavior, does not occur in isolation. According to systems theory, a change initiated in one component of a system (that is, hospital, public health agency, unit of an agency and the like) may, through a rippling or domino effect or direct contact, affect (1) other individual units within the system, (2) the entire system, and/or (3) adjacent systems. Specifically, a change initiated by an individual or group affects other individuals or groups that, in turn, may have consequences for other individuals or groups, and so on. For instance, when two nurses on a six-nurse unit resigned and were not immediately replaced, the remaining nurses were forced to assume additional work and responsibility. Since there was an inadequate number of nurses, the remaining nurses had to relinquish one of their 2 days off per week. Though they were paid overtime, the nurses could not be with their families as much as they previously had. Family members became resentful and expressed anger and resentment towards their mother/spouse for being insensitive to their needs. The children of one of the nurses even got into trouble with the police because they apparently did not have adequate supervision.

This chapter presents what a nurse should know to anticipate and to deal with the implications and consequences of change. First, however, a general discussion of the conditions influencing the prediction of change is presented.

CONDITIONS INFLUENCING PREDICTION OF CHANGE

Recognizing or predicting the implications or consequences of change is quite difficult. The problem of predicting the outcome or result of an actual (or proposed) change is complicated by several conditions: (1) the outcomes of change in individuals or groups are not necessarily uniform, (2) individuals can be irrational, (3) the ever-increasing complexity of society results in most changes eliciting multiple consequences as well as frequently unanticipated consequences, (4) technological developments are still new and their outcomes cannot be predicted easily or, for that matter, at all, (5) a perceived benefit or a change to one member of a group may be perceived as a liability to other members of the same group, and (6) the problems of prediction are complicated by the lack of behavioral tools for determining in advance the consequences of change. Elaboration of each of these conditions will be helpful in further understanding how one should best deal with change outcomes.

Uniformity of change outcomes

Frequently, a change that was successful in one group is tried in another. The logic is very clear; if the change has been successful in increasing productivity, quality, and/or nurse satisfaction in hospital A or county health department B, why not implement it in another facility. In actuality, however, the change may not elicit the same results; the outcomes may be either better or worse. The difference in outcome is related to several factors, of which similarity of populations is crucial. If the two populations differ significantly, it cannot be expected that the change that was implemented successfully in the first group will necessarily be successfully implemented in the second without some major alterations either in the strategies or tactics used to implement the change or in the nature of the goals of the change. Providing assertiveness training for staff nurses will not necessarily (or usually for that matter) result in turmoil on a unit, as occurred in the example cited in Chapter 3. Doubtless, assertiveness training can engender changes in the attitudes of nurses receiving it (as expected), but whether it takes the form of a negative or a positive consequence depends greatly on the target population. An older, more traditional staff is less likely to be readily influenced by a few nurses with some new ideas than is a younger, more liberal, less experienced staff.

As indicated above, a strategy or tactic used successfully to implement a change among one group of nurses may be totally inappropriate in another setting or even among another group of nurses within the same setting. Groups of nurses may have similar professional roles (that is, nurses) but have different backgrounds: educational (that is, diploma, associate degree, or baccalaureate degree), ethnicity, age, urban-rural, and so forth. Each condition that differentiates groups may not be a factor in whether or not the change can again be implemented successfully. In Stevens Hospital, a new 12-hour rotation work schedule was successfully implemented. The nurses, as indicated by the decrease in job turnover and number of sick days taken, were satisfied with the new schedule. The administration at Sandy Hill Hospital found out about the new "12 hours on—12 hours off" schedule and the documented decrease in job turnover at Stevens Hospital. In an effort to "please" their nurses, this new schedule was implemented at Sandy Hill Hospital. To the chagrin of Sandy Hill Hospital's administration, the new schedule appeared to have exactly the opposite effect: job turnover and sick days increased dramatically. Termination interviews clearly indicated that the nurses did not like the new scheduling. Furthermore, Sandy Hill Hospital found it could not attract new nurses. After 8 months, the hospital reverted to the old system. Why didn't the nurses at Sandy Hill Hospital respond as readily to the new schedule as those nurses at Stevens Hospital? The administration at Sandy Hill Hospital failed to recognize that the median age of the nursing staff at Stevens Hospital was 46 years of age; the median age at their own hospital was 27. Thus, the nurses' family responsibilities and personal lives were very different. Many of the nurses at Sandy Hill Hospital, as contrasted with those at Stevens Hospital, had preschool children. The 12-hour shifts did not coincide with the schedules of day care centers or spouses, and therefore the nurses were forced to seek employment elsewhere.

The receptivity to change of groups or individuals can change for a variety of reasons. The group's composition may change, the group or individual may receive new insights or new information, and the values and attitudes of the group or individual may change. It is not unusual for an individual to change role models and for this change to affect her inclination or resistance to change. The leadership of a group may change, from liberal to conservative or vice versa, which, in turn, may affect its receptivity to change. Certainly, changes in group or individual values and attitudes occur very slowly, but, nonetheless, change agents must be cognizant of the implications of changes of this kind. Thus, a group of nurses who had been resistant to change of any kind may become more change oriented when a new supervisor or nurse clinician assumes leadership of their group as a result of different attitudes or behavior on the part of the leader.

Irrationality

It is generally assumed that individuals are rational. But not all individuals are rational under all conditions and at all times. In highly emotion-laden situations, there is an increased potential for individuals to exhibit irrational behavior patterns. Thus, an individual or group may not choose to change in a manner that would appear to be most rational even when the implications of not implementing such a change are negative. A student, for example, comes to her instructor and complains about the poor grade she received on the physiology midterm exam. The instructor reviews the examination with the student, and it becomes clear that the student did not sufficiently learn some of the necessary material. The instructor tells the student that unless she studies more effectively, she will not pass the course. The student remarks that if she does study more she will be unable to pursue an active social life at the university. The instructor says she is sorry that studying may interfere with her dating, but she needs to perform better if she wants to pass the course. The student proceeds to fail the next exam for the same reason she failed the midterm exam.

Complexity of society

With the ever-increasing complexity of modern society, it is difficult to anticipate all the possible consequences a change may have on society. The problem is that a change in a large, complex system with a multitude of components will have an effect on many units therein. In a simple system, the rippling effect is limited by the number of components. For instance, in a rural community, the mayor decides that one of the two primary care clinics must be closed, resulting in the lay off of five of the twenty people employed there. This closing will have major implications for the persons laid off and for their families, for those employees still employed who must now be more productive to do the work of the persons laid off, and for all the patients who will be inconvenienced because of the increased travel necessary to obtain care and because of the long waiting periods before care is received. The consequences of a change of this magnitude are more easily assessed than if an industrial facility laid off 500 people. In other words, it is quite likely that in the case of this rural county health department, we could envision most, if not all, of the problems fostered by the lay off of five employees. On the other hand, in a large metropolitan community where many individuals were laid off, the prospects for a similar assessment are dim.

In their effort to anticipate the consequences of change, people attempt to develop contingency plans to eliminate most, if not all, unwanted outcomes. Again, the larger the social system and the greater the number of components, the more possible the number of unexpected and, possibly, unwanted outcomes. Conversely, the possible outcomes of a change introduced into a limited system (for example, a rural primary care facility) are determined by the number of people interrelated to the facility.

Technological development

What will be the long- and short-term implications of using hemo-dialysis machines? Some obvious implications are that (1) people who would otherwise die will be enabled to live, (2) families will have the job of caring for their loved ones for an additional period, (3) the financial well-being of families whose loved ones are receiving dialysis may be seriously, if not irreparably, damaged, and (4) nurses must be trained to assist patients (and their families) who use these machines. Did anyone anticipate that patients receiving dialysis might become so frustrated as a result of being dependent on a machine for survival that they might commit suicide to free themselves from the dependency?

It is reasonable to assume that the increased mechanization of health care has altered the traditional role of the nurse. We do not know, however, if the changes generated by technological developments have made nursing more or less satisfying and desirable. Likewise, we do not know if patients are more satisfied with their nursing care now as compared with a few decades ago when care was more personalized (and probably less effective).

Benefits and liabilities of change

There is an old adage that states that "one man's trash is another man's treasure," and in many cases, change falls under this kind of designation. Inasmuch as everyone does not have the same perspective (that is, interests, values, attitudes, and goals), people do not view any one situation in the same way. While an individual or group may perceive a proposed change as having positive implications for them, another may view it as having negative implications. Part of this discrepancy is founded on the fact that people have different vested interests that shape their perspective. If, for example, a hospital is considering making promotion to a supervisory position dependent on having a baccalaureate nursing degree, many registered nurses with associate degrees and diplomas will be unhappy with the proposed policy change because it will exclude them from possible advancement. Nurses with baccalaureate degrees, on the other hand, will be very positive toward the change because it will permit them to compete for supervisory roles. However, some nurses with baccalaureate degrees who do not wish to be supervisors may also find the proposal threatening since they might foresee a time or a situation when they are the only nurses eligible for promotion.

Culture also plays a major role in shaping a person's perspective. A nurse from one culture may have a different view of the implications of a change than a nurse from another culture. For example, a nurse from a minority group may view abortions and family planning as a form of racial genocide, while a nurse from the majority group coincides abortions as a necessary procedure to maintain our way of life. The minority group nurse may view abortions and family planning as a means to restrict the growth of the numbers of people in her group so that the group cannot compete for power (through group size) with the majority group.

Prediction tools

Predicting the outcome of change is a very risky business. Who, for example, predicted the high inflationary spiral initiated by Medicare and Medicaid; who anticipated the upheaval brought to nursing by the nurse practitioner role; and who predicted that when nurses stopped threatening to strike and actually engaged in work stoppage situations that they would get most, if not all, of their demands met?

Because prediction of the outcome of change is hazardous, companies such as the Rand Corporation, using the latest computer modeling techniques, attempt to develop contingency plans for every possible outcome of a change. Simply stated, the modeling procedure says: "If A is changed, what *possible* implications could this have for B, C, and D?" There is an attempt to discover in advance all possible permutations (that is, groupings or subsets) of change. However, with the most advanced technology, these efforts are not complete. Part of the problem in prediction is that computers expect a certain amount of rational behavior. When rationality is not used, the computer also has difficulty predicting the change.

Unfortunately, the average person does not have access to advanced computer modeling techniques for use in developing contingency plans for proposed change. If such techniques were readily available, many changes would never be implemented (or attempted) because the modeling procedure would show the futility or the ineffectiveness of the proposed change. Instead, people base their prediction of the success of a proposed change on their experience, intuition, counsel of others, and/or various behavioral science techniques. Unfortunately, they do not rely heavily enough on research theories and change theories.

Experience can be a valuable activity or practice for predicting outcomes. Experience is not, however, totally reliable because people's past experience does not always provide them with the appropriate information for dealing with the future as it is characterized by new events and conditions. Experiences are not always sufficiently similar so that they can be used to put the proposed change into proper perspective. People do not always recognize that the experience on which they are basing a decision about a current activity is not the same as the current activity.

Doubtless it is similar; surely, it is not identical. Nonetheless, experience is widely used by people in their effort to predict the outcome of a change.

Intuition is a mystical quality possessed by few but admired by many. It is commonly referred to as a "hunch." The statement, "we ought to re-align the emergency room staff because I believe that this is how it should be organized," is a frequent basis for change. Unfortunately, intuition as a basis for predicting the consequence(s) of change is more worrisome than its use in pari-mutuel betting. In the latter situation, the main con-cern is money; in the former, much more than money may be involved.

Should we (nurses) demand a larger pay increase than they (em-ployers) are offering? Should we (nurses) let the state nurses' association represent us in our collective bargaining or should we be our own bargain-ing agent? Should we (nurses) go on strike since it is obvious that they (employers) are not willing to meet our demands? Questions such as these are constantly being asked by nurses. To change or not to change, that is the question. Questions are frequently taken to friends and relatives who have ostensibly great insight and are willing to respond to the inquiry. The truth of the matter is that very frequently other people cannot pre-dict any better than we can what the outcome of a change will be unless, of course, they are using more scientific tools. How will they know what administration will do if nurses increase their pay demands? The obvious outcomes are not difficult; the unexpected ones are probably as hidden from the persons asked as they are from those of us who are asking the question. This is not to suggest that outsiders cannot address an issue from a different perspective. It is meant, however, to suggest that people mak-ing decisions about change must rely as much as possible on other re-sources (for example, expert consultants, behavioral science techniques, and the like) (see below) to assist them in predicting the outcome of a pro-posed change.

Friends and relatives may be inadequate in assisting people in making decisions about change, but appropriate consultants can be an invaluable resource in such endeavors. *Appropriate* means persons who have relevant knowledge in the area for which advice is needed. Consultants may be people from either inside or outside the institution or unit seeking advice. But to be effective, they must have information acquired through experi-ence and/or study to be able to provide insight that might otherwise not be obtained.

Perhaps the most effective mechanism for predicting the outcome of a change is to use one or more of the various behavioral science techniques available for such tasks. Included in this group are personal interviews, questionnaires, surveys, panels, and the like. They are all designed to obtain knowledge for the person(s) using them. But this knowledge, unlike that obtained through intuition and experience, is more likely to be closer to reality, if it is obtained correctly. For instance, if nurses want to answer their questions regarding the benefit of demanding a larger pay increase than offered by their employer, they can attempt to locate and survey other employee groups who have faced similar dilemmas to determine what happened in instances in which nurses have struck. Using an approach such as this will improve changes for predicting both the positive and the negative outcomes of change.

If the administration is interested in using two 12-hour shifts instead of the usual three 8-hour shifts, why not suggest that they survey a sample of the population that would be affected to determine what the outcome of such a change would be? Mistakes in using such tools can be made; in the 1948 Presidential election, Dewey thought he was going to be president, based on a survey of readers of a literary magazine that predicted an easy victory for him. No one realized at the time, however, that the readership of the magazine was not representative of the voting populace of the United States. Truman won the election. The point is that for behavioral science tools to be effective prediction devices, they must be utilized appropriately (for example, a representative group survey or spoken to).

CONSEQUENCES OF CHANGE
Speculating about consequences

The extent of the consequences of change depend on the size or magnitude of the portion of the system (for example, hospital, patient ward, nursing home, and so forth) involved in the change. The more components of a system that are affected by the change, the more far-reaching its consequences, for example:

1. The reduction of federal capitation funds in 1979 to schools of nursing had major implications for the entire nursing profession. After the original legislation was passed in 1967, most schools immediately sought to increase their enrollment so that they could take advantage of the generous abundance of "free" dollars awarded by the federal government to schools of nursing for increasing their student bodies significantly. To increase their enrollment, schools also had to increase the number of faculty members. Thus, when the government announced that capitation funds would be eliminated, many schools were caught in a bind: high enrollment and large faculties, but inadequate resources to meet their financial commitments.

2. A change in the curriculum at a single school of nursing, especially

one that is not recognized as a leader in nursing education, will have a negligible effect on the nursing profession. However, a change in the curriculum of a school that is in the forefront of nursing education would more than likely have a major impact because of the influence this school has in establishing models for nursing education.

3. The death of the dean of a school of nursing may have only insignificant implications for the nursing profession, while having grave consequences for the school at which she was dean. The difference being that the dean was the chief operating officer for the school and, in the capacity, controlled all school activities. Regarding nursing on the macrolevel, this dean may have been only one of many who did not have much national influence.

4. Finally, a major increase in the number of nurses with earned doctorates will have major consequences for the nursing profession. As more nurses earn doctoral degrees, the quality of nursing education and the production of nursing research will increase. As this occurs, nursing faculty members with less education will find themselves pressured to either return to graduate school or leave academic nursing.

Personal change has varying implications for the social system in which the person functions as the person undergoing change interacts with other members of the system. For example, a passive nurse who takes new assertive steps in her work environment may cause varying ramifications (that is, animosity, respect, and admiration) between herself and her co-workers. The nurse who becomes divorced or widowed may find that her new situation will affect her work on several levels. For instance, she may now need to find employment only during the daytime hours because she no longer has a spouse who can care for her children when she is working at night. She may attempt to change the professional relationship she has with some male co-workers so that she might develop another intimate relationship with one person.

The consequences of change must be viewed, therefore, within their proper perspective. They may be limited or systemic changes. That is, some change consequences affect only a small or limited segment of a larger social system, while others have a much larger (systemic) impact as they literally affect all or most of the components of a system; for example, the two nurses who received assertiveness training (Chapter 2). Their change in behavior had a major impact on their relationship with physicians and other nurses on their unit. But the change in their behavior did not have systemic implications; administrators, physicians, and nurses at other hospitals did not feel the effect of this experience or at least not directly. Perhaps, through informal discussion, their experience was relayed from one administrator to another; perhaps, through literature such as this, their experience is shared. However, in general, very few people or institutions were affected by the experience of the two nurses. Limited consequences also are much more easily dealt with by the change agent. In this case, the hospital resolved the conflict by (1) eliminating any further assertiveness training and (2) firing the two "troublemaker" nurses. Resolution of systemic change consequences are much more difficult.

A change occurring in one system may also have consequences for other related systems. For example, the board of governors of a major stock exchange decided to provide health care to members and staff during working hours. It was decided to employ a nurse clinician to provide this care. The nurse clinician developed a medical alert system requiring all stock exchange employees to provide her with a recent EKG tracing and other health data. Each person was then expected to carry a special identification card that included relevant personal health data to facilitate care in the event of an emergency. Significantly, many of the employees of the exchange responded favorably to the new attention given to their health. Some of them voluntarily joined weight management plans, others began regular exercise programs, and many made an effort to upgrade their nutrition.

The success of this experimental program had even broader implications inasmuch as other stock exchanges began exploring the possibility of using similar health care delivery systems. Furthermore, this example illustrates that people will alter their behavior (in this case, adopt a new health philosophy with accompanying behavioral adaptation) when they perceive the benefits of such a change to outweigh the possible liabilities. The example also points out that change can play a major role in people's behavior. That is, it was unexpected that so many people employed at the stock exchange would voluntarily change their personal health/fitness philosophy as a result of the introduction of a health program. Apparently, the employment of the nurse practitioner acted as a catalyst; people who were "ready" to introduce personal health changes did so as a result of the new emphasis placed on health by their employer and the ready availability of the service.

A registered nurse in Tennessee was working as a lay midwife in rural areas where she was in considerable demand for home deliveries. Mothers were very satisfied with the care she provided and were content to pay $150 for her services. This nurse was in conflict with the state's nurse practitioner act, however. Although the state of Tennessee permits lay midwives to practice without a license, the state board of nursing specifies that nurses can only act as midwives if they have received additional training and have been certified to practice as midwives. Lay midwives have had no training as a member of any health profession and are not licensed as a member of any health profession. Accordingly, this nurse's license was revoked by the board because not only did she practice outside the limits of the nurse role but she did not have the proper credentials or education. More importantly, the state board of nursing's decision to revoke the nurse's license may result in the nurse's decision to appeal to the Tennessee Court of Appeals and possibly to the Supreme Court of the United States. Ultimately, the court will be placed in the rather difficult position of making a significant decision about the practice of nursing, an area in which it surely lacks knowledge. This teaches us a lesson about social systems. They are so closely interrelated that the Tennessee State Board of Nursing's decision to revoke the license of a registered nurse who is working as a lay midwife may ultimately result in clearer differentiation between the behavior, expectations, and rights of a lay person and a professionally trained person. The decision of the Tennessee State Board of Nursing and subsequent litigation may have national implications: other professionals, for example, physicians, who are performing tasks for which they are not licensed, may find that their licenses may be in jeopardy.

A final example will further clarify this condition. The nurses in the public health clinics of a large urban center realized after long, frustrating, and fruitless negotiations with the mayor and the city council that the public health department would not meet their demands for better salaries, improved working conditions, and continuing education release time. Even though the city officials said they wanted to meet at least some of the demands of the nurses, they also said that they could not do so because of financial constraints. Accordingly, the nurses initiated several half-hearted work stoppage efforts, for example, demonstrations, threatened mass resignation, and the like. The results were not encouraging. In desperation the nurses decided to strike the public health clinics. As a result of their decision, more than 50,000 patients were unable to obtain care. Also affected by the nurses' decision were the families of the strikers, wholesale medical suppliers, laundry companies, and other clinic employees who were laid off as a result of the strike.

All three of the above examples indicate how a change in one system (stock exchange, the practice of a nurse, or public health clinics) can affect change in other systems (other stock exchanges, individual health, the legal system, the ability of other nurses to practice, businesses, and families tangentially related to public health clinics).

Now let us discuss what is, to all intents and purposes, a rather simple, straightforward social change. A large, urban hospital increased the salaries of its registered nurses. This action would appear to have major consequences beyond the impact it would have on those families receiving the increase. The increase in the salaries of the staff nurses at Green Hills Hospital might have two sets of consequences. One would be as follows:

1. Other hospitals in the same city would be forced to increase nurse salaries to attract new nurses, as well as retain their present staff.
2. Other Green Hills Hospital employees might decide that since nurses received a salary increase they should, too. To ensure that they would receive additional remuneration, these workers might threaten unionization and possible strike action.
3. Green Hills Hospital (and subsequently, other area hospitals that also increased wages) might be forced to pass on to their patients the higher cost of operating the hospital.
4. Since nurses were now receiving salaries considered to be equitable, more people in the area might decide that nursing is a viable profession and, accordingly, schools of nursing in the region might be beseiged with new applicants.
5. Many LPNs and nurse's aides might decide that the increased differential between their wages and those now received by registered nurses constituted a sufficient reason for them to go to nursing school so that they might become RNs.

Another set of consequences that might have occurred is as follows:

1. Other hospitals in the area might have decided not to increase the salaries of their nurses. This decision might have resulted in these hospitals being able to keep their daily room rates below that of Green Hills Hospital. Their rationale for this decision could have been that Green Hills Hospital could only hire a limited number of nurses, thereby forcing the majority of nurses in the region to accept less money if they wished to work at all.
2. Because Green Hills Hospital had to pass on the increased cost of its labor, its room rate was significantly higher than that of other hospitals, and patients were reluctant to go there. The subsequent decrease in the hospital's occupancy rate forced it to lay off some of its nursing staff.
3. As a result of Green Hills Hospital's decision to lay off some of the nursing staff, the overall efficiency and effectiveness (that is, quality of care) of the hospital dropped. The lower than normal quality of care being provided at the hospital resulted in several bad incidents that, in turn, resulted in an even lower occupancy rate. The economic picture blackened so greatly that the hospital adminis-

tration that had originated the idea of increasing nurse salaries in the first place was forced to resign by the hospital's board of directors.

This section illustrated that the consequences of change depend on many factors such as the size or magnitude of a system or portion of a system involved in the change. The extent to which the change actually penetrates a system may be limited or systemic. In the next section, attention is focused on different types of consequences of change, namely those that are expected by persons implementing changes and those that are not expected.

Expected and unexpected consequences

The consequences or outcome of a change may be expected or unexpected (unanticipated). Expected consequences do not constitute a major problem for the nurse who is attempting to assess the outcome of a proposed or actual change in behavior or procedure. If all consequences of change are expected, there would be no reason to write a chapter on recognizing the implications of change. Unfortunately, a considerable portion of the change that occurs is unexpected. In addition, the consequences of change may have either a positive or negative impact depending on the group or on the individual's perspective or vested interests. The change, in other words, may result in an outcome that is helpful or one that is not helpful.

The consequences of a change may be both positive and negative; positive for one group of nurses or one aspect of nursing, while negative for another group or another aspect of nursing. Thus, a strike by nurses may result in higher wages for them, but may also result in a significant loss in prestige and status for the profession. In addition, changing the nurse practice act to specify that only nurses with baccalaureate degrees will be defined as professional registered nurses will have positive implications for persons who can afford to enroll in a 4-year nursing program as opposed to a 2-year program. Persons who do not have the necessary time and/or resources to pursue a longer and more expensive education will be adversely affected by this change. Surely this change may also have positive and negative social consequences. For instance, this emphasis on collegiate nursing may improve the quality of nursing care. It may, on the other hand, set up further upward mobility barriers for lower-class persons. When an instructor changes the exam format from subjective to objective, we can also observe different consequences for different groups. Those students who are better able to complete objective examinations (for example, multiple choice, true-false, fill-ins, and so forth) will find this change much more positive than students who prefer subjective examinations (for example, essay, short answer, and so forth).

Whether the expected and unexpected consequences of change are positive or negative depends on the change and its relationship to the group affected by it. Typically, people think of unexpected consequences as being negative because they do not anticipate them and when they occur they somehow cause problems. This need not always be the case. Quite frequently, unexpected consequences surprise us; often times they are positive. For instance, a school of nursing decided to develop a graduate program in maternal and child nursing because of the apparent demands for nurse clinicians in the area. After the school's program was developed, the state in which this school was located granted the school a large sum of money to train additional clinicians. These funds were given to this school because it was the only one with a graduate program in maternal and child nursing that was beyond the developmental stages. The school changed its curriculum to include the graduate program without intending that its early decision to develop a program of this nature could result in a large financial windfall. In this case then, we have a positive, unexpected consequence of change. A negative outcome might be that if after the school had hired the necessary faculty to staff this new program, no students wanted to enroll, and the school was forced to pay the salaries of faculty who were not necessary.

An outcome of a change that is both expected and positive is the type of outcome that planners seek to achieve. This type of outcome generally occurs when individuals who are planning change have successfully considered the factors effecting change. As a result, the change that occurs, occurs as predicted. They rely on superiors, colleagues, subordinates, research literature, experience, outside consultants, and any other resources that may assist them in making a good decision. In essence, positive and expected consequences are outcomes that are identical to those that are planned for by the change agent. For example, directors of nursing, director of the hospital, staff nurses, and supervisors, after a thorough review of relevant nursing literature (for example, *American Journal of Nursing, Nursing Research, Nursing Outlook, Nursing Administration*) and various specialty journals and texts, changed the work schedule from the standard 8-hour shift to the innovative 12-hour shift. In this instance, all available information that could relate to this change had been received. There was also extensive input from all persons involved that reduced the chances for negative, unexpected consequences.

Sometimes change occurs in the way it was intended; at other times, the outcome is considerably different from that which was anticipated.

For instance, a primary care nursing center was recently established in a southern rural town. The center was staffed by a family nurse clinician who worked closely with a physician located 25 miles away. The major goal of the center was to provide primary care and health education to a population of 3000 people in the center's service area. Since this area was not serviced by a physician, the nurse clinician was not considered to be in competition with any of the physicians in the general vicinity. Treatment charges at the clinic were lower than those of any of the physicians in the area since the health care provider was a nurse. After 2 years of operation and apparent financial viability, the clinic's board of directors voted to replace the nurse with a part-time physician, because use of the clinic in its 2 years of operation showed that there was sufficient patient interest in it to support a physician.

The operation of the clinic with a nurse clinician intended to bring health care to the area. This goal was achieved. However, the nurse clinician was replaced by a part-time physician who worked only 20 hours per week (as compared with the 50 hours worked by the nurse clinician), and who charged approximately 40% more than the nurse clinician. After only 6 months, the clinic closed; patients were not using the facility and the physician was unable to meet his expenses. For unexplained reasons, no effort was undertaken to find a replacement physician for the clinic.

UNDERSTANDING THE NATURE OF THE SITUATION TO BE CHANGED: THE TASK OF THE NURSE–CHANGE AGENT
Change systems

According to Zaltman and Duncan (1977:18-19), the change agent can play either of two distinctive roles, depending on the change system. In one case, the change system (individual, group, or organization) requests that the change agent help to change some condition(s). In the second case, the change agent is attempting to alter the status quo of an individual, group, or organization without their consent. Zaltman and Duncan refer to the first change system as a "change client system" because the client brings on the change; the second change system is called a "change target system" because the change agent's goal is to change the system whether or not people in the system request help to change.

Before nurse–change agents can change a "change client system" or a "change target system," they must be able to diagnose the client's needs. Rogers and Shoemaker (1971:237-238) point out that frequently change agents are "more innovation-minded . . . (than) they are client-oriented. They scratch where their clients do not itch." In other words, the success of nurse–change agents is positively related to their knowledge of the individual, group, and/or organization they want to change. However, they will not be successful if they try to change situations that are defined by clients as not constituting problem areas. The clients must have a "felt need" for change, or a "felt need" must be created. Developing a feeling that something is wrong with a situation or organization is much more difficult than dealing with clients who already acknowledge that a problem exists. This effect of "felt need" was clearly evident in the case of employees of the stock exchange who altered their health behavior when the exchange introduced the nurse practitioner into the system.

Diagnosing a client's needs is considered by Rogers and Svenning (1969:171-173) as one of the seven essential functions of the role of the change agent. Change agents must perform this function if they are to ascertain the reasons for a client's dissatisfaction. The change agent can most effectively diagnose a client's needs by examining the situation the client defines as problematic from the perspective of the client. That is, change agents must attempt to put themselves in the place of the client and then view the client's dissatisfaction through the eyes of the client.

A client may define a situation as problematic, while the change agent may not define it as a problem. However, the client's perceptions are more important than those of the change agent. For instance, the director of nursing at West Hospital decided, in consultation with her staff, that there was an inordinately high turnover rate among her staff. To help resolve this situation, the director hired a nurse researcher to investigate the problem and to recommend ways for resolving it. The nurse researcher found that the 20% turnover rate among nurses at the hospital was not inordinate; in fact, most hospitals had much higher rates of turnover. Nonetheless, the director of nursing perceived the 20% turnover rate as problematic, which it was, especially when the cost of hiring and training registered nurses is considered. The nurse turnover rate at West Hospital was approximately 30% lower than that at other hospitals. But this fact does not eliminate the costs associated with the turnover rate. In this situation, the change agent informed the director of nursing of the hospital's turnover rate in relation to other hospitals. She also attempted to find out why so many RNs were leaving West Hospital's employment and what changes the hospital could make to reduce the number.

To determine why the turnover rate at West Hospital was 20%, the nurse researcher developed a research plan that looked at the entire picture, including the attitude and behavior of both the nurses and the administration. The nurse researcher spent time getting to know the nurses and their problems. She isolated the factors contributing most to the nurses' dissatisfaction by: (1) reviewing the extensive literature on nurse turnover, (2) conducting in-depth interviews with "key" staff and supervisory nurses, (3) developing an extensive survey instrument that was administered to a large sample of the staff, and (4) analyzing the results of the survey. Throughout this process, the nurse researcher consulted frequently with the director of nursing and kept her informed of the various decisions she had to make so that when the results of the study were submitted, the director would be cognizant of how she had arrived at them. This last point is extremely important because unless the client has confidence in the change agent's results, they will not be readily received. Therefore, the change agent must take whatever time and effort is necessary to discuss the progress of the research with the client.

The nurse researcher found that for West Hospital's nurses, dissatisfaction correlated most closely with low wages, poor working conditions, and inadequate promotion policies. She took the results of her research to the director of nursing and presented her findings and recommendations to her. The director of nursing was especially surprised that the nursing staff was dissatisfied with wages; she thought they were competitive with those paid to nurses at other hospitals. Although the director of nursing was sympathetic with the other concerns of her staff, she told the nurse researcher that she believed nothing could be done about them. However, she believed that the hospital would agree to increase nurse wages to "keep the peace." The nurse researcher realized that the results of her research were not fully utilized. She wondered why the director commissioned the study if she had no intentions of trying to change things.

Being a nurse–change agent requires much more than wanting to change some behavior. It requires that the individual understand the group that she wants to change, it requires that the individual develop a "felt need" in the target group (if one does not already exist), and it requires a plan for implementing the change. If these steps are not taken, the role of the change agent is likely to be a most unsuccessful one.

Informing, consulting, and building alliances

Introducing a planned change requires considerable organization. A plan must be devised to determine the best strategy for ensuring that the change will be successfully implemented. To enhance the chances that the project will be successful, certain people must be informed and consulted and alliances built before the change is introduced.

The ideal scenario is as follows. The director of nursing, in consultation with her staff, decides that Problem-Oriented Nursing Records

(PONR)[1] should be introduced into her hospital because it constitutes a better method of obtaining access to information about patients from their charts and documenting patients' problems. Additionally, obtaining accountability information from charts is also in evidence. The director of nursing assigned a nurse, who was working in her office, to the project. This person was selected because she is well known in the hospital, has excellent language skills, and relates to a variety of nurses. The object of the project is simple: prepare and implement PONR for the entire hospital. It is anticipated that there will be considerable resistance to PONR because most of the nurses at the hospital are familiar only with traditional charting practices.

The nurse–change agent decides that the best strategy is to include at least one person from each nursing unit in the hospital on the implementation committee. This committee will study and then orchestrate the introduction of PONR. She theorizes, then, that if these people are working to implement PONR, they will serve as project advocates in their own units. Thus, each unit will have one PONR advocate. The nurse–change agent goes to each unit and discusses the new project with each nurse clinician, head nurse, and/or supervisor. She asks the supervisory staff for the name of one staff nurse who might be influential in implementing PONR on her unit. The nurse–change agent then meets individually with each nurse selected for the committee and discusses the project with them. She tells them the advantages of PONR and requests their assistance in implementing PONR. She assures the nurses that committee meetings will be held during their regular shifts and that they will receive conpensation for any additional time. Once the committee is in place, an in-hospital advertising program, emphasizing how PONR will provide increased quality of care, is begun to inform and educate the hospital staff about PONR. A hotline

---

1. Problem-Oriented Nurse Records is a system of record keeping based on the Problem-Oriented Medical Records (POMR) developed by Weed (1969). This record-keeping system includes four parts. First, data are collected about a client using a systematic, standardized form. In the described setting, a Nursing History form was developed. This form clearly defined the information that was to be collected on the client by the nursing staff. The information collected in the Nursing History, along with information from other health team members, was used in the development of the client's Problem List for use by the nursing staff (the second part of PONR). Problems identified from this data base were numbered and titled. In the Progress Notes, the third part of PONR, each entry had a number and a problem label, corresponding to one appearing in the Problem List. The SOAP format was used. That is, the charting documented in the client's point of view. Next followed the staff member's observation about the client's appearance, activity, behavior, and so forth in relation to the problem under consideration. The Plan, the fourth part of PONR, documented the long- and short-term goals for the client, along with the proposed nursing care plans, to attain those goals.

number is also set up to answer any questions that staff members might have about the new program.

The implementation committee decides to bring in several nurses who are familiar with PONR as consultants. Since these people know this record-keeping system, it is thought that they can assist the committee in developing an effective plan for implementation. Committee members are requested to keep their fellow nurses apprised of the committee's progress. The nurse–change agent maintains close and continuous communications with supervisory level personnel. When PONR is sufficiently adapted for use in the hospital, a unit is selected for testing. The unit selected is one in which the nurse–change agent had very good relations with the nurse staff and that appears most enthusiastic about PONR. Staff nurse attitudes and behaviors are carefully monitored, and meetings are held very frequently to obtain staff input for improving the system. After about a month, it is decided that all anticipated problems have been worked out of the system. The implementation committee decides that PONR should now be introduced but only in several units at a time. This last step is taken to ensure that as problems arise, they can be resolved before they become a source of resistance. Within a year, PONR was being used on all units.

In retrospect, the nurse–change agent considers several steps taken as vital to the successful implementation of PONR. First, she kept all persons who were directly and indirectly involved with PONR informed about the goals of the system as well as implementation progress. She reported to the director of nursing on a weekly basis or more frequently if necessary. She kept the various assistant directors of nursing informed about the program through memos and presentations at administration meetings. She worked with the director of nursing to provide the director of the hospital and the medical director and their staffs with information about the project and how its implementation would affect different sectors of the health care team. The nurse–change agent met semimonthly with all nurse supervisors to provide them with details on how the project was developing. At these meetings, she not only answered questions but also anticipated questions that the supervisors (that is, head nurses, clinical nurse specialist, and the like) might have but did not ask. Finally, through the hospital's newsletter, she provided the hospital staff with information about the project.

Although the actual implementation plan presented here is highly representative of implementation plans, it should be noted that the nurse–change agent received considerable advice from the nurse consultants regarding the most effective way of introducing PONR. They provided her with ideas from their own experiences in introducing PONR in their own facilities. The nurse–change agent also consulted with members of the hospital staff whom she thought might provide her with insight that could ultimately reduce resistance to PONR. In particular, she received information regarding who was the most influential staff nurse on each nursing unit. The nurse–change agent recognized early that if the most influential person on each unit favored PONR, it would be much easier to successfully implement it. It should also be remembered that, as generalized by Rogers and Shoemaker (1971), the success of a change agent is positively related to high social participation by clients. In other words, if people participate in a social change they are much more likely to adopt the change than people who do not participate in the change process.

Forming alliances is an important function of the change agent. Forming alliances means that the change agent forms bonds or relationships with clients to assist the change agent in successfully implementing the change. In the case of PONR, the nurse–change agent developed alliances with the influential nurse leaders on each nursing unit. The influential leaders "joined" the alliance, even though they did not realize that one had been formed, with the nurse–change agent because they were made to feel important. They were part of a major change in the hospital, and they had been selected to assist in the transition. Also of importance is that these influential persons were at the source of information to which no one else on their unit had access. Their selection also conferred status on them; they were made to feel important in the eyes of their co-workers. Tradeoffs of this nature make for effective alliances. The change agent must have something to offer clients so that they will enter into an alliance; otherwise, they normally will not join in the relationship. Power and status are most often offered to significant clients with whom the change agent wants to establish alliances, and typically these are sufficient to draw clients into successful alliances.

SUMMARY

This chapter has discussed the following issues: (1) the difficulty involved in determining the implications of social change, (2) the various factors influencing the prediction of change, (3) the expected and the unexpected consequences of change, and (4) the role of the change agent regarding change consequences.

Chapter 5

STRATEGIES AND TACTICS FOR IMPLEMENTING CHANGE IN NURSING

If nurses are to successfully implement change in a social organization, they must devise a plan of action. Successful implementation[1] of a change is not generally achieved without considerable advanced thought and planning. Strategies and tactics incorporated into such an effort must be to overcome normal resistance to change.

In this chapter, we discuss the various strategies and tactics that nurses might use in their efforts to successfully implement change. We differentiate between strategies (master plans of action) and tactics (activities for implementing a strategy). We show that different strategies and tactics are required for different change situations, depending on whether an interpersonal or an organizational change is desired. Since strategies and tactics must be compatible with the attitudes, beliefs, practices, and knowledge prevalent among the change population, we discuss these issues with reference to theory and through examples. Finally, we present the different types of strategies and tactics to be used under varying circumstances and provide examples of circumstances in which each might be most effective.

DIFFERENTIATING BETWEEN STRATEGIES AND TACTICS

strategy A master plan for managing and directing the flow of change. Strategy deals with how the influence from the change agent to the change target is processed.

---

1. Successful implementation is defined to include utilization by the target system. In other words, a change in data collection procedures that is not utilized by the staff is not regarded as successful implementation.

tactic An activity planned and designed to carry out a portion of the plan aimed at implementing change.

Thus, a strategy may consist of a variety of tactics. Both strategies and tactics take many forms and depend on the style in which the change agent envisions the implementation and on a variety of circumstances, particularly the nature of the setting in which the change is to take place. For instance, if the nursing staff is aware that the head nurse resists change, an appropriate strategy would be for the staff to (1) adopt attitudes that would make the head nurse comfortable and not feel as if she is under attack and (2) implement the change in such a way that the head nurse might think it was her idea in the first place. The actual activities for putting this strategy into effect are the tactics. The tactics used would obviously vary depending on the style of the different staff nurses who implemented the change. A meaningful tactic might be to say to the head nurse, "I read such an interesting article yesterday that related to the issues we are discussing. I brought a copy of it for you to read." This is a disarming tactic that most people cannot resist, particularly if they want to appear to be reasonable, knowledgeable, and change oriented. The follow-up tactic would be to inquire a few days later what the head nurse thought of the article. If the answer is "possible," it provides a bridge to action.

STRATEGIES AND TACTICS BASED ON THE TYPE OF GOALS TO BE PURSUED

A long-range goal or a goal that is of sufficient magnitude that its achievement would require fairly sophisticated preparations would, in turn, probably demand fairly sophisticated strategies. They would also have to be detailed and sufficiently diverse to allow for varieties in responses. A short-range goal that has few if any permanent implications requires much less preparation and certainly very different strategies.

As one prepares to design strategies to implement short-term change, one needs to weigh very carefully what the cost of implementing such change is. Change that does not have permanent implications may be costly and may not be very cost effective. An example of such a change might be to change the charting process when one knows that computerized record keeping will soon be implemented in each nursing unit. Thus, staff members will have to change the chart twice with the first change being only temporary.

Another basic dimension in developing effective change strategies and tactics might be measured by temporal criteria. Is the change to be quick or slow? An excellent example for a change that is going to be slow and of long duration is weight loss. To expect individuals to quickly change their eating habits, lose weight, and change their entire life-style is unrealistic and totally unwarranted. Both the provider of health care and the recipient (in this case, the obese person) need to be very realistic about this aspect. There are no true shortcuts to losing weight, and there is a great deal of documentation that indicates that people who lose weight through fad diets usually gain all of it back and more. This is a change that requires a strategy that has a long temporal dimension. It demands careful planning with a timetable that enables the individual to contemplate changes on a daily basis. Similarly, it requires tactics that fit the individuals' personal needs. For example, by gradually acquiring new eating habits, eliminating certain foods from the diet, and acquiring a taste for certain new foods, the change may eventually take place. Thus, tactics used in a long-term change must be sufficiently meaningful to counteract boredom created by events that are necessary to implement the continuity of the change. An example of this, as it relates to obesity, is the tactic of being inventive in developing dietary novelties. If one expects the individual to eat the same foods every day, it might soon become wearying and boring and result in abandonment of the diet altogether.

Short-term changes or quick changes, changes that require a quick decision and must occur quickly, on the other hand, need to be implemented through strategies (plans) and tactics (activities) designed to achieve those ends. The instructor who observes the nursing student giving injections day after day in a cumbersome, awkward way, resulting in more discomfort than necessary to the patient has a number of options as to what to do. She may use the strategy of giving the student instructions as she gives the injection. A second strategy might be to assist the student to change her injection method by giving directions at the last minute so the student does not have time to think about it and become upset or emotional about it. A tactic could be for her to stand next to the student and say, "Now, this time, how about holding the syringe in this manner and injecting it in this fashion." She demonstrates it and then has the student repeat it. The student has not had time to worry. She observes a different way of giving the injection and experiences the advantages of this method. It is a quick change, requiring a tactic that one might almost call "surprise," and is extremely effective. The student responds to positive reinforcement, and without ever having contemplated changing her way of administering an injection, she now does it and does it very well.

Lastly, one needs to think of the change in terms of the magnitude of the system that it may involve. For instance, if one wishes to institute primary care nursing in a hospital of 500 beds, a large number of nursing stations, nurses, patients, and other staff will be required. It will, indeed, revolutionize the delivery of nursing care in the institution. The strategy for this change will take a long time, as will its implementations. Developing goals for a change of such magnitude will require careful planning and participation by all involved. There is no shortcut to successfully implementing such a macrolevel change.

Thus the strategy that is needed to implement a change of this magnitude must be directed toward the individuals on the management level who will be involved: (1) whose permission must be obtained, (2) how many levels of management need to be invited to participate in this change, and (3) what resources can be used to develop the change process. All these strategies are of long-range planning. They have diplomatic and political overtones, and they certainly take into consideration that to make a basic change like this there will be numbers of people who will have to be persuaded and influenced effectively (through equally effective tactics). Strategies that are used in this situation will require documentation to justify the plan for such a change. Such documentation may have economic as well as resource dimensions and will certainly be related to quality. One would suspect, therefore, that it would be important to understand that strategies for a change of this nature are complex and have a variety of purposes. A change of major magnitude will be discussed later in this chapter.

DIFFERENT STRATEGIES AND TACTICS BASED ON SYSTEM CONSTRAINT
Legal

Any change within an institution of health care delivery, whether it be in an inpatient setting or an ambulatory one, needs to be considered from the perspective of its legal implications. As our society becomes more and more dependent on services, the legal constraints become more and more pervasive. The kinds of considerations imperative today are very different from those of 50 years ago when the control of services in the health care delivery system depended to a great extent on the contract between the patient and the provider. This is not so today. The issues of privacy, informed consent, and the right of individuals to share in the decision making have all now been translated into laws. Thus, strategies that deal with change in any part of the system must be carefully examined to provide the kind of outcomes that are legally acceptable and, at the same time, congruent with desired goals.

A good example in another area is the need to change nurse practice acts before nurses can practice in new nursing roles. Although a population group may be extremely desirous of having nurses function in the new roles, a great many difficulties may emerge for both provider and consumer if the legal prerogatives have not been aligned accordingly. Thus the strategies for implementing the delivery of services by health providers who heretofore did not exist, such as nurse practitioners, would be sorely lacking if the legal constraints of the pertinent nurse practice act were not incorporated into these strategies. As legal issues appear with increasing frequency and intensity, nurse–change agents must acquire an awareness for this component of change and make it an integral part of their strategies and tactics.

Social norms

Anyone attempting to implement change without an understanding of those norms prevalent in a system would indeed be making a very serious error. In society, behavior is guided to a very large extent by a set of norms that are translated both overtly and covertly, from generation to generation, and that are diffused among the society in ways so varied that they could not all possibly be described.

Social norms in a health care setting are particularly significant because of the rigidity of the environment. For many years, a key norm has been that physicians are not only the "captain of the ship" in the therapeutic sense, but also situated at the apex of the hierarchical pyramid, where no member of another discipline was their peer. In other words, the physician's position was virtually untouchable. Physicians were given decision-making powers and the opportunity to pass judgment in all facets of the operation of the hospital and the health care delivery system regardless of whether these decisions were within the confines of their actual knowledge base. Physicians made decisions on nursing, nutrition and diet therapy, and behavioral interactions, and yet had no training in any of these areas. They were expected to counsel, pass judgment on the projects of others, and participate in decision making in areas of management and education in which their competence certainly was not establishable. Yet no one questioned their eminence in these areas. What emerged was a social norm that placed the physician on a pedestal with a level of prestige and status that no one else shared.

The nurse–change agent would need a great deal of support in changing the social norm that accorded physicians their almost omnipotent expertise. One or more change strategies and tactics might be used in altering how physicians address nurses. The problem is that physicians address nurses by their first name, while nurses address physicians as "Dr. Smith." The strategy: to change how physicians address nurses. The tactics: a nurse could do it directly by saying to Dr. Smith one morning,

"Good morning, Joe," without blinking an eyelash and waiting for a response. Most nurses would not be sufficiently risk taking to do this but are receptive to another tactic that is also effective. This tactic would not interfere with an existing relationship but would change the address format whenever a new physician or resident was in a unit. Dr. Smith would hear a nurse call another physician by his first name, which would give him the opportunity to think about it and consider the implications of such a change. The response may not be uniform. Some physicians to whom fairness is important and who are aware that we live in a different time might say to nurses, "It has occurred to me that you are calling me by my last name after all these years. Don't you think we are good enough friends that you could now call me Joe?"

Other physicians might observe with horror the demolishing of this social norm. An appropriate tactic for changing their orientation might be: "Good morning, Dr. Smith. I have given serious thought to the way in which we talk to each other. It has occurred to me that there is something very uncollegial about the fact that you address me by my first name, while I call you Dr. Smith. Thus I have decided that, as of today, I shall address you as Joe. Please don't be surprised." Needless to say, Dr. Smith will be surprised. This nurse has chosen to approach an existing social norm in a direct, open manner. Her decision to assume the initiative has put her into the position of being a decision maker and probably, thereby, quickly establishing herself on a collegial level with the physician. Whether or not the physician will appreciate the nurse taking this approach, and thus changing his behavior, depends to a great extent on the physician.

Considering how the health care settings in our society are fraught with behaviors reflecting social norms, one can well understand that implementing change requires much thought on the part of the nurse–change agent. It is significant that changes occur in society at large much sooner and are accomplished infinitely more rapidly than in certain structured systems, such as health care delivery systems. It has been said that health care establishments in the United States are vast vestiges of feudalism in the social sense, and this is probably still true. However, nurses are making changes and they are making change rapidly by means of strategies and tactics that permit those who are most seriously affected by the change to consider that such change is indeed a humanizing process.

Nurses as change agents confront the many social norms in the health care system. To promote change, they ultimately must use strategies that also have official effects. These strategies must be applied in an effective, predetermined manner, and above all, their continued implementation is of great significance. If, for example, physicians are not immediately receptive to nurses addressing them by their first names, the nurses should evaluate their strategy from the perspective of their overall goal. If this goal is to call all physicians by their first names if they so address them, the nurses should consider another strategy. If on the other hand, their goal is to change the address relationship with physicians only when physicians are inclined to do so, they achieved their goal.

The second tactic for the nurse whose goal is to address all physicians by their first name the way they address her is to confront the physician. This is an open approach, without the usual "game playing." This nurse might approach Dr. Smith one morning and say, "Good morning, Dr. Smith. I have though a lot about how we address each other and it has occurred to me that it is really not very collegial for me to call you by your last name while you address me by my first. Thus, I would like to propose that you make the choice. If you prefer for me to continue addressing you as Dr. Smith, then I would ask you to call me Mrs. Jones. If on the other hand, you prefer to address me as Mildred, I will then start addressing you as Joe." This collegial tactic has the advantage of not taking the decision making totally and unchangeably from the physician. He now has the choice. The nurse who proposes this tactic has considered that she will continue to work with this physician, and that while he has usually adhered to conservative practices, he has shown the capacity to change in many instances.

A third tactic might be considered the most assertive and egalitarian; in this case the nurse would greet Dr. Smith in the morning and state that she had decided to be addressed by her last name, since that was the way she addressed him. Therefore, as of this day, would he please address her as Mrs. Jones. This gives Dr. Smith no choice, at least not initially. He could of course ask her to reconsider and suggest that they both should be on a first-name basis. It would be counterproductive for Mrs. Jones to address Dr. Smith by his first name on the first day of her change tactic period but then go back to her old ways on the second or third day.

Resources

The third system constraint regarding the development of strategies and tactics for change relates to resources. Resources include materials and humans. There is a limit placed on all these resources, but different institutions view the relative significance of these resource categories differently. Also, values vary considerably regarding the need to add resources for the sake of change. In one hospital, the need to institute primary care nursing was expressed by many nurses. The director of nursing was interested and somewhat supportive of the project. The staff met repeatedly with a number of consultants and utilized these resources in an excellent manner. All went well until it became apparent that additional nursing staff was needed. The primary care nursing project could not be instituted without it. The director of nursing withdrew support at this point. Rather than going out of her way to assist in the provision of additional staff, she simply indicated that while she supported the adding of staff, such individuals were currently not available, and therefore, nothing could be done about it. This approach to resource constaint, heavily sabotaging a program by denying resources, indicates other phenomena that are in operation. The change agent must know what these phenomena are before deciding whether or not to pursue the program. In other words, resources are not necessarily controlled as part of a master plan or within the context of reason. Nor are they always controlled with a view of the overall institutional goals in mind. Rather, resources oftentimes become the tool or the leverage to assert power, exercise control, or sabotage a challenger who introduced change that, because of its merits, was officially approved, indeed promoted. The control of resources requires an understanding of tactic selection; control of resources may require the most complex of all tactics needed to implement change. The first of these tactics, currently considered by many as the appropriate tactic, is that of the *contract*.

Contracts can be oral or written. It is difficult for employees to approach their employers or their supervisors for a written contract. However, it is strongly suggested that this idea be kept in mind when developing the contract tactic. One modification of the written contract is the use of memos in an affirmative way. Thus, one would send a memo to the individual who is controlling resources, spelling out the necessary conditions. In the above example of primary care nursing, the change agents might have sent a memo to the director of nursing early in the deliberations of the project, stating clearly that the institution of primary care nursing could only be accomplished if additional staff was secured at the time of the initiation of the demonstration project. Such a memo would be forwarded to the director of nursing, a copy of it would be kept in the nurse–change agent's file, and references to it would be made.

Only if the director of nursing does not agree with the nurse–change agent's memo will she respond that additional staff cannot, will not, or may not be employed. An investigation into the reasons must be undertaken. What may emerge are reasons why additional staff cannot be hired or why the hiring of additional staff is deemed inappropriate from other perspectives previously unknown to the change agent. Either way, however, the nurse–change agent is duly forewarned that additional nursing staff will not be available unless other negotiations and possibly further contractual arrangements are undertaken. The nurse–change agent then must decide if it is appropriate to continue in the development of the primary care nursing project or whether the project itself needs to be set aside until such a time when agreement on the hiring of additional staff can be secured.

In some ways, the nurse–change agent is fortunate if the control of resources is a predictor that the attempted change will not be supported by the administration. This is a concrete component of the change process, a component without which change cannot take place and, therefore, a component that can serve as a realistic and necessary fulcrum around which to center the discussion regarding the implementation of the change. Many times, tacit agreement for the implementation of a change is given when the basic approval of the change has not been given. Administrators find it difficult to say "no"; they also feel sheepish because they may recognize that the implementation of this particular change may be desirable, particularly if the change represents one that is not unique, but rather replicates changes in the system that have already been adopted in many other institutions. Certainly, primary care nursing falls into this category. Thus, to say openly, "I don't want to do primary care nursing in this institution," would not make the director of nursing appear to be a very well-informed or sophisticated nursing service administrator. It is easier, then, for her to say, "Well, we really want to institute primary nursing but we were unable to secure additional nursing staff, and therefore we had to stop for the time being. As soon as we find more staff nurses, we certainly will move on with this project." In reality, however, finding of staff nurses is not the issue.

Tactics of dealing with resource control are particularly significant when they relate to interpersonal relationship skills. Experience has shown that to deal with administrators on a fairly open level is no problem until resources enter the picture; then, all of a sudden, the openness disappears. At this point, typically, there is constraint; information is withheld and very definite control management takes over. Somehow, in organizations of this nature, resource allocations and controls gain greater significance than their face value would indicate. Almost without exception, we find that the control of resources enters into all facets of the political sphere of the institution.

Tactics, therefore, must center around an open and honest approach based on the contract that enumerates the necessary resources. The project director of the primary care nursing project might have said to the director of nursing, "I regret that it is not possible for you to attract staff nurses for the primary care project. I wonder, therefore, whether it would not be best to discontinue the planning for the project and allow me to spend time on determining how the staff recruitment program is conducted by our personnel department. I have a good many data that indicate that there is ample supply of registered nurses available in this region of the country." It may then emerge that the overall recruitment program of the institution is faulty or that there is no intention of recruiting more people because the cost is not feasible or desirable. This latter strategy on the part of the management is not disclosed because it would incur disapproval. Thus, the nurse–change agent finds herself having to make decisions regarding: (1) should recruitment per se be examined, (2) should the recruitment for this particular project be discussed and analyzed, and (3) is the issue of recruitment only the tip of the iceberg (that is, the part of the problem that shows)? Is the iceberg (that is, the problem itself) much bigger and still submerged? What really is the reason why management does not wish to see the primary care project flourish? Very similar tactics must be developed regarding other resources. Frequently, they are a matter of the redistribution of power, and then their utilization needs to be carefully analyzed. The following will explain this further.

Still using the example of the primary care nursing project, the nurse–change agent might discover that the director of nursing really does not mind the idea of instituting primary care nursing. What she does mind, however, is that the project gains a great deal of attention throughout the institution and that this attention is positive and represents approval on the part of the nursing staff regarding this change. The director of nursing may be sufficiently insecure regarding her own capabilities and contribution to the well-being of the nursing department that she may not wish to have someone else (that is, the project director) get credit for a successful innovation that obviously will be well received. Even her actual use of power to stop it or to subvert it represents not so much a need on her part to control resources, but through the control of resources a need to fortify her position in the work setting. The nurse–change agent must be aware of the possibilities as they develop, and she must use appropriate tactics of communication that allow the director of nursing to continue negotiations regarding this project and at the same time also save face. If the change agent leaves the director of nursing no alternative, she has lost the round, because administrators do not respond positively to change if they find that in the process of instituting such change they themselves have either lost power or control or are perceived as not being truly in charge.

It is imperative that the nurse–change agent deal with the issue of resources from the perspective provided by a sound data base. It is much more difficult for an administrator to deny the continuation of a project that she approved initially, especially if the constantly supplied data base supports the development and implementation of the change. The circumspect nurse–change agent, however, will not only examine the resources themselves, but will also go beyond to find out the history of resource allocation and resource utilization within an institution. An organization history of interest in providing human resources for innovation serves well to contribute to the argument that another such event is about to take place. It can be considered precedent setting. On the other hand, if it can be historically determined that human resources as a product of quality services received low priority because the institution essentially was directed toward material and conspicuous consumptive goals, the nurse–change agent needs to guard against undue optimism that a different approach to the utilization of human resources could indeed become a reality.

A good example of this kind of issue is the utilization of ward clerks and other clerical personnel in the nursing unit, which was received with a great variety of responses at its inception. Some institutions found it very easy to relieve nurses of clerical tasks by employing ward clerks; initially, they covered one shift, but soon were covering two shifts, working on the weekend and so forth. On the other hand, there are some institutions today in which the utilization of human resources is of little concern. In these institutions, nurses, who are paid wages higher than ward clerks, are expected to perform the tasks of such clerks, thereby yielding significant nursing tasks. These nurses are still unable to persuade their administrators that the employment of ward clerks would ultimately not only be economical of human resources, but also financially profitable.

There is a most important point to be made about the administrative constraint of resources and how to respond to it as a nurse–change agent. We are referring to the tactics of "doing one's homework." None of the decisions that a nurse–change agent tries to promote can be supported unless the nurse–change agent has the knowledge and understanding of historical events. This knowledge and understanding enables the nurse–change agent to convert a past negative into a positive or to make a past positive into a present one. Using this information about the past can make it supportive of the change. Once this has been established, other data regarding the utilization of resources can be useful in indicating how resources are to be used in the most meaningful and productive manner.

Resources are always interrelated. The utilization of human resources eventually has economic implications. The redistribution of economic resources eventually has human resource implications and many times reflects on the redistribution of inanimate resources. If, on the other hand, inanimate resources are the principal target of opposition for a change, it has to be clear that inanimate resources certainly have economic resource implications and, many times, human ones. Thus any discussion of resources needs to be directed in such a way to allow the administrator to see all interrelationships. By so doing, the case for the innovation can be made more effectively, and it also becomes more institutionally oriented. The interrelationship of resources unfortunately is not as readily perceived by some as it is by others. It is the individual who is highly skilled in strategy (that is, the planner) who sees the "whole picture," who will determine the interrelationship of all resources. If the nurse–change agent can be such an individual, the issue of how resources are to be dealt with may become the focus of more meaningful and rational rather than emotional, analysis leading to change.

STRATEGIES AND TACTICS BASED ON THE OPPORTUNITIES AVAILABLE TO THE ORGANIZATION
Target population acknowledges need for change

When instituting change, the group that will be most personally and significantly affected by it is called the *target population*. Thus in the example of the primary care nursing project, the target population is the staff on the nursing unit where the change is to be implemented. This staff includes not only the nursing staff but also the physicians, aides, ward clerks, and so forth—everyone who has direct or indirect contact with the care of patients on that particular unit. The implementation of successful change requires not only approval but also enthusiasm on the part of target populations. The communication instituted with those groups is of primary importance. If the target population believes that it has not been appropriately consulted, that the change is "being put over on them," that information about the change was withheld to control the group, or a variety of other similar perceptions, their response to the proposed change will be at least negative, if not obstructive and outright resistant. The nurse–change agent then has two options: the first is to win over the target population to the contemplated change, and the other is to act as if the idea for the innovation had come from the target population itself.

The best strategies for winning over a target group to a change is to determine what the different members of the target population know about the proposed change. For instance, who has heard about primary care nursing? What have they heard? If primary care nursing is known to members of the target population, what attitudes do they have toward this method of providing nursing care? Once this is known, the nurse–change agent develops tactics to persuade the target population that this change would indeed be desirable. Target population persuasion may be simple, it may be difficult but achievable, or it may be almost impossible. Target population persuasion is effective. In many instances, it may be the best tactic to accomplish the change.

An example in which persuasion through information is an effective tactic is the institution of a computerized information system on the nursing unit. Initially, people are suspicious of computers; but if they are persuaded by example and demonstration that a computer terminal on the unit will be beneficial to them, they will show interest in the computer. Properly provided incentives will eventually make most staff members experience a great sense of pride in their ability to deal effectively with this innovation. If on the other hand, the administration places the computer in the unit without first informing or consulting the staff, the staff will very likely undermine it. Computer printouts will be considered faulty and inefficient, and the entire utilization of the computer will be a series of unsatisfactory events that prolong and delay, rather than speed up, its operation.

It is not possible to introduce the use of a computer through the strategy that implies that the innovation was the idea of the target population. But there are other instances when this strategy can be used. In these situations, the nurse–change agent assumes the role of the implementor at the request of the target population, or so it is made to appear (see Chapter 3 for a detailed examination of this role). This certainly has been the case in many instances regarding the institution of primary care nursing. Staff nurses heard about primary care nursing at professional meetings or workshops, they read about it in the professional literature, and they said to their head nurses, and certainly to each other, "Wouldn't it be nice to have primary care nursing in this institution?" As a result, the change is implemented at their behest; they have acknowledged the beneficial potential of this change, and it is up to the nurse–change agent to elicit their support. The change will assume a greater significance than if they were only an informed target population.

Sometimes, a group asks for a change without so stating. Rather, there may be expression of a need to abolish a current ineffective system or procedure, for instance, when a group is overtly dissatisfied with the charting system. This then provides the nurse–change agent with the opportunity for subsequent change implementation. The administration is not responsive to the nurses' demand for changing the charting system. The nurse–change agent can use this demand effectively by turning to primary care nursing. She can make a statement such as, "One of the great advantages of primary care nursing is that it is responsive to the utilization of the patient-oriented record. Therefore, let us ask the administration to permit us to use patient-oriented records on this floor, even though the entire institution has not adopted this method." The staff then has the feeling that a change requested by it previously is indeed now being considered and experimentally implemented. There is the feeling of having been heard, and support of the primary care nursing concept will be greatly enhanced.

Ability for change to occur without conflict and resistance

A discussion of the role of conflict or resistance to change must take into account the nature of the climate in the institution. Is it conducive to conflict resolution? An institution that reflects an inability to deal constructively with conflict and that has an attitude of smoothing over conflicts in an effort to avoid facing the basic issues will probably not be readily susceptible to a change. Once nurse–change agents are aware of how conflict is handled in the institution, they can develop their tactics accordingly. For example, one tactic might be to sensitize individuals who are to participate in the change to a different mode of conflict resolution. Once this is accomplished, change may gradually occur.

Institutions in which conflicts rarely occur, because communication is sound and because the resolution of conflict is constructively preserved, do not fear these conflicts. Under those circumstances, the need to avoid conflict in the contemplation of a change is not nearly as great. Few changes can be implemented without conflict. Whether or not conflict needs to be avoided must remain the decision of the nurse–change agent. Avoiding conflict at any cost is as unproductive as is the artificial creation of conflict. Anticipatory preventive measures regarding conflict are meaningful and usually highly desirable. Conflict and resistance to change are a part of everyday behavior.

Tactics used in conflict situations includes: (1) leveling, (2) control, and (3) denial. *Leveling* is an honest approach to the issues at hand; calling things as they are perceived and, subsequently, openly attempting their solution. As soon as conflict arises, the individual in power will use *control* as a tactic of resolving the conflict. *Denial* is the least desirable tactic for resolution. If the conflict is denied, the nurse–change agent must be realistic about how to deal with the denial. Accepting it and believing that nothing else can be done about it is not productive. It never results in the resolution of the conflict and thus cannot lead to the sound implementation of change.

STRATEGIES AND TACTICS FOR DIFFERENT NURSING SITUATIONS

Interpersonal change is probably one of the hardest changes to achieve, and yet one of the most needed. Interpersonal relationships in institutions have been slower to change than interpersonal relationships in the larger society. Of all the areas of potential change within the society, interpersonal change is lagging. Slowly, informality and openness replace formality and deviousness. Institutions of health care delivery have certainly not distinguished themselves as being proponents of this change. In hospitals and other health care institutions, one still finds vestiges of the traditional, inequitable, almost feudal interpersonal relationships. There are a great many games being played, the most prevalent of which is: "I don't really believe that you know what you are doing, but I will not let you know that I think so. In fact, I will manipulate you in such a way that you do the right thing and that you believe that you were the initiator of that action" (Stein, 1968). This is principally the game nurses play when confronting physicians and their supervisors.

To deal meaningfully with consumers, health care providers must learn first to deal openly and honestly with each other. The greatest problem in the health care industry has been the exalted position of physicians. The physicians of old were the lords of the manor. They gave instruction, set the rules, and made the decisions. They asked for opinions and advice when they chose, but were never called to account either for not accepting the advice or for pursuing actions based on opinions that were inappropriate or outmoded. The "lord of the manor" syndrome is declining. The most important device to support and speed this decline is open communication. Once interpersonal relationships are built on honesty, directness, openness, and mutual respect, this change will be reflected in the entire realm of interpersonal relationships. The relationship of physicians to nurses will soon indicate competencies nurses possess that physicians never knew about. Next, physicians will build on these competencies in their interactions with nurses, which, in turn, will enable nurses to put their competencies openly into the picture. Much better planning for patient care will be the final result.

One of the newest and most successful strategies of supporting change in interpersonal relationships is that of open exchange of information, opinion, and feelings. Once an individual develops this strategy, it is almost impossible to abandon. Of all the changes we would like to see in the health care delivery system, the change of interpersonal relationships directed toward providing openness and collegiality among all providers probably holds primary importance. Personality, socialization, and norms are just some of the factors that will determine the ease or the difficulty with which a change in interpersonal relationships can take place.

Certainly, there is a wave of change in interpersonal relationships within the society. It is manifest in the church, in the relationship between parents and children, in educational institutions, and now in the health care delivery system. Nurses can play a major role in promoting this interpersonal change because they comprise the largest number of individuals involved in the delivery of health care. Their attempts to change the system have already met with success. They have taken the initiative nationally. Their utilization of approach strategies to achieve this change will support and increase this success.

What tactics do nurses use in achieving change in interpersonal relationships? First of all, they account for competence. In the past, nurses have underplayed their own competence and relied too heavily on the competence of other professionals, notably physicians. Today's nurses know that they are competent, and furthermore, they know that it is their competence that makes such a major contribution to the care of people. To bring this competence into the interpersonal relationship has been difficult, but perhaps the major difficulty is the very professional socialization nurses have experienced. They have been successfully indoctrinated to view themselves as least important when compared with the physician and therefore to discount their professional competence. No wonder, then, that individuals who have little esteem for their own competence do not view themselves as worthy of an egalitarian relationship with someone whose competence is highly respected and constantly admired by society. Nurses can deal with this; in fact, they must. Once the first step of identifying their own competence has been achieved and they have learned to put it "into the picture," recognition will result. The most important component of this tactic of interpersonal relationship is practice.

Another tactic relates to establishing a one-to-one relationship with physicians. Although the physician addresses the nurses by her first name and expects her to address him as Dr. Smith, she now must practice calling him Joe. This is not easy and many times causes flustering and insecurity on her part. Yet, it is one behavior that is recognized as being a key to a change leading to other components of change in this interpersonal relationship. The physician who criticizes the nurse for addressing him by his first name when he addresses her in this manner has given a very clear indication of his attitude toward her. She then has the choice of asking him to address her by her last name or to practice the above course. However, if her initiative of addressing him by his first name is simply followed by his continuing his relationship with her without even mentioning the change, she knows that she has scored the first point in changing their interpersonal relationship. Thereafter, it becomes easier and easier. Instead of saying to the physician, "I think you might like to consider changing Mrs. Jones' sleeping medication because she apparently has not slept well during the last few nights," the statement may go as follows: "It will be necessary to change Mrs. Jones' sleeping medication because she has not responded well to the current medication." The difference implied in the second statement may not seem very significant, but it represents the change from a nurse who acts as a penitent to one whose action makes her the patient's advocate and whose statement is based on knowledge and competence.

One cannot close this discussion without reference to the barrier to good interpersonal relationships provided by sexual differences. In this society, men deal with women in a certain way and women deal with men equally specifically. However, these rules are now definitely changing. Therefore, it is time to assume that they also can change in subsystems of the society such as the health care delivery system. We believe that the most propelling reason for a change in interpersonal relationships is that it will result in better patient care. As collegial relationships improve, better communication will follow with patients deriving increased benefits.

MAKING STRATEGIES AND TACTICS COMPATIBLE WITH THE ATTITUDES, BELIEFS, PRACTICES, AND KNOWLEDGE PREVALENT AMONG NURSES AND/OR NURSE ORGANIZATIONS

Unless the nurse–change agent understands current behavior patterns, values, and practices, the introduction of change will fail. Individuals who are not only accustomed to doing things in certain ways, but who have developed emotional commitments to doing things in a certain way, are easily upset when it is pointed out to them that they could do things differently, albeit better. Attitudes toward change have been discussed before, but attitudes that need changing are a different matter. Nurses are generally considered to be fairly conservative, rigid, and here-and-now oriented. They are threatened by the idea of change. This latter concept has been considered as such an insurmountable barrier to change that attempts at modifying these attitudes (or order) to become receptive to change have until recently not been a major thrust in nursing organizations.

The attitudes of nurses to change can be affected in many ways, but it is of primary importance that the nurse–change agent understand the basis for attitudes that are in conflict or present barriers to the introduction of new ideas and change. The most significant barrier to the acceptance of a changing world is the submissiveness of most nurses. They expect that direction for their activities will be set by surperiors and/or physicians. It appears almost as an act of treason to many nurses when someone suggests that they initiate the introduction of change rather than wait until someone else does.

Attitudes toward new ideas and toward individuals who introduce them need to be changed. We know that the status of the individual who suggests new ideas seems to have great bearing on the manner in which new ideas will be accepted. A change tactic that all nonchange-oriented nurses need to be subjected to is a systematic raising of consciousness. This tactic is no longer new, yet it is probably still frowned on in many instances. However, unless nurses are introduced to new ideas and, perhaps most significantly, to the fact that they can generate new ideas and that they themselves have ideas that are worthwhile, their ability to deal with change and with the subsequent benefits they will derive from any kind of exposure to change will not be very meaningful. It is suggested, therefore, that the beliefs of nurses be carefully evaluated to determine their ability to see the need for change. Do they possess the realization that they have meaningful contributions to make and that there are a number of constructive and ultimately rewarding activities in which they can participate to effect change?

The nurse who believes that things must stay the way they are might be invited to participate in the following exercise: to develop tactics to change an activity deeply steeped in an attitude. An example of this situation is the belief that only nurses can transcribe physicians' orders. The tactics for getting this nonchange-oriented nurse to change might be to have her first list all the things she wishes she could do for her patients if she had the time. Once this task is completed, the next tactic is for her to list all the things that she is currently doing that are not on her first list. One would expect that transcribing a physician's orders would appear on the second list. The third tactic requires the nurse to select activities in the second list that someone else might be trained to do. This will free her to apply herself to the tasks on the first list. This exercise should result in a self-examination on the part of the nurse regarding her distribution of time; it should reveal the patient care effectiveness that this distribution of time engenders. If the exercise is carried out under conditions of sympathetic appreciation of the problems faced by the nurse, there is a good chance that many nurses heretofore opposed to change will now participate.

Another desired attitudinal change relates to the denial by nurses regarding their obligation to affect improvement of patient care. Thus if it is suggested that nurses participate in making changes that are for the benefit of patients, it is only possible to move them from an attitude of noninvolvement to one of recognizing their responsibility to be involved by a change of their attitude. A good example is the serving of meals. In most institutions, meals are served by dietary personnel at certain pre-arranged times. Usually the scene is as follows: the dietary aide brings the tray, places it on the overbed table or the bedside table, and leaves the room. It has been frequently observed that no smile or word was ex-changed. It does not seem to matter whether or not the patient can reach the tray, if he can feed himself, or if he is able to enjoy the meal. It is the nurses' responsibility to have the patient ready for a meal, and if the pa-tient needs assistance with eating, to provide such support; however, rarely does this happen. The staff is often not available. Many times, pa-tients cannot reach their meals, which become cold and thus not eaten.

The basic problem in this situation is that the administration decided to split the task of meal service and feeding, and to divide it not only be-tween individual practitioners, but between departments and major func-tion holders. The individuals who bring the trays and the individuals responsible for seeing that the patient consumes the food do not com-municate. The end result is a patient who is not enjoying a meal and who does not receive the kind of service he deserves. Two things need to be changed about this situation. First, the procedure itself needs to be reeval-uated. It must be determined whether this is the best way to provide meal service for patients. Second, the attitude of those involved in bringing the tray and assisting in the meals must be changed. The first step in chang-ing these attitudes should be for the nurse–change agent to develop a strategy of communication that provides unity of purpose and, perhaps more significantly, a sense of pride in a jointly achieved task. Neither of these is currently the case, and thus the outcome of this particular en-deavor is poor at best. The second step would be for the nurse–change agent to actually develop tactics for implementing a change.

When aiming for new behavioral attitudes, an analysis of the current ones is necessary. In this example, a dietary aide is expected by her super-visor to do the following: take the tray to the right room, place it next to the bed of the correct patient, and leave. The aide is not to worry whether the patient is able to reach the tray and consume the food or whether the patient needs any assistance. By attaching this negative directive to the task, the dietary aide never has to question whether or not she is doing the job because she was, in accordance with the directions she had been given. The nurse's responsibility most likely is described in more positive language. The nurse is indeed expected "to have the patient ready for the meal" and see that he receives assistance if he needs it.

For some reason, nurses often do not believe that providing mealtime supervision and assistance is a significant task for which they are responsible. Thus one can see them hurrying all over the place in an effort to take care of a variety of matters rather than assisting patients with their meals. New behavior attributes need to be introduced to both these functionaries. They need to be matched with agreed on goals (to see that patients get warm meals), and they need to be introduced in such a way to provide sufficient interest by those who are to acquire them. One tactic might be to have the functionaries of these two departments meet together and work on a simulated patient care situation: "How do you wish to meet the patient's needs during mealtime?" It would be interesting to see the variety of ideas presented in the process of solving this particular problem. Basically then, the change tactic would be to provide individuals with ways of looking at a task to remove the stigma or negative association that obviously exists regarding it (the serving of meals). By so doing and by having a new overall series of steps to follow, it would be possible to develop new attitudes that would be more constructive for the patient's sake, but that also would be more rewarding to the functionaries.

TACTICS USED TO ACHIEVE SPECIFIC GOALS

Some types of change strategies and tactics are shown in the following outline:

    I. Coercion
        A. Threat of force
        B. Exercise of power
            1. Economic
            2. Political
            3. Shame
            4. Guilt
    II. Persuasion
        A. Inducements
        B. Incentives
        C. Rewards
        D. Strike
        E. Work slowdown
        F. Demonstrations and informational picketing

III. Reeducation
    A. Education process
        1. Lectures
        2. Demonstrations

Coercion

Everyone knows what it means to use force as a tactic. We are certainly aware that force is a tactic used significantly all over the world. There is always a country taken over by force, either by another power or by a faction within it. Thus the tactic of using force, particularly if the force is mighty and if the tactical implementation of this force can be accompanied by a measure of surprise, is not new. Many times it is successful, at least temporarily. But at what price?

The use of force in the hospital is exercised frequently. A surgeon can simply sit down in the operating room, cross his arms, and state categorically that he will not perform the operation until a certain instrument has been included on the instrument table. The nursing staff can reply, "we do not provide this instrument for this particular operation, so please proceed with your surgery," or sterilize the instrument and add it to the available equipment. In most instances, it is only the latter behavior that will show results. The nursing staff is usually not willing to call the physician's bluff. Furthermore, it is common knowledge that were the physician to complain to the hospital administrator, it would indeed be the nursing staff who would be criticized for having the operation delayed. This use of force is a coercive means whereby individuals in an institution impose their will on others and succeed in having it carried out.

Force in institutions is not only carried out by individuals. It is also carried out by groups of individuals who use tools of force such as policies, directives, and procedures that are formulated and adopted by a few and yet affect the entire institution. This use of force is rarely countermanded because it is so difficult to determine where it originated and who is in a position to eliminate it. Thus the memo that is delivered from the hospital director's office, even though it carries the director's signature, many times will be used by another group such as an executive committee or a board committee. The point to be understood is that force is used by individuals or by groups to impose their will on other members of the organization and that the tool, namely a tactic by which this force is introduced, is well tested and well known to administrators and politicians all over the world.

The threat of force. It is not always necessary to implement a decision or a directive by force. Frequently it is sufficient to use tactics that propose or imply a threat. This will cause individuals who are so threatened to comply and modify their behavior as desired. Threats are used in many ways within a nursing staff. The most common threat is the use of a name of a superior by a middle management individual when confronting an individual of lower hierarchical level. For instance, the supervisor will say to the head nurse: "The director of nursing wants you to do this and therefore, it needs to be done." Never will the supervisor say "I want you to do this." If she did, the threat might not be sufficiently strong or powerful to prevent the head nurse from confronting the supervisor. The use of the name of the organizational head is an effective threat and the game has been won. Compliance follows.

Threats are also used by nurses in patient care. Patients are told innumerable eventualities that might occur if they do not conform to desired behaviors. "If you do not drink enough water, we will have to catheterize you." "If you do not get up and walk around, you may get an inflammation in your leg." Sometimes the "may" is actually expressed as "will," and patients already weak and tired by the very nature of being ill will not question such statements and comply.

Threat or force has also become an educational tactic to achieve compliance. The student who is told that if she does not carry out procedures as indicated, she will be supervised more closely and thereby "forced" to do things as she is supposed to do them. Such threats are tactics used by individuals who wish to change the behavior of others to suit previously set purposes. They find these tactics effective because they preclude dialogue and thus exposure of ignorance or wrongness. These tactics are in the category of maintaining the status quo within an institution.

Dealing with threat as a change tactic is very difficult for an individual. Certainly it takes a great deal of self-esteem and autonomy to attempt to counteract this particular use of force. This explains why such tactics are so successful.

Exercise of power in several ways

ECONOMICS. The strategy of using economics to obtain the desired behavior is certainly not new. The most common and widely used economic tactic is that of salary raises. Under the cloak of merit increase, salary increases are given to individuals who indeed comply with expectations and who do not question the execution of certain demands. Economic persuasion or force also is exercised on groups. We certainly learned this lesson from our national political scene, where economic assets are removed from constituents who have not properly played the political ballgame; the assets are shifted to those who have. In institutions such as hospitals, the same thing is true. A head nurse who has been loyal and who submits to institutional rules and regulations will have a much easier time getting a new piece of equipment for her unit or obtaining economic advantages for herself and her staff. The head nurse who has been rebellious will find that she cannot replace her equipment or send a member of her staff to the continuing education workshop. Thus strategies of economic origin are widespread and widely used, and their tactics are effectively implemented as long as those who are affected by them have not found ways to counteract them.

POLITICAL COERCION. This is a parallel strategy and is used every bit as much on Capitol Hill in Washington as in the hospital or the community health agency. Concomitant tactics include developing alliances in institutions that allow individuals to have political clout. The departmental director who wishes to introduce a new salary scale is wise to develop political allies among other department chairmen before proposing the idea at the executive committee meeting. After gaining assurance of support, the director will be able to move into action and get the proposal approved at a considerably greater degree of certainty. Politics in an institution are more complex and devious than they are in government because it is much more difficult to find out where institutional power resides, who possesses it, and how to obtain access to the power structure. But once this has been ascertained, the use of political maneuvering to obtain certain goals is a widely used strategy in the institutional power group. The hospital's power group operates like any other political group. This is true about the manner in which it arrives at decision making, the way in which goals are identified, pursued, or displaced, and certainly the way in which self-interest is interjected into the entire decision-making process.

SHAME AND GUILT. Nurses must learn about the strategy and tactics of shame and guilt to become effective change agents. Nurses have operated submissively since the beginning of the profession. There is no group more susceptible to accepting guilt placed on them than nurses. A good example is the situation in which the head nurse informs the day nurses that the night nurse has called in sick. "One of you," says the head nurse, "has to work the night shift tonight." The nurses are uncomfortable about this. Every nurse believes that she should probably make the offer to work despite the fact that she knows how tired she will be after her regular 8-hour shift. Also, many things need doing at home. It does not occur to any of the nurses to suggest that the hospital have a list of substitutes, as do school systems. Nor do any of them say: "I cannot be responsible for providing patient care for 24 hours. I can only be responsible for a certain number of hours a day, and I am here doing my share during those hours.

It is the administration's responsibility to find staff for the other shifts."

Another example of control through guilt is when nurses are told repeatedly how expensive consumable materials are and that they should be more conservative in their use. This warning reaches the extent where nurses actually believe that their use of equipment is part of their own behavior structure, and that they must account for the use of equipment as if they had used it for their own purposes. At no time does it occur to them to say, "I used these things to take care of my patients. My patients need them. It is part of their contract of care received in this institution that this equipment be provided for them."

The use of shame and guilt as coercive tactics works as long as the group over which they are exercised has low self-esteem and feels powerless. As nurses become more assertive and acquire a greater sense of self-worth, it will be increasingly less possible to use these tactics as coercive forces.

Persuasion

Many types of persuasion are effective tactics of change, including rational, emotional, factual, and fallacious persuasion. The rational tactic persuades individuals through reason. It is effective if used with individuals who are oriented toward reason and who have the ability to deal reasonably with everyday situations. More common, however, is the emotional tactic. Nationally, this is particularly true in times of crises such as war or disaster, but it is operational at all times. For nurses, it is couched in loyalty: loyalty to the institution and loyalty to one's profession. The emotional tactic is used as a way of having individuals comply with directives that, if examined rationally, would probably not be accepted. Fallacious tactics are not used as frequently. Nevertheless, we know that fallacy at the beginning of an argument has made its way frequently into the argument. Perhaps one of the most common fallacious tactics is the use of the term *socialized* in relation to medicine. Very few people, if asked how to define *socialized,* are able to do it. These very same individuals will state categorically that they oppose socialized medicine, because it has been presented to them in a negative way and their entire response is emotion ladened with no reason or rational explanation provided.

Changes are created by tactics (or activities) using reasoning, urging, and inducement. Tactics of reasoning induce behavior based on a stated reason to comply with the request. The use of urging is effective in individuals who are flattered by such urging and who respond to this tactic simply because they have no reason not to do so. It is unfortunate that urging can be as effective as it is because, in the long run, it induces people to engage in an action for which they have no reasonable basis in terms of their own conviction or competence. Inducement, on the other hand, is used as a tactic when an expectation of some reward for suggested behavior exists. Nurses must believe that a time-saving procedure indeed does save time, and to be induced to try it, the time-saving component is presented as an inducement. Once such an inducement is found to be true, it proves an effective tactic. Inducement can be honest and sincere, and if used with discretion, obtaining a meaningful goal should be considered a desirable change tactic. The difficulty arises when inducement is used to achieve behavior that is not functional, for instance, when nurses are asked to work extra shifts and the inducement is a higher pay scale for this overtime. This is basically immoral. People should not be expected to work excessive hours because it affects their health and in this situation does not give patients equity of service. No one can perform as well on a second 8-hour shift as on the first.

To suggest a change of procedure by using an inducement of better quality, higher efficiency, better results, and more rewarding effect is a *positive* way to use this tactic. This is helpful in any situation in which nurses are attempting to implement change. It is important to understand the inducements are only meaningful if they are part of the overall value system. If a nurse–change agent in an institution of high moral standings introduces an inducement that will suggest tampering with the law or bypassing the law, the inducement will not be effective. It is important for nurse–change agents to understand how to use a tactic of inducement, how to structure inducement in positive and creative ways, and how to suggest their use.

Reeducation

Literally, reeducation means that the educational process that had resulted in certain behaviors needs to be redrawn to have the individual change the previously acquired behavior. A good example of this in nursing is the use of computer facilities for the administration of drugs and nursing treatments. The nurse who has never used the computer in patient care needs to be reeducated in the sense that she give up the previous method of doing these activities. This method had been taught to her as a student and become part of her nursing consciousness. When using the computer for drug administration, the basic procedure has changed drastically. In fact, the only thing that remains is the part that occurs at the bedside. Furthermore, it is much more difficult to look back to see if the patient had the drug at the previous administration time. The only way this can be done is by asking the computer to make a special printout; otherwise, the printout for drug administration occurs every 24 hours. Once reeducated, the nurse will handle this procedure appropriately.

The steps in the process of reeducation begin with the nurses familiarizing themselves with the computer procedure, which involves going through the stages of learning how to operate the terminal. They will learn how to utilize all the new information provided. They will then understand how to operate the computer and will have a certain amount of confidence in this ability. However, before it is possible to do this effectively, the nurses must have an opportunity to change their attitudes regarding drug administration. Many nurses find it difficult to view this procedure in any way different from their original ideas. Furthermore, it is true that the computer is an intermediary between the nurse and the activity. The computer requires certain service to respond in the way desired.

Unless the nurses are able to meet the requirements of the computer components of drug administration, they will not be allowed to administer the drug to the patient. This may be very frustrating. Also, everything that we said before about resistance to change and the mechanism in which people use it is operational here. Thus, the nurse needs to have ample opportunity to understand the advantages of a computerized drug administration system, how it contributes to the overall operation of the modern hospital, and how it increases safety and accuracy as well as saving the nurses' time. The new behaviors required regarding the operation of the computer will also provide the nurses with a new set of checks and balances that make their activities safer and ultimately facilitate their accountability. The acquisition of this perspective will take time and is achieved through carefully worked-out educational experiences. Reeducation is not a simple matter—it is a complex process that requires the application of educational principles pertinent to this particular situation.

If one looks at this process of reeducation, one realizes that knowledge about the computer and its operation is one kind of educational input, while the different procedures, in this case, the operation of the computer, constitute another kind. The reestablishment of attitudes and the integration of the change occurs as the nurse becomes more and more comfortable with the use of the computer in relation to this procedure. After a while most individuals find it interesting, challenging, and rather gratifying to participate in a reeducation process; they enjoy having acquired skills and facility in the implementation of change. Reeducation, then, is a strategy of major significance in the implementation of change within institutional settings. Change, if it is truly to be implemented on an institutionalized basis, involves many individuals. To have the change implemented correctly, there must be a way whereby many individuals can become sufficiently acquainted and reeducated to participate in the change effectively and meaningfully.[2]

STRATEGIES USED TO ACHIEVE SPECIFIC GOALS
Nonviolent strategies

These are plans for implementing significant change for large numbers of people. The strategies to be discussed here are demonstrations, work slowdowns, and strikes. Many times they all are used for the same goal: to bring about a major change in working conditions. This does not necessarily mean only those conditions immediately affecting the employee. It also means an overall change of conditions within which the work takes place.

Demonstrations and informational picketing. These two strategies are used to bring to the attention of the public what workers, in this case, nurses, wish to convey. They could be used to indicate to the public that nurses recognize that the equipment in an institution is dysfunctional or that conditions in an institution are such that safe and effective nursing care cannot take place.

Two examples of demonstration strategies with subsequent tactics that took place in a large, metropolitan, publically supported hospital a number of years ago will serve as examples. In one case, nurses were told that there were no more funds available to purchase toilet paper. This was an unacceptable condition to the nurses. They conferred with their supervisor in the administrator's office, but to no avail. Their change tactic was for all nurses to bring a role of toilet paper to work. Moreover, they did it in such a way that their action was easily noticeable. When questioned about it, they explained what compelled them to engage in this demonstration. This is an example of a peaceful demonstration. Also, it is not necessarily reminiscent of mob action, because the nurses came to work at different times and certainly in no more than small groups or as individuals. Furthermore, it was not accompanied by any kind of hostile or violent behavior such as shouting or marching. Yet it was a demonstration of considerable impact, attracting the desired attention of the public and the press.

The second example of a change strategy occurred at the same hospital. The strategy was designed to demonstrate how understaffed the hospital was at that particular time. The tactic used was that all nurses, regardless of whether they were off duty that day or whether they worked

---

2. Toffler (1970) draws a similar conclusion.

on another shift, appeared at the hospital for the noon meal and proceeded to feed patients who could not feed themselves. They called it a "feed-in," and its purpose was to show how many nurses it would take to feed all the patients at the hospital who needed that service. Even though the number of nurses on the premises was more than threefold that which would have been there under ordinary circumstances, there still were a good number of patients who had to wait for their meals. The press, television, and radio reporters were there, communicating the nurses' behavior to the community. Both the strategy and the actual tactics were highly effective.

Strikes. The manner in which a strike is carried out as a nonviolent strategy to obtain a certain goal is as old as the labor movement itself.[3] For many, striking is an emotional-laden concept. Until recently, it was considered incompatible with professionalism. Thus, it was not deemed an acceptable strategy of nonviolent behavior. During the last 30 years this has changed, and today physicians, school teachers, engineers, and nurses have engaged periodically in strikes to communicate most effectively a grievance that they considered unbearable. It is important to understand that these strikes are not self-serving. Nurses strike because they have exahusted every other way to communicate to those in power that working conditions are incompatible with professional practice. A strike is a nonviolent strategy that embodies the right of a group to exercise prerogatives that are available in a democratic society. Nursing has gained a great deal of autonomy through strikes. Thus the strike is a potentially and realistically effective strategy, nonviolent in nature, that is to be used as a last resort to obtain a major and significant change.

Work slowdown. Work slowdowns are another peaceful strategy to demonstrate a grievance or a lack of satisfaction within the work situation. It seems to be more acceptable to both employer and employee than the more drastic strategy of the strike. Work slowdown, for instance, as used by airport control tower operators, means that adherence to rules that otherwise are somewhat overlooked results in slower conduct of work. Nurses might do the same. Their tactics would be to walk instead of run and to do everything exactly as it should be done instead of participating in many of the shortcuts that a busy day seems to impose on a nurse's activities. If slowdowns are nonviolent, they are also a strategy of somewhat passive aggressiveness, and frequently, they take a long time to be effective. In fact, they are sufficiently hard to notice that their full effect is of delayed manifestation; participants might get tired before their goal is reached.

---

3. Miller (1975) and Miller and Dodson (1977) discuss the major issues, ethical, political, economic, and sociological, surrounding nurses' right to strike.

THE STRATEGY OF USING STRATEGIES

It is obvious that as one looks over one's armamentarium of strategies and tactics, decisions consistently have to be made. Thus looking at the last type of example, a group of nurses working for an institution where grievances prevail would have to choose between demonstrations, work slowdowns, and strikes. If the first choice is not effective, it is important to recognize this and substitute an effective one. We have talked about planning before. It is a component of the use of strategies that cannot be overemphasized. In the selection of strategies, timing is of great significance. Thus, setting a time limit when instituting a strategy and then assessing the effectiveness of the strategy within the time limit is crucial. Once the time limit has arrived and the strategy has not been effective, the decision may well be to use another one. It should also be noted that the strategy may be appropriate, but the tactics used for implementation may be ineffective and/or inappropriate.

The best strategy involves the least amount of accommodation by the organization, staff, and one's colleagues

Strategies that require changes in behavior are most difficult and most expensive to use. One would not have to refer to the computer example to validate this statement. Obviously, the initial purchase, rental, or installation of a computer is extremely expensive. But over and above that, the accommodations necessary to have the computer operate effectively and to have all systems participate in it properly is most likely extremely great. Thus the amount of accommodation required needs to be calculated before the change is implemented. It is a significant strategy in itself to do this before making the decision that such a major accommodative modality is desired for the changes considered.

Values and behavior must be consensual between change and target population

The change contemplated is explained to those who participate in it (target population). It is important that they understand immediately that the purpose of the change and the behaviors necessary to implement it are consistent. Thus when the computer is explained to a group of nurses, it is important that reference is made to the purposes of the institution, namely patient care, to the manner in which the computer will increase the institution's ability to meet these purposes, and how the individual staff will enhance the utilization of the computer and therefore, goal achievement. If a computer company came to the hospital and said to the nursing staff, "we are bringing in this computer because we want to see how people who have no computer training work with computers," the indignation by nurses would be justified. Their purpose of working in the hospital is not to meet technologists' interests; rather, technology must be modified to meet the interests of the hospital.

Complexity of strategy is inversely related to the facility of implementation and may reside in a possible breakdown of the change

The simpler a strategy is, the easier it will be for people to acquire its contents. The more complex it is, the more discouraged people become in implementing it. Simplicity of strategies can be achieved by breaking down a complex strategy into its component part: the tactics. We can use the computer example again and indicate that there are a number of tactics to engage in before the computer itself is introduced. Thus making the learning of computer activity simpler is making it more effective. The first step that many computer systems now require is the change of language. Rather than using the traditional computer language, computers in hospitals are now using English. This facilitates their use considerably and certainly makes it a much less strange machine with which to cope. Before the computer is instituted, the forms in the hospital must be changed and the nurses must begin to deal with coding systems. They are sequential or branching in nature so that the way in which computer language ultimately forces them to operate will not be new.

Complex uses of the computer can also be broken down by having practice sessions so that individuals can learn each component of this activity separately. However, some organizations have refused to complete a computer learning period and have thereby lost the opportunity to implement the change meaningfully. In reviewing the tactics whereby the computer was introduced to a certain staff, it became evident that the educational orientation, which is complex, had not been understood. Rather than using simple tactics that could be mastered and could yield a good deal of personal reward and gratification, complex tactics were introduced but not learned. The computer remained the nurses' enemy, rather than becoming the friend it should be.

Implementation effectiveness increases with low risk and certainty of strategy

It is obvious that the lower the risk involved in making a change, the greater the possibility of implementing and adopting the change (Rogers and Shoemaker, 1971). Most individuals are not high-risk takers; most changes appear to be high-risk oriented. The idea then is to reduce risks to the lowest possible denominator. Once this is accomplished, the certainty of success of this strategy will have increased. A good example of this might be the strategy of demonstrating by means of bringing toilet paper or having a feed-in. Neither of these strategies involved high-risk tactics because they were positive actions. How can one fault a nurse who brings toilet paper to her patients? Particularly, when it is documented that this is a needed commodity? How can one fault a nurse who comes in on her day off to feed the patients? These are low-risk tactics, and by being low risk, they increase the certainty of effectiveness for the individual participant. The overall plan of this kind of strategy obviously needs to compute its effectiveness by separating it from the risk and by enhancing it through all available means. In the case of these two strategies, the use of public communication media was a significant way of ensuring certainty of the effectiveness of the strategy and making it low risk.

Implementation increases if the results of a change strategy are visible

If members of an organization are becoming aware that a change strategy is paying off, their attitude toward the change itself becomes increasingly more positive. This attitude, in turn, results in more interest in participating in the implementation process. If a good thing occurs, it encourages the occurrence of additional things. As good things continue, the overall attitude toward the innovation become increasingly more positive. A good example of this is the implementation of the problem-oriented medical record. Initially, most large institutions viewed this system as cumbersome, difficult, too different, and simply "not right." Even today, this attitude prevails, and the innovation never had a chance. In those institutions, however, where there was someone who was either sufficiently powerful or sufficiently skilled in developing strategies and tactics of implementation, the change in attitude toward this particular innovation was dramatic. The number of "believers" increased with an almost unheard of rapidity. Today, most institutions that have undertaken the implementation of this recording system find that it has definite advantages and is preferred to the traditional method of patient management charting. Thus the issue is: should one start implementation of an innovation to give the innovation a chance? Success breeds success, and nowhere is this more apparent than when a meaninful innovation is the result of a well-implemented strategy (Rogers and Shoemaker, 1971).

Multiple strategies are not always compatible

In developing the strategies of change, it is important for the nurse–change agent to realize that one strategy at a time will be the most effective way of implementing change, for example, the strategy of persuasion and the strategy of coercion. If used concurrently, the persuasion strategy will disappear because the coercive strategy will be more threatening, and more attention will be paid to it by the affected individual. The compatibility of strategies employed must be estimated and calculated. Only if it appears that strategies would reinforce each other, should they be used together.

Divergent subgroups are likely to respond to different strategies

If we think of nursing staffs that consist of professional nurses and nurse's aides, we are dealing with a very heterogeneous group. The orientation of each staff group is different. There is perhaps a certain commonality of goals in terms of patient care, but there are many divergent personal goals and different career orientations. Thus the implementor nurse–change agent must take the time to determine the nature of the different subgroups and their needs. What will appeal to the nurse's aides in the nursing staff may be almost anathema to the professional nurses.

A good example of how groups differ is the method of salary payment. In one institution, it was decided that employees should be paid on the last day of each month, thus receiving 12 paychecks a year. The professional nursing staff was quite pleased. They believed that this method of payment was indeed representing professionalism. By receiving a larger sum of money once a month, it was easier for them to budget their income and to plan their spending. They liked the idea of being able to bank a sizeable paycheck and then draw against their checking account. The nurse's aides on the other hand, receiving a much smaller salary, believed that being paid once a month was not to their advantage. They had a hard time budgeting their income and found themselves without money during the last week of each pay period. They preferred to be paid every 2 weeks, which adds up to 26 paychecks a year. Their ability to manage their household expenses in this manner far exceeded that with which they had to cope with a monthly payment. Hospital administration had to decide which group's needs to meet; the decision was to accommodate the nurse's aids, since they operated on a much smaller salary.

The best nurse–change agents are the individuals who are most efficacious and skillful in their knowledge and use of change strategies and tactics. However, it is quite obvious from the above discussion that the knowledge of strategies for the implementation of change alone is not enough. Strategies must be selected carefully and weighed meticulously in terms of their benefits and potential cost. Above all, they must be viewed from the perspective of how effective they will be. Being a nurse–

change agent means having an armamentarium of strategies. Understanding these, being able to evaluate them, and having the ability of deciding which strategies are appropriate for a given situation is of crucial significance. These are difficult decisions for the nurse–change agent to make. The nurse–change agent must also supervise the application of appropriate change tactics and keep track of how well strategies and tactics are implemented and the responses of the affected individuals. The ability to do all this and to exchange strategies as indicated, because one did not work and had to be replaced, requires an unusually skillful person.

Use of specific interpersonal tactics

Some of the tactics reported here have sufficient track records to be applied routinely. Nurse–change agents may find that having a variety of tactics at their disposal gives them the opportunity to select them according to their use and then plan their use as indicated. This will make the plan for a particular implementation maneuver more securely fixed in their mind and also more meaningful in terms of expected outcomes. The selection of appropriate tactics ahead of time also gives people an opportunity to practice them, which is important in many instances. A person must have the chance to understand how a tactic can be used to ensure an outcome of a questionably successful endeavor. Several types of tactics and their usefulness over a wide range of possible situations are discussed below.

The ego sandwich. The ego sandwich is an effective interpersonal relationship tactic because it permits the individual using it to say something not too pleasant and yet terminate the interaction on a positive tone. It goes as follows: first, something pleasant or positive is being said, then a critical message is included, finally the completion of the interaction is accomplished with another pleasant message. For example, the head nurse might say to the staff nurse, "Good morning, Jean. I am so glad that you told me about Mrs. Jones' decubitus ulcer. It was an excellent time for you to discover it because it is at an early stage and we will be able to handle it in as short a time as possible. I wish that you had put it on the chart, though, because Dr. Brown has already been here and I think it would have been helpful had he been able to read about it. However, I told Dr. Brown how well you reported it to me, and he understands. If you get it on the chart before he comes back later, I think that he will feel better." The positive message was meaningful and sincere, and the negative message was justified. The nurse certainly should have put this observation on the chart. The conversation was terminated on a positive note that should make the nurse think that the head nurse is on her side.

Stroking. Stroking is a contemporary term; it means giving a person praise in some form. It certainly is one that we need to consider in the health care delivery system. We have a great tendency to be critical and to let people know when we think negatively of their work. Less frequently are we prepared to give people good feelings or to tell them about the positive side of their performance. The stroke is a positive statement that is relevant and justified. It is important to remember that tactics such as stroking lose all effectiveness when it is discovered that the positive statements are not justified. To tell someone that she looks well in a new dress, when indeed the person knows that the new dress has been a big mistake, is not stroking, it is hypocrisy. This makes no positive contribution to the interpersonal relationship between these two people. If one does not like a person's dress and feels the need to comment on the person's appearance, one should find something else to talk about; but it must be based on an honest observation. Stroking is most meaningful at work if it is directed toward performance. Thus, for the same head nurse to say to the nurse who identified the decubitus ulcer, perhaps after 2 days of management, "I looked at Mr. Jones' ulcer, it certainly is almost gone. What a good job you have done in taking care of this," is a very welcome comment. It is based on fact and is directed toward the individual's competence. Stroking is always desirable. People have a tendency to think that individuals who are functioning on the top level of a hierarchy do not need strokes; nothing could be further from the truth. A well-spoken stroke is always appreciated. The tactic of stroking is a meaningful and welcome component of a relationship between two or more persons. Strokes are effective with groups; a teacher may give one to a class, a head nurse may give one to her entire staff.

Appealing to priorities. This tactic involves concentrating on the cause for a needed change, rather than on the change itself. A significant tactic in change implementation is to understand how the individual who would be affected by the change would respond to the change in terms of her particular perspective. An individual who works at the hospital is concerned with the world at work there and does not necessarily look at a needed change from the perspective of the entire institution. She may look at it simply from the perspective of her own position. The head nurse who has not had a vacation for an entire year and who has looked forward to and planned her vacation is certainly not going to understand why the urgency of an innovation has to be pressed on her 2 days before she leaves. In fact, she would be very unconcerned about it. A tactic of significance then, would be to say to her, "I understand that you are going on vacation and that our having orientation sessions to introduce the new computerized delivery system does not come at a good time for you. Let's sit down and figure out what we can do to work it out so the process will not be delayed. I know how important it is for you to go on vacation. We want you to be comfortable." This tactic has significance within this interpersonal relationship. It indicated that the work of the institution must go on, but that the needs of the individual and the perspective of the individual also must be taken into consideration. There is always the possibility that if these two individuals work together, they may make things work well.

Induction. This tactic is a transmission of an idea regarding a change. One describes the change and its positive effect but does not tell the individual directly that she could change; rather, one waits to see if the individual takes the hint. For instance, the assistant director might say to a head nurse, "We have now budgeted for a clerk to be on the night shift and the new clerk will probably start next Monday. Much of the paper work that is now being done by nurses on the night shift will be done by the clerk. One of the things to be done is the orientation of the night nurses toward leaving work for the clerk. We hope that this will result in more nursing care delivery to all patients on the floor. It is the reason why we are making the change." The head nurse listens to this but offers no comments. The assistant director did not say to the head nurse, "Get the night people together and orient them to this clerk." She made the assumption that the head nurse would act in accordance with this information. In this way, a person can deal with a change according to her own choice. The change was obviously directed by top management in the nursing department, but the manner in which each staff member is to get the message is left up to the head nurse. The assistant director will note how the head nurse handles this situation so that when another change of this nature occurs, the assistant director might use the same tactic or decide to use another one, if this one was not effective.

Bargaining. This tactic is probably the oldest one known to humankind. The precept on which bargaining is based is: "if I give you this, what will you give me?" Bargaining serves a good purpose in a situation in which the individual who suggests the bargain has a definite goal in mind and is interested in making the bargain on an equitable level. When bargaining is used inequitably and when there is an inclusion of force, it ceases to be bargaining and becomes a coercive force that we will discuss later. Bargaining, to be effective, must be honest. It must be without coercion or other strings attached, and, above all, it must give the individual to whom the bargain is proposed complete freedom to accept it or reject it. The assistant director may say to the head nurse, "Francine Jones came to us with the hope that she could work in Pediatrics. We told her at the time that there was no vacancy in Pediatrics, but that there was a vacancy on your unit. That is why she came to be interviewed by you. You both agreed that she would work on your unit. Now, there is a vacancy in Pediatrics, and in all fairness, I must inform Francine of this. However, if you would like to talk to her and see if she is sufficiently happy here so that she would be willing to forfeit her place in Pediatrics, that would be fine. If you would rather not do that and simply interview a replacement for Francine, I have a number of people on my list that I can ask to come in to see you."

The assistant director bargained with the head nurse in an effort to: (1) keep her own commitment to Francine, but (2) allow the head nurse, who most likely would be very unhappy if Francine left, to find out if Francine wanted to stay. To have a choice of accepting the bargain as offered or allowing the assistant director simply to proceed with an administrative procedure into which she, the head nurse, would not be included was a fair way to do it. The head nurse could accept the bargain on a number of levels. She could say, "I think you had better talk to Francine, because it is only fair that she go to Pediatrics. But I will not have her leave until I have found what I consider a suitable replacement." That means that the assistant director has to keep the position in Pediatrics vacant until Francine is ready to take over. Or the head nurse might say, "I would prefer to talk to Francine, because it gives me a chance to persuade her to stay on this unit, which I would really like. I believe that Francine has been so good that she will be hard to replace." Either way, the head nurse wins even though she is now faced with the possibility of losing a good nurse.

Power through command. The tactical command is losing popularity very rapidly. Professionals do not consider it justifiable to be commanded to do anything. Translated in the world of work, it depends on how different individuals function in terms of their perception of what constitutes a command and what constitutes a recommendation. Many times, it is the manner in which a statement is made that makes the difference. If a director of nursing commands her assistant directors to have budget requests in by a certain date, it will not make them feel that they are her collaborators as she has pointed out in the past. If on the other hand, she says, "I have to see the Chairman of the Board on March 1 about the budget. Usually I find that it takes me at least 2 weeks to get all my budget ideas together and develop a good rationale for my presentation. It would really be helpful if you could have your budget request in no later than February 10. Will that cause any hardships for you? Will you need to see me before you bring the budget request in so that I can deal with all your questions?" In this situation, the individuals concerned believe that they are part of a process of decision making, rather than having been commanded to do something over which they have no control.

At times, there is a real place for a command tactic. About 30 years ago, the director of one hospital had to issue a command that said, "Patients of different races will be placed into the same room as of this date. If one complains about the race of the other, it is the complainer who will be moved out of the room, *not* the individual about whom the complaint is filed." This was a command; there was no question that the power of his office enabled the director to issue this command and that anyone who would question it would have to deal with him rather than simply overlook or ignore the command. Subsequent investigation indicated that without the command, the procedure would not have been followed.

Rewards and punishment. The tactic of using rewards and punishment to effect change is well known. However, individuals who use these tactics are not always aware that they are using them. To use salary as a tactic of reward and punishment makes the employees not only uncomfortable but puts them at a disadvantage if they are not able to verbalize what these manipulations mean to them. If an employee whose work is poor is told that there will be no raise in salary without telling her why, she is not being given a fair chance to improve her work and thus her chance to receive a subsequent raise. Withholding a salary raise as punishment in that manner is not very effective. The same is true on the positive side. Without telling an employee that she is receiving a salary increase because she has done a good job and to indicate why it has been determined that she has done a good job does not assist her in validating her work standards and thus strengthen her professional identity. Professional people need to have their own understanding of what constitutes a competent practice. They must be able to discuss this with their peers and with their superiors. It is on the basis of that judgment that rewards or punishments are meaningful.

When one tactic fails, use another one. This dictum is as true for tactics as it is for strategies. When one realizes that one tactic does not work, it is very unwise to continue to use it, certainly not in the same situation. The decision to carry out a subsequent plan of tactical use needs to be viewed from two perspectives. Will this tactic work somewhere else even though it has not worked here? Since it has not worked here, chances are it may not work anywhere else and therefore it won't be used again. This is a difficult decision, and the outcome of it cannot always be predicted. Thus, the nurse–change agent must decide whether or not to try it at all or whether another situation might prove to be different and offer more success.

INTERACTION OF STRATEGIES AND TACTICS

In concluding this chapter on strategies and tactics, it is important to remember that all strategies and the tactics they include need to be evaluated before they are used again. Unfortunately, most individuals operate on the basis of applying a set of tactics repeatedly without built-in evaluative observations. Even though a tactic has not been effective, it has been used over and over again. This is the way in which people and innovations get reputations. The supervisor who will talk about a head nurse behind her back and does not confront her with criticism is certainly perceived as being dishonest and not very helpful. Even though she knows that she is viewed this way, she still is not changing this tactic and has not made an effort to acquire an approach of confrontation and leveling. Until she is ready to evaluate her behavior and undertake the necessary changes, she will remain ineffective as a change agent.

The same is true of matching strategies with tactics. If a strategy is known to be unsuccessful, it does not necessarily mean that the tactics selected to implement it also need to be discarded. Rather, as a new strategy is drawn up, tactics should be selected based on this "new fit," which may include tactics that were also included in the discarded strategy. For instance, when nurses selected a nonviolent strategy of informational picketing to achieve improvement of working conditions at a hospital, they used slogans as tactics to gain visual recognition, for example, "We would rather fight than switch." When the picketing did not work, they changed this strategy to one of work stoppage, but kept the slogan because community feedback informed them that it had been effective.

SUMMARY

This chapter has focused on various change strategies and accompanying change tactics that nurses might use in their efforts to implement an idea, program, skill, or process. We showed that different change situations require different change strategies and tactics depending on whether the change is of an interpersonal or organizational nature.

Chapter 6

HOW THE NURSE–CHANGE AGENT IMPLEMENTS CHANGE

Change occurs through the action or behavior of an individual or group. Although this statement may sound hackneyed, it is very significant for understanding the nature of change. Social change does not occur without human involvement. The development of new roles in nursing does not occur spontaneously like a fire in a grain elevator or a fire in a hot, damp, junk-filled attic. New roles were developed through the extensive efforts (that is, research and evaluation) of many people such as Loretta Ford and Henry Silver (1967) in the initial stages. If people do not decide that something needs to be changed, there is little likelihood that change will occur. People are, in other words, the force (engineers) behind social change. Without people, there can be no change. Social change should not be confused with ecological or physical change. Obviously, the seasons and the weather change without human involvement, earthquakes occur in spite of people not wanting them to, and people become sick (a change in physical condition) without collusion from others or even their own blundering. In this chapter, the focus will be on the role of the nurse–change agents. How do they effect a change? What are their considerations and concerns, and how do they implement change? What are their goals? As they cope with these questions and plan their actions, they use strategies and tactics (as discussed in Chapter 5) to meet the demands and goals of the planned change.

One major goal of nurse–change agents is to assist people in developing a need for a change. They must make people (patients, other nurses, administrators) aware of the relative condition of their situation so that they can determine whether or not they should be dissatisfied or whether their situation has inadequacies that can and should be remedied as compared with other persons. One might say that the nurse–change agent has to make people unhappy with the status quo and simultaneously convince them that they can alter things for the better. For instance, nurses may be unhappy with the working conditions at their place of employment, but unless they recognize that some nurses are content and that nurses have means at their disposal for getting changes in their work setting, conditions will not change. Likewise, nurses may appear content with their work setting until a nurse–change agent informs them that, relatively speaking, they are much worse off than other nurses. Accordingly, the nurses begin to feel "relative deprivation" and try to do something about changing their situation, especially after the nurse–change agent guides them in the mechanics of change. Before nurse–change agents can make people want to change, they must understand the various "factors associated with the change target that must be considered in planning for change" (Zaltman and Duncan, 1977:225). This chapter examines many of these factors and indicates how the nurse–change agent can deal with them. (The Appendix contains three case studies recounting how change agents accomplished their goals.)

ASSESSING THE CHANGE TARGET SYSTEM

For change agents to competently decide what changes will best suit a target population, they must have a thorough understanding of the nature of the target system. The change agent must be sufficiently knowledgeable about the target population not only to be able to know what change(s) will be beneficial but also to use strategies that employ methods for introducing change that will be effective. In other words, effective implementation of social change involves a two-pronged approach: (1) the change must be relevant to the needs of the target population and (2) the strategies used in introducing the change must be consistent with the target population's values and needs. Some examples may be helpful in understanding how to assess a change target system.

The administration of the South Side Hospital, a 500-bed, teaching hospital, decided that a significant annual sum of money could be saved by replacing the hospital's present intravenous (IV) system with another brand. The hospital's administration informed the nursing staff of the reasons for their decision and set up comprehensive orientation classes so that the nursing staff could learn how to use the new IV setup (both the procedures and equipment were different, the new system used bags and the old one used bottles). Although the administration hoped for a fairly easy transition, there was considerable resistance to the change by the nursing staff. Nurses complained constantly about the new IV system, the staff reported an inordinate number of problems, and many of the new IV setups were contaminated because ostensibly they did not work correctly. When a sample of the nurses at the hospital were questioned about the new IV system, the majority said they did not understand why a new system was necessary. Most believed that the old IV system was quite adequate and in fact superior to the new one, which in general they knew little about. None of the nurses interviewed believed that the financial savings to be gained justified switching to the new system. The amount of the financial saving had not been made known to the staff.

The public health nurses at City Public Health Clinic were informed by the assistant commissioner of public health that passage of Proposition 13 by the voters (legislation designed to reduce property taxes and thereby effectively reduce the tax income of municipalities) had forced the county to initiate a job freeze. The job freeze, in turn, prevented the department of health from replacing any worker who retired, resigned, or was fired. However, all nurses remaining with the department of health would have to increase their work load (as necessary) to compensate for the void created by the loss of nurses. The commissioner also said that the number of clients using the department would not decline because of the reduction in the department's budget nor would the loss of nurses force the department to reduce the services it provided. The response of the nurses to the commissioner's dictum was totally unexpected: they went on strike. The nurses did not support the administration's decision because they felt totally excluded from the decision-making process. No one in the department of health had sought their advice regarding various alternative plans of action. The administration of the department of health assumed that most, if not all, of the public health nurses would support the city's decision to maintain the present service level. But the callousness of the health department in assuming that there was no need to inform the nurses of the situation or to consult with them regarding the various alternatives resulted in the nurses' decision to strike.

It is obvious from these two examples, that change agents, whether they consciously acknowledge their role or not, may not sufficiently understand the nature of the target system to be able to design an effective change plan. An effective change plan is a method or procedure for effecting social change(s) in a group that will take place as the change agent designed its occurrence. In the case of South Side Hospital, the plan was to introduce the new IV system to the staff by means of an orientation program, conveniently set up so that nurses on all shifts could have access to it. However, the change agent (frequently there is a change agent team) did not anticipate or think to assess whether or not the nurses thought a change of this dimension was appropriate. The change agent was given the assignment of getting the nursing staff to accept the new IV system. She did not have any input into the decision to implement a new IV program, nor was she able to assess how the change would be received. Her only responsibility was to get the new system, already decided on, into use. Therefore, she used the best strategy at her disposal: she designed an orientation program to prepare the staff nurses for using the new system and did not go through the entire process required to ensure a satisfactory change.

The staff heard about the hospital's decision to introduce the new system from their supervisors who were uninformed about both the advantages and the disadvantages of the new system as compared with the old and the necessary data concerning the cost of the systems. Wouldn't it have been better if a change agent team had visited each unit or grouping of smaller units and explained the reason for the hospital's decision to implement the new system? Wouldn't this type of approach have had the added benefit of reducing nurse anxiety about the new system since the team could fully explain the new system, the cost, and the reasons for the change and anticipate any problems? The personal approach takes more time and involves added expenses for the hospital, but the benefits surely outweigh the liabilities. For instance, the nurses would have felt more involved with the plan to introduce the new IV system if their importance to the success of the plan was acknowledged by the change team. Staff cooperation is much more likely when a direct appeal is made from a change agent than an indirect appeal from the director of the hospital (by means of a nurse supervisor). Furthermore, the approach used tended to cause the staff nurses to build resistance to the new system before they went through orientation because of the inadequate manner in which the new system had been introduced to them. In other words, many of the nurses felt threatened and antagonistic toward the system because they did not know anything about it. The change team could have very easily reduced these emotions by fully informing the nurses about the system.

Another strategy that could have been used at South Side Hospital was for the change agent to orient all the nurse supervisors to the new IV system before it was introduced to the staff nurses. Although the nurses would have felt more important to the success of the new system if the change agent had directly sought their cooperation, this approach reduces the information problems that might otherwise exist if the supervisors are not completely knowledgeable about the system when they introduce it to their staffs. Whichever approach is used, the cost/benefits will be different. If the change agent approaches the staff and seeks their support, the likelihood of successful adoption of the change is increased. This approach costs more than the other approach in which the nurse supervisors participate in early orientation programs so that they can assist their staff in preparing for its own orientation. Certainly the least expensive approach is for the nurse supervisors to announce the new system to the staff and for all nurses to undergo orientation together. While this latter approach may cost the hospital less in the short run, how does one calculate the cost of nurse anxiety, frustration, and feelings of little self-worth, the cost of destruction to equipment, and the cost of patient injury when the new equipment functions incorrectly as a result of human error?

Each change to be introduced may entail a completely different change plan. But before change agents can decide on the best or most appropriate change strategy, they *must* assist the change target system to determine basic information about its attitudes, beliefs, knowledge, and social practices as they relate to the social change that is to be introduced.

Attitudes

Attitudes are the result of a person's beliefs about given objects, events, and issues. They are also "a general disposition to respond to an object in either a favorable or an unfavorable way" (Middlebrook, 1974: 111). Attitudes serve to guide a person's thoughts, behavior, and/or feelings toward people and objects and play a significant role in one's decision to accept or reject change (Lauer, 1977; Zaltman and Duncan, 1977). Attitudes, like most other social behaviors, are learned through membership in groups (for example, family, school, peer groups, sorority). Persons usually believe certain things or think certain ways because of the influences of the group or groups to which they belong. If an individual changes her attitudes, values, or behavior significantly, she will probably come into conflict with the groups and individuals that are now in opposition to those beliefs. Groups do not tolerate well significant deviance of thought or behavior among their members. They will, however, tolerate some divergence, but not such an amount that will cause a serious disruption in group solidarity. Accordingly, individuals are very reluctant to alienate themselves from their group by changing their attitudes or behavior unless they undergo some significant transformation in their attitudes and values.

Conservative physicians, for example, who were raised in upper class or upper middle class conservative families are unlikely to advocate a national health plan. If they were suddenly to champion the transformation of medicine to the point where most health care is underwritten by the government through taxation (as in Canada), they would probably be ostracized by some individuals or groups to which they belong. On the other hand, it is much more conceivable for these same physicians to support catastrophic health insurance or the American Medical Association's national health insurance plan, which do not disturb the status quo.

Lack of information does not preclude individuals from forming attitudes. In fact, many attitudes that individuals have are based on incomplete, distorted, or erroneous information. A person's attitudes toward racial and ethnic groups (stereotypes) are frequently based on inaccurate information. Attitudes may also be based on cultural traditions, which may have little correlation with the present situation. Individuals in American society frequently express personal opinions about events, conditions, issues, or behaviors in public opinion polls and surveys. They very seldom say "I do not have enough information about that particular subject, therefore, I cannot express an opinion." Instead, they answer the survey because it is socially acceptable to say that they favor/disfavor, like/dislike one candidate, issue, or group over another one. Even professionals fall prey to this phenomenon. Conservative physicians would probably be negatively inclined toward the expanded role of the nurse not necessarily because they were aware of the potential and actual benefits of this role for the provision of care, but because they had heard (or read) that it ostensibly threatened to take away from physicians some of their control over the health care delivery system. In other words, these physicians might very well be threatened by a condition that they do not fully understand. But, interestingly enough, lack of information does not prevent them from developing an attitude toward the expanded role of the nurse that may result in some behavioral action (for example, discrimination).

Attitudes change. The major process through which a person's attitudes change is persuasion. Persuasion may be effected through either individual personal influence or life circumstances. *Persuasion* is the process by which one or more persons influence the attitudes, values, and/or behavior of another person or persons. We will discuss the issue of persuasion later in this chapter.

Life circumstances cause attitudinal change when, for example, an individual joins a new group with attitudes and values different from those to which he had previously been exposed. Frequently individuals do not anticipate the impact of life circumstance changes on their attitudes and values. For instance, does the registered nurse who, after several years of working in a hospital setting, decides to become a nurse practitioner or nurse clinician, anticipate how changing careers will affect her attitudes toward other health care providers, patients, and national health insurance? Does she foresee how a drop in income and interaction with other nurses and graduate students will affect her personal perspective on life? Even if the nurse does not anticipate these changes, the results will be the same: an increased likelihood of a breakdown of attitudes and values and replacement with new ones.

The impact of life circumstances on attitudinal change occurs specifically and directly through peer pressure. The research of Asch (1955), for instance, illustrates that individuals can be dramatically influenced by their peers even when the group's request for conformity is most incongruous. Attitude change can also be effected through the reference group. This is a group of individuals to which an individual belongs or wants to belong and, as a result, uses this group as a standard of reference "for expressed attitude and action . . . for comparison with others and a perspective for viewing the social environment" (Hollander, 1976:23). Nursing students, for example, frequently use registered nurses as their reference group and accordingly exhibit attitudes and behavior similar to those they think nurses should have. In this respect, the nursing students will alter their values and attitudes to fit the model they have fixed in their mind as that of the "registered nurse." Similarly, when students become registered nurses, they may change their attitudes and behaviors to conform to those of their new reference group: other registered nurses. It is not unusual, however, for a member of one group to use another group as its reference group. Under this condition the reference group becomes the standard for the person's attitudes and behavior. An example of a nurse who fits this description is the one who uses physicians as her reference group because she was brought up to think that physicians are always right and know best. Therefore, she typically has many attitudes and values different from her nurse colleagues about the role of the nurse in relation to the physician. These differences may generate considerable conflict as the group of nurses attempt to persuade this nurse to conform to the group's attitudes and values regarding the appropriate role of the nurse.

Beliefs

Beliefs are a component of attitudes (Kothandapani, 1971). Beliefs are ideas that develop from experiences; they are what people have been told and have seen. Beliefs help people function in society because they establish certain "givens," that is, they establish what individuals can expect from situations in which they interact. Kramer (1972) shows that nurses who have baccalaureate degrees have trouble adjusting to the role of the hospital nurse because their beliefs about the role of the nurse differ dramatically from the current reality of the role.

Beliefs tend to "organize what we see" (Middlebrook, 1974:112) and, as such, establish what people *will* see or experience. If, for instance, a nurse believes that one group of patients is inferior to another, she is likely to pick out specific things about patients from this group that support her beliefs. Similarly, the elderly nurse who believes that primary care nursing is inferior to functional nursing will resist the efforts of nursing service to change the direction of nursing care. For this nurse's belief pattern to be changed, it is essential to assess the reason she dislikes primary care nursing. Is it because (1) she feels threatened by this new approach with which she is unfamiliar, (2) she does not feel competent enough to assume full responsibility for a patient's total nursing care, or (3) she has found some major flaws in primary care nursing? If this nurse's beliefs about primary care nursing are to be changed, the nurse–change agent must determine the basis of her beliefs.

It should be noted that individuals frequently do not disclose to administrators and/or investigators the real or complete reason for their beliefs. Individuals sometimes are more at ease providing socially acceptable reasons for their beliefs and behaviors than the actual reasons. The use of socially acceptable answers to questions and/or surveys is evident in analyzing the results of hospital employee terminating questionnaires[1] that were conducted by researchers not affiliated with the hospital. In a study conducted at Vanderbilt University Hospital, the results indicate that nurses tend to say they are resigning their position because of marriage, family difficulties or illness, family mobility, and the like rather than indicate that they are leaving as a result of some interpersonal disputes with co-workers or supervisors or a lack of concurrence over administrative or nursing procedures on their unit or in their institution. Three of the major reasons why people give "socially acceptable" causes for leaving, rather than the true one, are (1) they fear retribution by the disclosure of their true feelings (for example, future letters of recommendation will not be complimentary), (2) the person seeking information asks questions in such a manner that the interviewee is forewarned about how the interviewer would like the question to be answered (for example, "You like working in this department, didn't you Ms. Miller?"), or (3) the individual decides to answer the questions in such a manner so as not to adversely affect anyone (or perhaps, to adversely affect someone) or to "rock the proverbial boat." Ajzen and Fishbein (1972) have conducted relevant experiments on this latter situation.

Knowledge

It is essential to determine both the extent and the quality of information or knowledge that persons have about a particular issue or behavior

---

1. These interviewers are used to determine why nurses and other employees leave their positions at the hospital.

before a change can be effectively initiated. There are exceptions to this case: the hospital administration, for instance, can force acceptance and adoption of an innovation by its staff even if the administration does not know anything in advance about the staff's perception of the innovation. In other words, individuals can be forced to use a new piece of equipment or follow new policies or procedures. But that does not mean that they will not consciously and/or unconsciously work to subvert the innovation. If the new procedure introduced in a nursing home is perceived (correctly or incorrectly) by the nursing staff as ultimately affecting their job security, the nurses may tacitly cooperate in initial efforts to implement the procedure. However, they may then work diligently to undermine the very effectiveness of the new procedure. The point is that unless people faced with a social change *accurately* understand the full implications of the change for them, they are likely to respond in unpredictable ways; subversion is a very common response.

Employers can eliminate much of the grief that frequently accompanies the introduction of social changes by obtaining, through interview or survey (formal or informal), employees' perceptions of a proposed change or even their reaction to a hypothetical situation. Tactics of this nature allow the change agent (employer or representative) to anticipate the type of response the change will have. With this knowledge, the supervisor might introduce procedures that will reduce anxiety. For example, many hospitals have recently introduced promotion procedures (for nurses) based on the concept of the career ladder. Older nurses, who were trained in diploma schools of nursing, might perceive this type of promotion system as discriminatory against them. Promotion from step to step is based on proficiency at lower levels; nonetheless, nurses with more education are typically vaulted to higher steps than nurses with less education, regardless of proficiency. To forestall anxiety over this issue, the director of nursing must develop an employee education program (for example, group meetings on all units during all shifts that are led by someone from nursing service) whereby everyone is informed about the proposed new promotion system and its anticipated impact on employees. These meetings should also be designed to reassure different groups that their advancement and job security are not adversely affected by their type of nursing education. The only criterion that will be considered is an individual's performance or achievement at each level.

Lack of knowledge is instrumental in resistance to change if, as mentioned, the change agent does not know how much information the target population has about a particular issue or policy or if the target population has incomplete or erroneous knowledge about a proposed change.

In the latter case, the target population may have inadequate knowledge even though the change agent considered it to be sufficient. This assumption is dangerous and should not be made without assessing the knowledge base of the target population and its disposition for or against the change.

A change agent can determine a target population's knowledge in a variety of ways. One of the best tactics is for the nurse–change agent to meet with supervisors and/or a representative sample of the nursing staff who can serve as informants. These individuals can inform the change agent about the probable responses of the staff to the proposed change. They can also advise the change agent on ways the proposed change should be modified if it is to receive a favorable staff response.

Finally, it is not unusual for a change agent to survey an entire target population to obtain informaton from them regarding their knowledge of various issues, job satisfaction, future behavior, and the like. Surveys of this nature must be conducted in a forthright manner to ensure anonymity. Confidence in the anonymity of the survey can be achieved by the change agent by using an outside research firm to conduct the survey. Whether the change agent or an outside firm conducts the survey, the questionnaires themselves should not contain any information that could identify the respondent. When, for example, there are only a few subjects on each unit being studied, organizational position should probably *not* be requested, because it is obvious that specific individuals could be identified by their responses. In this regard, it should also be pointed out that the institution's Human Subject's Committee should be allowed to scrutinize all research, even in-house research, to protect human rights.

DEVELOPING A NEED FOR CHANGE

Prior to adopting a social change, the organization's administrators must perceive the existence of a change or an innovation and identify a need for an alteration in the status quo.[2] Similar conditions are true for individuals who may adopt behavioral (personal) changes. According to Zaltman and Duncan (1977:226), it is not entirely clear whether the change process or sequence perception of a possible change must precede a need for change or whether a need for change must precede the perception that change is possible or necessary. Do nurses return to nursing school to become nurse practitioners without (1) knowledge of the exis-

---

2. Obviously, some changes begin with the employees, but compared with the proportion that are initiated from the top of the organization (administration), this is a very small number.

tence of this type of role and (2) direct or indirect awareness of the employment needs for nurse practitioners? It is not significant whether perception precedes need (or the reverse), but only that both conditions are
present for an organization or an individual to adopt a change. In other
words, a hospital is likely to introduce a policy of open admissions only
when someone in the facility becomes aware of this type of program for
increasing hospital census *and* when enough significant people in the
organization recognize that something should be done to increase patient
census.

    The recognition of a need for change is a problem when "specific
symptoms are not associated with specific causes or not assigned a high
priority for remedial action" (Zaltman and Duncan, 1977:136). The nurse–
change agent can use various strategies in this effort; the major ones are
reeducation and persuasion. Persuasion and reeducation programs are
used to help people to recognize the need for changing some behavior,
condition, or situation (for example, to stop smoking, decline premarital
sexual relations, breast-feed, eat specific foods, or work more effectively).

    Persuasive strategists use an incentive as the main ingredient in
influencing people to change. When, for example, a hospital administrator wanted to get all the nurses in her hospital to apply only the best
antiseptic procedures, she decided to use a persuasive strategy. She
decided that those units with the lowest infection rates would receive
financial remuneration in the form of a bonus at the end of the year. But
interestingly, the plan was only successful for a year; after the initial
enthusiasm, interest in the program and in the bonus money declined.
Part of the problem with persuasive efforts is that most do not have an
enduring effect (Middlebrook, 1974:192). Unless the behavioral change
is reinforced with additional persuasive efforts, permanence is very
unlikely. The hospital administrator continued her program but now
gives bonuses every 4 months. The results were encouraging. Not all
persuasive strategies are successful; many plans using persuasion do not
work at all (Lee, 1975; Bryk, 1973). Part of the problem is that persuasion
seems to work most effectively with persons less open to change (Kasulis,
1975).

    Reeducation strategies, according to Zaltman and Duncan (1977:111),
typically "involve the unlearning or unfreezing of something prior to
the learning of the new attitude or behavior." This approach assumes
that people are rational beings who can differentiate fact from fantasy
and, as a result, alter their behavior to fit the facts. In other words, reeducation is an approach using unbiased fact to provide individuals with

a "rational justification for action" (Zaltman and Duncan 1977:111). The use of unbiased information differentiates this approach from persuasive strategies. Zaltman and Duncan (1977:122) also pointed out that this approach is most useful when the target population "requires extensive information and skills" before the change can take place. It is also a valuable method for providing people who would be motivated to change if they were provided with appropriate information.

Reeducation is frequently used when people have been made to change their behavior through an administrative decision. For example, the head nurse on a children's unit recently told her staff that she believed it was improper for them to smoke on the unit, even while on break. She believed their smoking provided a poor role model for the young patients. Following her mandate, she had the staff survey the patients about their attitudes toward smoking. The results showed, among other things, that children were likely to smoke if people they respected smoked. Next, the head nurse began showing nonsmoking films to the staff and conducting small group discussions about the liabilities of smoking. The staff, at first very angry with the head nurse's dictum, calmed down considerably when they realized just how harmful their smoking was for themselves and for the children whom they influenced. Many of the nurses gave up smoking entirely after the reeducation plan was initiated. A reeducation strategy has the additional advantage of getting people to change for a lengthy period.

The nurse–change agent can use both reeducation and persuasive strategies in change programs (Chapter 5). A reeducation approach is used first as the principal method for informing the target population about the nature of the problems and the reasons why they "need" to change. The nurse–change agent follows this with a persuasive program designed to obtain the desired change in attitude, condition, or behavior (Zaltman and Duncan 1977:121). In a small, midwestern city, the public health nurses wanted to organize a health fair. In their effort to ensure a large attendance at the fair and to effect positive health-seeking behavior, the nurses decided to use a combined reeducation and persuasion strategy. Their plan was as follows: the nurses prepared several public service announcements for radio and television. These advertisements informed the public about the need for early detection and gave them information about the health fair, including what was provided, the location, and the times it was open (reeducation strategy). At the health fair itself, the nurses attempted to persuade (1) persons who did not have any specific health needs to have a medical checkup every 6 months and (2) persons with problems, including high blood pressure, positive Pap smears, sugar in their blood, and the like, to become aware of the severity of their problems and to immediately consult a physician about treatment. Various tactics were used to achieve these goals. They included: (1) health films, videotapes, and audiovisual presentations concerning the most common illnesses and abnormalities were shown continuously to patients waiting for interviews with physicians or nurses, (2) a diversity of pamphlets was handed out, and (3) each patient met with a physician or nurse who reviewed the results of their health evaluation and strongly urged them to follow a particular health-seeking behavior pattern.

Most likely, an organization (or an individual) will be aware of the existence of a possible change (for example, new expanded roles exist in nursing and graduates from any of the three different nursing programs are eligible for most of them, work stoppage action is a viable alternative for nurses when they are dissatisfied with the status quo, hospital supervisory role vacancies can be filled successfully with RNs from other than baccalaureate graduate pools) even though it has not identified a need for adoption of the change. Need identification is, then, perhaps the single most crucial task of the change agent. If people do not acknowledge their needs on a conscious level, they will not seek means for changing their situation so that their needs can be satisfied.

Differences in people's perception of a problem "will produce differences in opinions about the appropriateness of a given advocated change" (Zaltman and Duncan, 1977:228). Two groups of nurses, then, may perceive the role of the nurse practitioner very differently; one group might oppose it, while the other both favors and encourages its spread throughout nursing. This difference, which need not be based on fact, may result in the first group perceiving the nurse practitioner role as threatening to their own job security (for example, nurse practitioners will ultimately displace all nonextended role nurses), while the second group may envision increased social status for the profession (and themselves) as concomitant to greater health responsibilities being accorded to nurse practitioners.

CREATING A PERCEPTION OF A PROBLEM

In the initial stages of getting an organization or individuals to change their behaviors, the nurse–change agent must stimulate perception that (1) a problem exists and (2) the problem can be solved. The duality of this process is clear in Rosenstock's (1966) *health belief model*, which contends that health-seeking behavior is more likely to be initiated by an individual if he has (1) a high perception of the severity of a disease and his susceptibility to it, (2) a low perception of the presence of barriers to taking recommended action, (3) a high perception of the benefits of taking a recommended action, and (4) been given suggestions for action.

Developing an awareness in an organization or in individuals of the existence of a problem is not always an easy task. Quite frequently, people do not perceive problems as problems. People sometimes may not define a prevailing condition as problematic because they do not perceive the problem as rectifiable. Moreover, people tend to retain their traditional values, which support the status quo. Koss (1954) in his extensive study of health in Regionville (NY) found that a large proportion of people with acknowledge lower back pain did not define their back pain as a problematic illness. When questioned about this discrepancy between their definition or a condition and its actual presence, the general response of the people was that they did not define the condition as illness because their parents, grandparents, and most of their friends who worked in the mines also had the condition. Similar situations exist in nursing: the American Nurses' Association apparently does not believe that small staff nurse representation in its membership is a problem (Miller and Flynn, 1977), even though Miller (1977) reports that staff nurses appear to be forsaking membership in the ANA for membership in nurse special interest groups. Similarly, some nurses may not be easily convinced that nurses are inadequately paid. If they hold this belief, it may be because (1) they have always found nurse wages to be rather modest since service was more important than wages and (2) they do not believe hospitals make much money and, therefore, neither should they.

As mentioned earlier in this chapter, accuracy need not be positively correlated with a person's beliefs. Individuals frequently believe in ideas, conditions, and situations that are not based on sound data. It is the nurse–change agent's role to make people aware of discrepancies between assumptions and reality and to use a change strategy that circumvents this problem (for example, persuasion). At the same time, the nurse–change agent must be able to assure the target population that once they have defined a condition as problematic there are mechanisms for resolving it. Both of these components of the nurse–change agent's role are directly related to efforts to create a need for change within the target population. If nurses (target population) believe, for example, that their employers are committed to guaranteeing them highest wages and, therefore, they can relinquish their responsibility for wage and benefit monitoring, the nurse–change agent will have to help them see the absurdity of this belief. She might illustrate that employers have another more important responsibility to the larger organization, which is to optimize profits for proprietary facilities or to control costs for nonprofit facilities. The employer, to be a fully responsible administrator, must hold down costs, including the salaries of nurses. The nurse–change agent may have to rely on historical experience to clarify the fallacious nature of the nurses' beliefs about employer responsibility. Even if the nurses can be convinced that they must work more aggressively to improve their wages and benefits, the nurse–change agent must present the nurses with a plan by which they will be able to actualize this. In other words, helping nurses to define a need for change carries with it the added challenge to the change agent to have a reasonable plan of action ready for the nurses to act on once the need has been established.

OBJECTIVES OF CHANGE

In developing a plan to implement a social change, it is essential that the change agent conceptualize very clearly the objective(s) of the proposed action. Change for the sake of change, as pointed out in an earlier chapter, is wasteful, inappropriate, and dangerous. However, change with a specific aim or end (objective) allows for optimization of the change. In other words, a change should only be initiated after the change agent and all other persons involved directly and indirectly in planning for the change have agreed on the outcome(s) of the change. It does not follow that nurses who want higher salaries and better employment benefits will gain their objective by going on strike. Perhaps, the demands of the striking nurses will be too expensive for the hospital to pay, and the hospital, like the 60 public general hospitals that closed in the U.S. between 1975 and 1977 (The Nation's Health, 1979), will close. In setting an objective of a change, caution must be used to make sure that the objective is realistic (that is, reachable). If the nurses are successful in organizing a work stoppage, which ultimately results in their losing their jobs, it will not be difficult to imagine how bitter these nurses will be toward this type of change process. Conversely, people lose much of their hesitancy about change when they observe that it is not a personally dangerous phenomenon.

At Status Hospital, one nursing unit was highly ineffective (for example, low staff morale and patient satisfaction and high employee turnover). The administration of the hospital found that this unit was less effective in its cost containment efforts than others in the hospital. As a result of its cost-containment ratings, which were conducted weekly by the management firm managing the hospital, the administration decided to change the organization of the unit by replacing the clinical specialist with a head nurse, replacing three RNs with an LPN and two nurse's aides, and so forth. Even though these and other organizational changes were made in this unit, no significant changes appeared in the cost-containment ratings. Apparently, the administration did not have a clear conceptualization of its objectives before initiating these changes. Perhaps the administration should have asked some of the following questions: "What is the goal of the unit?" "Are the problems in the unit possibly connected with hospital policy instead of with the unit's organization and management? "Could the number and type of patients on the unit (oncology and neurology) be related to the observed problems?"

Further analysis of the above problem ultimately disclosed that historically this unit had placed considerable emphasis on patient-service objectives. The seriousness of the illness of patients on the unit prompted the nursing staff to place low emphasis on profit objectives if not almost disregard them altogether. When the hospital's management was taken over by an outside management firm, renewed emphasis throughout the hospital was placed on profit objectives. One result of this change was that many of the staff on this unit (as well as other staff in the hospital) felt betrayed. They believed that the hospital was now trying to put a price tag on the "right to live." Demoralization increased and staff members showed increased resistance to being accountable for all the supplies required by their patients.

Problems with this unit continued until management realized that even though they changed the organization of the unit, and they did it several times, the problem was more deep-seated than purely staff organization. Progress was made, however, when the administration brought in a psychologist who specialized in death and dying to provide the staff with some group therapy sessions so that they could discuss some of the ethical issues related to working with dying patients. Even patient satisfaction ratings increased as a consequence of the staff's receiving counselling.

POSSIBLE INDIRECT CONSEQUENCES OF CHANGE

The nurse–change agent is responsible for assisting people (for example, patients or staff) to adjust to a social change. But the nurse–change agent must realize that frequently people, even though removed from the direct impact of a change, may experience much uneasiness over possible consequences of the change.

According to Toffler (1970), many people have difficulty in coping with change, especially with rapid change. Whenever a new change program is initiated by a hospital, public health department, nursing home, or any organization, many people related to the organization become uneasy. People express anxiety over social change, regardless of a program's innocent appearance, because past experience, direct or indirect, has shown them that change can have very broad implications.

Quite frequently, some change programs that are directed at a specific target population arouse great anxiety and uneasiness in other members of the organization or society, even when the change will ostensibly not affect these persons. People are reluctant to put a great deal of trust in the word of an organization that tends to abide by the popular cliché of "where there is smoke, there must be fire." In other words, when Smithville Hospital began laying off RNs because of the low patient census, other employees thought that they too would probably be laid off. Naturally, employees become quite insecure when they hear about fellow employees losing their jobs because they wonder when they also will receive their severance notice, even if their employer denies that further lay offs or firings are anticipated.

In another example, a department of health decided to reorganize some of its 30 nurse practitioner clinics located in rural areas. The department decided to improve the administration of nine of these facilities by having one administrator for groupings of three clinics. Prior to this decision, the nurse practitioners at the clinics served as their own administrators. All the employees reported directly to the nurse practitioners, of whom one usually held supervisory status. Under the reorganization, the administrator was to take control of all aspects of the clinics. The nurses would now report to the administrators, even though they usually had no health care experience. The staff at the nine clinics to be changed were quite concerned about the implications of the change in administration. The nurse practitioners were particularly uneasy about it because they believed that the new administrators would not be sensitive to either the health care needs of the patients or to their own professional needs. Just as anxious about this change in administration were the nurse practitioners at the 21 clinics unaffected by the change. Most of the nurses at these clinics believed that this change was but the first step in a plan that would ultimately affect the entire clinic system. Like their colleagues in the clinics that received new administrators, they strongly resented the nonhealth background of the administrators. This group also believed that their clinics required more than a part-time administrator. Although the head of the health department contended that administrators were provided for the nine clinics to correct disorganization and inefficiency, the nurse practitioners could not be appeased. Many of these nurses indicated job dissatisfaction and said they might seek employment elsewhere.

Nurse–change agents have at least two alternatives for dealing with the implications of a change program for persons and/or groups other than the target population. They can choose one of two strategies: (1) not to address their attention to these groups and let them work out their anxiety and concern as best they can, or (2) identify these persons. If the change agent elects the first strategy, the repercussions may be more explosive than anticipated. The reaction of the nontarget population may be so severe, even though without a valid basis, that the entire social change program may have to be revamped or discarded. For example, Smithville Hospital, which laid off some nurses, found that the rest of the staff began to make a mass exodus for other jobs to forestall being laid off. As a result, the hospital was so short staffed that it had to deny further patient admissions. This situation also caused an additional financial shortage that resulted in the hospital's laying off additional employees. The hospital did attempt, unsuccessfully, to hire new staff members to maintain the proper nurse/bed ratio as well as sufficient support staff. Whether or not a self-fulfilling prophecy occurs (that is, staff members not layed off believe they will be laid off and because of their activities are eventually laid off), it is imperative to understand that allowing the nontarget population to become anxious can have serious organizational implications.

Although most change agents probably do not intercede with nontarget populations, their doing so would be a highly desirable procedure because it would ensure the success of their change program. A well-conceived, well-planned, and well-implemented change program should not fail because of the emotional reaction of the nontarget population. The nurse–change agent should follow these steps in dealing with this issue: first, the change agent should attempt to identify, before the change is implemented, which nontarget population might feel uneasy about the change. Second, the nurse–change agent, anticipating some reaction from specific nontarget populations, should meet with these groups to explain the nature of the change program, its parameters, and its consequences. The change agent should be ready at this time to answer all questions posed by the nontarget population to reduce anxiety. If the issue is macroscopic enough, the change agent may find it valuable to request that a top level administrator be available for input at these discussions. Finally, the change agent should maintain communication with the nontarget populations to keep them informed of the progress of the program and, at the same time, to be able to assess their reaction to it.

DEVELOPING RAPPORT WITH THE TARGET POPULATION

Unquestionably, change is not always greeted with enthusiasm. People tend to fear change because of the uncertainty of the consequences for them (that is, loss of job, alteration in job status, change in habits) even when they are advised that the change will have no major impact on them. Nurse–change agents can play a major role in modifying the concern people generate over a proposed social change. It is the change agent's responsibility to reduce their fear and anxiety and to prepare them for the change. They can accomplish this by first establishing rapport with them. If, for example, the target population trusts the nurse–change agents and their motives, it is more likely to be much more cooperative in accepting the change program. If, on the other hand, the target population distrusts the change agent, there is a greater chance that it will resist the change program. Several factors influence the nurse–change agent's ability to establish rapport with the target population, including (1) the effective use of two-way communication, (2) the ability to empathize with others, (3) homophily with the target population and with the change team, (4) the ability to work through opinion leaders, and (5) credibility.

Effective two-way communication

Two-way communication is communication through which the change agent provides information to the target population and it, in turn, shares its ideas and feelings with the change agent. Two-way communication is effective if what is being communicated is meaningful to both parties. The change agent should recognize that only giving "lip service" to the philosophy of two-way communication will not satisfy people's needs for active involvement. People are most positive toward a change program if they have had some meaningful input into developing the program.

Empathizing with others

Empathy refers to the change agent's ability "to identify with others, to share their perspectives and feelings vicariously" (Zaltman and Duncan, 1977:193). If the change agents can empathize with the target population, they are more likely to select the best strategy for implementing the change program as well as interrelating with team members and with the nontarget population.

Homophily

Homophily exists when the nurse–change agent has personal and social attitudes and characteristics that are similar to those of the target population. Homophily assists in effecting better communication because common meanings, attitudes, and beliefs are shared to a greater degree than when heterophily exists (Rogers and Bhomuk, 1971:529). The difficulty for any one change agent to be "all things to all people" makes the change agent team an ideal method for establishing rapport with a diversified target population. The change agent team is useful since nurses with varying backgrounds (for example, 2-, 3-, and 4-year program graduates) and characteristics can work with different target population subgroups with whom they share homophily. It is also advantageous for the nurse–change agent to be at least partially homogeneous with the members of the change agent team.

Opinion leaders

An opinion leader is an individual in a group (there may be more than one) to whom other persons in the group look for advice and information. People look to opinion leaders when they are uncertain about a situation or a decision. If the opinion leader(s) advocates nurses working 12-hour shifts instead of 8-hour shifts, the so-called "rank and file" is very likely to concur. To obtain the support of the opinion leader, the nurse–change agent may have to make her a part of the change program so that she will have a vested interest in its success. An opinion leader can greatly facilitate (or hinder) a social change program. The nurse–change agent must identify these individuals and convince them to support the program.

Credibility

It is essential that nurse–change agents develop truth and technical credibility with the target population if they are to establish rapport and ultimately be able to implement the change program. Truth and technical credibility are different. *Truth credibility* refers to whether or not the target population thinks that the nurse–change agents honestly believe the change they are advocating is appropriate (Zaltman and Duncan, 1977:203). *Technical credibility* refers to whether or not the target population believes that the nurse–change agent has "the requisite information and skills to acertain that the change advocated will in fact work" (Zaltman and Duncan, 1977:203).

The more the nurse–change agents use the above factors, the greater the likelihood that they will be able to establish rapport with the target population. The following scenario illustrates how one nurse–change agent used many of these factors in her efforts to change the status of an obstetrics unit. The nurses in Metropolitan Hospital's obstetrics unit were told by the director of nursing (nurse–change agent) that the number of women having children at the hospital had decreased dramatically over the past few years and, as a result, action needed to be taken to reduce the amount of money lost. She explained to the nurses on the three shifts how much money the hospital was losing and also discussed the rather bleak future for obstetrics units in the city since the birthrate had dropped 20% in the last decade. The nurse–change agent told the nurses that neither she nor the hospital's administrator wanted any of them to lose their jobs; the hospital felt a strong obligation to its employees and would find other positions for them. She further explained how the hospital had dealt with similar situations in the past and even provided the group with the names of nurses whose positions had been terminated but who had been retained. "We have nurses working at Metropolitan Hospital for over 20 years, and we are very dedicated to you all," she said (credibility and empathy). She also told the nurses that she understood their uneasiness with the situation because she had a family she supported and thus she knew how important their job was. She also said that she respected the fact that all nurses do not like working on certain shifts and in certain units. "No one," she said, "would be arbitrarily moved. Everyone would be given at least one or two choices of units where there is an opening." She then went on to say, "Before we make a decision about closing or altering this unit, we would like to get your suggestions on what you think would be the best solution to this difficult problem (empathy and homophily). If you have any ideas on how we can retain this unit, let us hear them. I have decided that there are a few people on each unit to whom I would like you to give your ideas. Tell them orally or in writing what your ideas are, and I will meet with them next week. After our meeting and after I have had sufficient time to assess your ideas and other options open to us, (for example, seeking federal funds), I will come back and discuss the situation again (opinion leaders and communication)."

DEVELOPING REALISTIC EXPECTATIONS FOR GOAL ATTAINMENT

According to Watzlawick, Weakland, and Fisch (1974:110), basic to any successful change program is "a clear definition of the concrete change to be achieved." Implicit in their formulation is the call for concrete and "reachable goals." Unrealistic, and therefore unreachable, goal setting results in the problem of the target population not really knowing what its goals are regarding changing a situation. Vagueness about goals make achieving them twice as difficult. For instance, the nurses at University Hospital were dissatisfied with their job situation and called the representative from their state nurses' association to help them. When the nurse–change agent (representative from the state nurses' association) asked the nurses to specify the change they wanted in their job situation, they responded as follows: "We want better communication with nursing service and the hospital's administration, increased job benefits, and more satisfaction from our jobs." When the nurse–change agent pressed the nurses for more specific goals, they were unanimous only in regards to "higher wages and elimination of day-shift assignments based only on seniority." This example illustrates the problem the nurse–change agent can encounter when the target population has not sufficiently framed its goals. Ideally the reframing of poorly conceptualized goals should take place during the planning stage of the change program.

The wise nurse–change agent will appreciate a target population's need to discuss goal development. Time spent in doing this is time well spent. The better a target population's focus on a goal, the more efficient and effective the process of change implementation, and this in turn results in a more effective change.

SUMMARY

In this chapter, the process of implementing a change was discussed. By building on the material discussed in Chapter 5, the change agent proceeds to implement change. She starts by assessing the change target system, realizes if there is a need to create a desire for change or if that desire already exists, and develops objectives, which is followed by a discussion of indirect consequences of change. This chapter also discusses the need to develop rapport with the target population and the development of realistic expectations for goal attainment.

Chapter 7

AFTER THE CHANGE HAS BEEN IMPLEMENTED

Nurse–change agents may wonder whether the change programs they have planned and implemented will become a permanent part of the social system or if they will disappear shortly after they have relinquished their change efforts. Unfortunately, little evidence is found in the literature regarding how many change agents can ensure the survival of their change programs after they have moved on to another project. Few change agents sufficiently understand the process by which change endures. In fact, Lippitt, Watson, and Westley (1958:218) concluded that "Probably more time, money and effort are lost at this point in the change process than at any other." Even though this statement was made in the late 1950s, there is little evidence to suggest any increased interest in the problem of change stability; most books on social change do not discuss this topic. This chapter will discuss what Lippitt, Watson, and Westley (1958) consider to be the final two stages in the change process: (1) the stabilization of change and (2) the termination of the change relationship. This chapter will also discuss those conditions or factors that work to prevent the survival of change and the termination of the change relationship.

STABILITY OF CHANGE AND PREVENTING DISCONTINUANCE

A variety of factors affect the achievement of stability of a change program. Some of these factors cannot be directly influenced by the nurse–change agent, while others can. Those outside the nurse–change agent's influence include: (1) whether or not the change spreads to other neighboring systems or subsystems of the target population, (2) whether or not the change program receives a positive, that is, effective, evaluation, (3) whether or not the target population initially experienced a painful and difficult change process, and (4) program inertia. The major activities that the nurse–change agent controls are: (1) making the change program visible and (2) providing all members of the target population with information about the consequences of the change.

Nurse–change agent in control

Making the change program visible. Change program visibility is usually the task of the nurse–change agents. They are responsible for publicity and, accordingly, must develop a sufficiently innovative advertising plan to raise the visibility of and the familiarity with the change program. If people are familiar with a change program, they are likely to be less resistant and more at ease with it. The more publicity a program receives, the more likely the target population is to perceive the change program as a part of its environment. After the target population has been thoroughly bombarded (and therefore indoctrinated) by the publicity, it is less likely to reject the change as something unusual or new.

In one instance, nursing service at a Veterans' Administration hospital wanted its staff members to participate voluntarily in a program designed to improve their understanding of nursing service and the hospital. The administration proposed a 3-day workshop. A nurse in the department of continuing education was given the responsibility of attracting the nursing service staff members to the workshop. To ensure participation in the workshop, the nurse–change agent developed the idea of an owl as the logo for the program. All literature about the program included a picture of the owl and frequently included sayings attributed to it. The staff was also told that at the conclusion of the workshop they would receive an attractive button with the picture of the owl on it that they were encouraged to wear as a symbol of accomplishment. The program successfully attracted staff members to one of the workshops; apparently, everyone wanted to display the owl button. Only a few nurses did not care about being identifiable in their unit or service as lacking the owl button.

Other methods for publicizing change programs include the use of posters and other visual aides placed where the target population is likely to see them. Many nurse–change agents use staff, faculty, or other in-house institutional bulletins or newsletters. This method is effective because persons who receive bulletins or newsletters from organizations with which they are affiliated usually read them. Even a personal letter or memo from an administrator (for example, a dean, director of nursing, or hospital/nursing home administrator) may be helpful in increasing the target population's knowledge and understanding of the change program.

Providing information about the consequences of the change. The nurse–change agent must realize that the results of some change programs may be more easily perceived by the target population than others. Yet it is the responsibility of the nurse–change agent to make the results of a change program as conspicuous as possible to all members of the target population. The more a target population is thoroughly informed about the successful outcome or result of a change program in which it participated, the more likely it will accept the change as a permanent part of its social system. People tend to support programs that they believe[1] to be successful because of their personal satisfaction in knowing that a program is worthwhile and because they played a part in its development and success (Lippitt, Watson, and Westley, 1958).

One method of helping the target population assess the impact of a change program is for the nurse–change agent to have the target population recall the state of the system before the change program was introduced (that is, what was the unit like before it was reorganized, or how whites related to blacks prior to the implementation of the new program designed to reduce racial tension, and so forth). According to Lippitt, Watson, and Westley (1958:229), research feedback allows the target population to contrast conditions before and after the change. The nurse–change agent must question the target population about whether or not the change has corrected the problem and contributed to an improved state. One nurse–change agent, for example, was having difficulty convincing her staff that the physical renovation and rearrangement of the unit was a success. The nurses on the unit (target population) seemed to think that the previous arrangement was better than the present one. They complained that they had difficulty finding the new location of equipment and supplies. The nurse–change agent called a special staff meeting and had the staff describe the physical arrangement of their unit before it was changed. The staff recalled that the decision to rearrange the unit occurred because it did not provide adequate security for drugs and, because some patient rooms were inadequately furnished. The staff also indicated, after further discussion, that these problems had been resolved by the rearrangement and renovation. The nurse–change agent agreed with the staff that the difficulty in locating equipment and supplies was troublesome but suggested that after they become familiar with the new storeroom and drug supply location, they would be happy with the arrangement. Following the meeting, the nurse–change agent noted that the number of complaints about the rearrangement of the unit declined markedly.

---

1. The *actual* success of the program is irrelevant.

When a target population is small, as in the case of a single nursing unit, the nurse–change agent will find it easy to keep the target population informed about the change program by holding regular evaluation meetings. At these meetings, which can be part of a regular meeting or held as a special meeting, details of the change program, that is, methodology, data interpretation, and so forth, can be shared with the group.

Nurse–change agent without control

The spread of the change program to other systems or subsystems. If a change introduced on one unit in a hospital is adopted voluntarily by one or more units, the staff on the original unit (target population) will exhibit increased likelihood to perceive the change as worth sustaining. The opposite does not necessarily hold true: innovations that one group adopts, but others do not, are not automatically discarded. But when one group adopts another group's change, the first group feels very proud that it had the insight to introduce and accept the change first. Under this condition, then, it would be unlikely for the change to be rejected.

In the early 1970s, a few schools of nursing changed their administrative organization from departmentalization to a division-program arrangement. The schools taking the lead in these programs adopted the change because, among other things, it eliminated the power of the department chairperson and offered the school more faculty and program flexibility. During the 8 years since some schools adopted this innovative organizational system, other schools have also examined and adopted this same organization. Interestingly, some of the schools that originally adopted the new organization began to grow weary of it. In at least one school in which the dean and her cabinet were discussing a return to a departmental type organization, many faculty members questioned how it would look for the school to do this when it had been instrumental in helping other schools to adopt division-program organization. As a result of the ensuing discussion, the faculty and the administration decided to keep the division-program organization. Thus a change was retained despite the fact that it was deemed less desirable than the condition existing before it took place.

The program receives a positive evaluation. As mentioned earlier, a target population is more likely to accept a change that it perceives to have positive outcomes. Informing the target population about the results of the program evaluation is one mechanism for illustrating program success (or failure). Unfortunately, nurse–change agents cannot assure target populations that change programs will have successful consequences; they work for this outcome, but it does not always come to fruition and thus cannot be predetermined as a definite occurrence.

When the program is successful, it is the change agent's duty to inform the target population about the success. A program that is considered successful is more likely to be institutionalized than an unsuccessful one because the target population develops ownership over a successful change, promotes it, and assists in persuading others to adopt it. The best indicator of successful change is its exhortation by those affected by it, rather than its promotion by the change agent.

Effects of a painful and difficult change process. Lippitt, Watson, and Westley (1958:230) observe that a target population that has experienced a very trying change program "will probably want to keep the fruits of its labor." In other words, the greater the target population's vested interests in a change as a result of expended energy, anxiety, or stress, the more likely the target population is to maintain the change.

In many weight management programs, participants (target population) are forced to spend a sizable amount of money to join the program. This contribution ostensibly establishes the participants' vested interest in completing the program because they will receive all but a minimal amount back at the conclusion of the program if they participate in all phases of it. How effective is this? Since it is common knowledge that weight reduction is one of the hardest changes for people to undertake and, even worse, to maintain, one's expectations have to be modest. Yet weight reduction experts seem to believe that a financial investment serves as both a commitment and an incentive.

At New Hospital, the administration found that the morale of the unit clerks and managers was inordinately low. It was decided that something had to be done to improve this condition. After considerable discussions, it was discovered that the clerks and managers not only felt inferior to the nursing staff but that this feeling adversely affected their job performance. The administration decided that by giving the unit clerks and managers a status symbol, they would feel less insecure and work more efficiently. It was decided to require all unit clerks and managers to wear blazers, which were to be purchased from the hospital. The purchase price, however, would be returned if the person changed positions or employment and could no longer wear the blazer. The hospital administration believed that by requiring unit clerks and managers to purchase blazers they would have a greater vested interest in wearing them (and in exhalting their importance) than if the hospital gave the new "uniforms" to them. After all, the reasoning went, other employees at the hospital also purchase their uniforms; therefore, this procedure did not constitute preferential treatment. The action of the hospital's administration apparently was successful since measured job satisfaction and job efficiency increased among this group and the turnover rate decreased.

Program inertia. Lippitt, Watson, and Westley (1958:230) have observed that "a changed state of affairs produces changed expectations and satisfactions (among persons affected by a change) and these in turn tend to maintain change." In other words, if some unit or group is drastically altered (for example, a 25% increase [or decrease] in one group compared with another group, a 20% increase in the birth [or death] rate, and the like) some changes will occur in the orientation, values, attitudes, and/or goals of the group. In turn, these changes will alter the group's expectations and/or satisfactions. Since the group's expectations or satisfactions have changed to meet its new orientation, values, attitudes, or goals, the group will attempt to maintain these changes because of their congruence with the new status quo.

For example, the director of nursing at Hillside Hospital increased the percentage of graduate nurses with baccalaureate degrees on the hospital's three medical units. She had heard from colleagues, later reinforced in a journal article she read, that nurses with baccalaureate degrees were better prepared to make difficult decisions than nurses with only diplomas or associates degrees. Furthermore, the literature seemed to suggest that nurses with baccalaureate degrees were also more ready to take on responsibility than other nurses.

The director of nursing gradually replaced all the nurses without baccalaureate degrees on these units. There was no overt reason to make this shift except to keep nurses with baccalaureate degrees together. The director believed that nurses with baccalaureate degrees adversely influenced the behavior and attitude of other nurses in regard to the hospital's administration, and she wanted to avoid a mix of nurses. The head nurses on these units, who also had baccalaureate degrees, soon noticed a major difference in their staff's orientation to nursing, in "taking orders" from physicians, and in the "tried and trusted" ways of doing things. The nurses with baccalaureate degrees questioned everything: how supplies and drugs were dispensed, the value of primary care nursing over other methods for giving care, the use (and abuse) of LPNs and aides, the distribution of days off and day shifts, whether physicians were adequate, and so forth. They were also quick to point out how they had improved the quality of care on their units. Overtly and covertly, they indicated that they liked the idea of having only nurses with baccalaureate degrees on their units.

After 6 months, several of the nurses with baccalaureate degrees resigned because their husbands' jobs required relocation. The director of nursing could not find replacements. She told the head nurses that they had a choice: take a nurse with an associate degree, a nurse with a diploma, or wait until a nurse with a baccalaureate degree was recruited. The head nurses and the affected staff voted unanimously to wait for a nurse with a baccalaureate degree.

This example is presented to illustrate how a change can act to self-perpetuate itself. The nurses with baccalaureate degrees felt more comfortable with their "own" and, accordingly, were willing to be short on staff to ensure their unit's homogeneity. This example indicates that the response to change is similar, regardless of the makeup of the target population.

ACHIEVING A TERMINAL RELATIONSHIP

The role of the nurse–change agent is a temporary one; when individuals accept this position, they must have a mutual understanding (with the target population or whoever hired them) about the length of time "the relationship will last and about the kind of work each partner will be expected to do" (Lippitt, Watson, and Westley, 1958:223-224). Nurse–change agents must terminate the change relationship with the target population for two major reasons: (1) other change programs that require attention and (2) the target population is ready to develop some of its own problem-solving techniques. The amount of time they will work with a particular change program depends on (1) the nature of the change and (2) the level of resistance to stabilizing the change: the more a target population resists adopting a change, the longer the nurse–change agent will have to work with the group.

Nurse–change agents cannot "nurse" the target population indefinitely. At some point, they must elect to withhold additional assistance to allow the target population to make its own adjustments. This does not always present a problem because sometimes the target population rejects the change agent's assistance. Frequently, however, nurse–change agents find it difficult to terminate a relationship with the target population. They may enjoy the relationship with the group, and they may fear that a break in their association with it will jeopardize full institutionalization of the change program. On the other hand, they probably recognize that by remaining with the change program longer than necessary, they will establish an even closer and more dependent relationship with the target population (Lippitt, Watson, and Westley, 1958:234).

Nurse–change agents typically perform their change agent tasks part-time. They usually have other full-time jobs such as head nurse, nurse supervisor, director (or assistant director) of nursing, staff nurse, and director of continuing education. They cannot devote all their time and effort for an extended period to the change program because of other job responsibilities. Only infrequently is the nurse–change agent a full-time role; in that case, the person is probably an outside consultant because most organizations do not use funds for full-time support of such a role. However, a few hospitals do employ a nurse researcher who frequently acts as change agent.

If nurse–change agents do not terminate the change relationship with the target population, the latter may not be able to stabilize and maintain a change in the future without a similar close relationship. Foresightful nurse–change agents know that the change relationship with the target population will end; they are likely to help the group develop some of its own "problem solving methodology" (Lippitt, Watson, and Westley, 1958:235). They might, for example, teach the methodology of problem and need diagnosis. The advantage of greater target population involvement in the change process, which occurs only when the change agent intends to end the change relationship, is that it "will serve in the future to help (the target population) . . . meet the problems which will continue to arise as long as the . . . (target population) whether individual organism or social system exists" (Lippitt, Watson, and Westley, 1958:236).

An interesting example of a nurse–change agent who did not want to relinquish activities with a particular target population occurred at Silvan Park Hospital. The director of nursing found that many of her head nurses and nurse supervisors were deficient in effective communication skills. She decided to provide a series of communication workshops for this group. At a staff meeting, she explained to the group why she believed that they needed to improve their skills in this area. She did not point out individual deficiencies; instead, she developed the issue of "need" as a managerial problem requiring constant upgrading. The entire staff accepted the director's challenge to take the workshops. Almost without exception, they indicated that the workshops were highly relevant and worthwhile. Before and after the series of workshops, they were required to take a brief written test of their knowledge of communication theory. The testing showed that the group had no solid understanding of communication theory before the workshops and had learned a significant amount from them. The director was not satisfied with the results of the evaluation, however. She reasoned that observations of how the nurses actually handled communication would be indicative of the effectiveness of the workshops. She decided to assess this herself by making a series of observations on each of the units.

During the following month, she spent a total of 85 hours making observations of head nurses and nurse supervisors. The head nurses and supervisors were unnerved by the constant presence (their perception) of the director of nursing on their floor. In fact, many thought that the director was spying on them instead of "evaluating" their interpersonal communication skills. Many of the nurses were also concerned because problems that needed the attention of the director of nursing (for example, personnel, incentive raises and the like) were not being attended to. "She was too busy seeing if we communicated appropriately to communicate effectively with us," said one head nurse. The situation became so chaotic that the nurses requested a meeting with the director. They told her of their concerns and said that her activities were causing more distress among the staff than the previous state of their communication. The director did not initially understand that her presence, or "mothering of the change program," was problematic. After it had been pointed out to her that her constant presence on their unit was not good for staff morale and that they thought that she was not doing her own job effectively, the director realized that she had involved herself too extensively and inappropriately in the change program. Yet, the evaluative idea was sound.

Nurse–change agents may not want to terminate the change relationship with the target population because they value the emotional rewards of being a leader and/or because of their idea that the target population is not yet ready to be on its own. On the other hand, the target population is likely to reach a point at which it will decide that it wants to stand on its own feet because it is "capable of carrying through the planned changes (itself)" (Lippitt, Watson, and Westley, 1958:345).

As indicated, it is essential that nurse–change agents deliberately terminate the change relationship with the target population. They may, however, experience some difficulty in this endeavor because of the part-time nature of their role. In most cases, nurse–change agents continue to interact with the target population after they have terminated the change relationship simply because they are around. Under this circumstance, it would be easy for them to lapse back into the change agent role unless they make a concerted effort not to do so. They must tell the target population that even though they are still available for consultation, they are no longer acting as a change agent. Obviously, a nurse–change agent who does not have contact with the target population after ending the change relationship does not have to contend with the group's "cry for help."

In the process of terminating the change relationship, nurse–change agents may find it helpful to remove themselves from the relationship slowly, as opposed to terminating the relationship all at once. During this process, they must clearly explain to the target population that it is time to end the change relationship with the group. They should inform the group that even though they will no longer be directing the change program, they intend to continue to consult with the group and periodically examine the progress of the change.

To make the transition easier from having a nurse–change agent to not having one, nurse–change agents might train an individual or individuals in the target population to take their place. This person would, in essence, be an apprentice change agent whose first change role would involve her own group. Thus, it is important that this person be accepted by the group and have demonstrated an ability to relate well to it. This person would not only be able to help effect the change, but she would also be able to learn the nurse–change agent role.

RESISTANCE TO CHANGE

A discussion that does not consider resistance to change "leaves an incomplete picture" (Zaltman, Duncan, and Holbek, 1973:85). Many efforts directed toward implementing change programs, including the spread of new information or procedures, fail because the perceived ratio of benefits to liabilities is not sufficient to induce people to accept the proposed change. It is also fair to say that many proposed changes do not succeed in being adopted by the target population because they just do not do what they are purported to do. In this section, some of the most important factors and conditions influencing resistance to change, especially implementing and stabilizing the change program, will be discussed.

Resistance to change can easily be recognized as the hallmark of many institutions and individuals in our society. While nursing may not collectively be resistant to change, it is nevertheless a reality that many nurses and many administrative structures in which nurses function are indeed characterized as resistant to change. If we believe that professions are committed to the welfare of the recipients of their services, it goes without saying that resistance to change is a contradiction to that principle. One cannot be resistant to change and at the same time be concerned with progress and the welfare of the recipient of one's services.

Two of the reasons why nurses have a wide range of change orientations is that the occupation involves at least two generations in age and includes three major routes of preparation. These two factors account for a wide variation in background and a great disparity in age and socialization, all resulting in a diversity of outlooks.

Resistance to change is reflected in one's sense of security. Yesterday's woman was not very secure, particularly not when functioning in the labor market. Thus, her resistance to change may have been exaggerated.

Today's woman finds herself in a different situation. Being in the labor market is becoming increasingly more acceptable, even desirable. Being a woman who makes it on her own has suddenly become a measure of consciousness that is shared by large segments of the nursing profession. Thus resistance to change is probably more visible because there are many more who would overcome this resistance and move forward demanding and implementing change. On the other hand, it is also known that as one's resistance to change becomes an object of conflict, the resistance itself represents a perspective that is tied socially to oneself and one's self-respect. Proclaiming the need for change may intensify the resistance of those who do not wish to change.

Zaltman and Duncan (1977:63) define resistance to change as "any conduct that serves to maintain the status quo in the face of pressure to alter the status quo." But as Zander (1966:544) points out, "all behavior which opposes change is not necessarily resistance." Change that is opposed for logical reasons that are based on well-supported facts is not resistance but rational behavior. For example, a nurse clinician with an earned doctorate in pharmacology is told that a new drug procedure is to be used in the hospital. She vigorously resists the change because she knows from her own research and reading that the new procedure is inferior to the present one. According to Zander, this nurse clinician would not be a change resistor because a resistor fights change in an effort to protect herself "against the consequences of change . . . ." Certainly, from the above example, we cannot know if there were other underlying reasons for the nurse clinician's resistance, but given the information we have, it appears as if she is not resisting the change to protect herself against the change but because she considers it dysfunctional.

Any proposed change that threatens the beliefs, attitudes, values, or behaviors central to a target population is likely to result in resistance by the target population (Rokeach, 1968). By and large, changes of this dimension threaten the target population's prestige, power, authority, security, financial viability, traditions, and so forth sufficiently so that it feels compelled to initiate some protective action to shield or guard itself from the consequences of the proposed change. For example, an attempt to change the color of the nurse's uniform would meet with greater resistance than an attempt to change the shape of the nurse's cap. While the color white has been associated traditionally with nursing and thus is central to the nurse's self-concept and professional image, the shape of the nurse's cap has not been so venerated. When nursing students propose changing the shape of their school's cap to improve its safety or attractiveness, there may be some resistance but not an overwhelming amount because nurses do not feel highly threatened by the change

(Bevona, 1980). On the other hand, changing graduate nurses' uniforms to navy blue, particularly in the hospital, would meet with much resistance, both by nurses and the public they serve.

Where resistance starts

Resistance to change can be caused by: (1) behavior of the change agent, (2) unclear change program, (3) forces favoring or opposing change, (4) maintenance of the status quo, (5) ignorance, (6) past experience, (7) lack of goal consensus, (8) lack of felt need and insufficient economic resources, and (9) passive resistance.

Behavior of the change agent. A major factor, easily neglected in attempts to determine the nature of change resistance, is the behavior of the change agent. According to Zaltman and Duncan (1977:62), change agent error may be more instrumental in eliciting target population resistance to a change than is commonly recognized. Little is known about change agent error because the change agent is likely "to attribute 'blame' or 'fault' for resistance to the client or target group . . ." (Zaltman and Duncan, 1977:62). The change agent can commit a variety of errors that might have a negative impact on the change program. However, it is unlikely that anyone would suspect that the reason for the target population's resistance was caused by the change agent. Only infrequently is the target population asked why they are resisting the proposed change. Change agents, on the other hand, are usually required to account for a target population's resistance to a change and it would be most unusual to identify themselves as the problem. Some of the errors nurse–change agents might make that could lead to target population change resistance include: (1) no communication of the nature of the problem or its relevance, need, and/or expected consequences, (2) no communication of trust or competence, (3) appearance of "looking down" on the target population, (4) lack of understanding of the extent of the target population's capacity to implement the change (Zaltman and Duncan, 1977:62).

Resistance to change increases when the nurse–change agent makes the target population feel that the proposed change is neither their own nor to be run by them. In other words, when the target population thinks it is responsible for initiating and implementing a proposed change, quick adoption can be expected. Nurses are very likely to resist an innovation that they do not feel any responsibility for or that does not provide for their input; usually the more involvement from them, the increased likelihood that they will adopt the new program, skill, and the like.

Many innovations have been rejected by a nurse target population that felt alienated from the entire change process. For example, at Central Hospital, staff members on several units were told by a nurse–change agent to use standardized (or structured) nursing care plans. (These are care plans that have been developed by someone other than the nurse providing the care for patients with particular conditions. Unstructured nursing care plans, on the other hand, are developed by a staff nurse for particular patients.) The staff members of the units affected by this change, almost unanimously, told the nurse–change agent that using standardized nursing care plans made them feel like robots; there is little professional judgment involved in following the direction of a card instead of one's own knowledge and experience. When the nurse–change agent persisted in her efforts, the nurses sought the assistance of the district and the state nurses' associations. With the assistance of these groups, the staff nurses were able to pressure the director of nursing into bringing in an outside review group to assess the advantages and disadvantages of the standardized nursing care plan. The review group concluded that the unstructured nursing care plan was superior to the standardized plan if the nurses using them were capable of preparing their own care plans and making them more specific and flexible to meet their patients' problem(s).

Unclear change program. Nurse–change agents can expect resistance to the change program if they do not clarify the nature of the change (and its consequences). Although we have already indicated the importance of communicating the expected consequences of the change program to the target population, it will be restated again through several examples.

At City Hospital, a change in billing procedures required one department to relinquish some of its responsibilities for processing Medicare and Medicaid billing. The responsibilities were now to be shared with another department. The change was announced in a brief statement sent to the department by the hospital's administrator. The reaction to this change was immediate; the members of the first department deplored their having to give up some of their responsibilities. The employees were reacting to insufficient information: was their work unsatisfactory? Was the department going to be eliminated and would they lose their jobs? Since no one took the time to inform them of the reason for the change, that is, the government was requiring additional justification of Medicare and Medicaid bills that could be better supplied by an office composed of people who understood patient records, the target population immediately jumped to conclusions that resulted in resistance to the change.

In West General Hospital, a small rural hospital, the head nurses, charge nurses, and nurse supervisors were provided special training in human relations techniques. The director of nursing thought that a course of this nature would assist her administrative staff in treating their personnel better. All indications from the nurses taking the course were that they liked it. The director found, however, that few of the nurse administrators actually used any of their new skills on the job. She said, "They know human relations techniques but don't use them, and I don't know why." She decided to survey the target population to try and determine why they were not using their new techniques. The reasons included: (1) they were not convinced that the consequences of using human relations techniques would actually benefit their units, (2) they were satisfied with the status quo, and (3) they felt insecure in "coddling" their staff. Even though the hospital had spent a large amount of money developing a human relations course for its administrative staff, it forgot to clarify all the actual and possible goals, issues, and consequences of the program.

Forces favoring or opposing change. Although this condition may not sound as if it is prevalent, it occurs frequently in health care settings. Competing forces in a hospital, nursing home, public health agency, or school of nursing compete with one another for both scarce resources and power and influence. One major avenue through which one competing force strives to obtain more power and influence than another is by championing or challenging newly proposed ideas, programs, or processes. In other words, change programs and processes are used as pawns in the efforts of these groups to achieve their goals, that is, more power and influence. They evaluate a change proposal, not in terms of how it will enhance the organization, but how it will benefit their own interests. This competition for power can be explained through the following examples:

1. The administration of a hospital, after evaluating the work schedule of the 12-hour day, 7-day week, 1 week on and 1 week off, decides that it is better (for administration) than the traditional 5-day week of 40 hours. Accordingly, the administration launches a campaign to convince employees of the benefits of the new working schedule. The union to which most of the employees belong, except for the registered nurses, decides that it does not favor the new program because it did not think of the idea and management did not discuss the advantages and disadvantages of it before suggesting the change to the employees. The union, therefore, begins a campaign denouncing the proposed change. Employees do not know what to do; they are bombarded with conflicting reports regarding the benefits and liabilities of the program. Not until the union and the administration of the hospital met to discuss the issue were the employees free from the competing forces of the two groups.

2. A nurse practitioner employed by a school of nursing wants to spend a portion of each week practicing nursing while the school's

dean wants her to concentrate her efforts on teaching and research. The dean believes that the nurse practitioner faculty member can best serve the school as a teacher-researcher, while the nurse practitioner believes that she needs to practice to optimize her practice role. Although the nurse practitioner tells the dean that it is more important for her to develop her nursing skills than to teach, the dean refuses to compromise and the nurse practitioner resigns.

3. A registered nurse wants to attend graduate school but is told by the faculty that it is better to work and get some nursing experience before entering graduate school. Although the nurse meets with the admission's committee, she cannot change their view toward the value of experience. Therefore, she applies to another graduate program and is accepted.

Maintenance of the status quo. Nurses insist on maintaining the status quo because it is representative of a position, of a span of control, or of a status that might have to be abandoned if change were to occur. Because many nurses find it difficult, if not impossible, to change, they deny the ultimate benefit from such change not only in terms of improved patient care, but also in terms of their own status. They lack confidence in their ability to participate in change and, therefore, find themselves relegated to the only role that they understand and have experience in: resisting the change. Thus, vested interest may be based on reality-oriented conclusions or, perhaps more frequently, on conclusions that are not found in reality but that are based in fear of the unknown and in lack of self-confidence. In addition, nurses may resist an innovation (". . . an idea, practice or object perceived as new by the individual" [Rogers and Shoemaker, 1971:19]) because they think that it may have some negative influence on their social or employment situation (compare with Zaltman, Duncan, and Holbek, 1973:86). For instance, nurses may perceive outsiders as a serious personal threat. Consultants are frequently placed in this category even if they are nursing consultants. Consultants are seen as posing a threat because they may be critical of the nurses' role performance or they may suggest an alteration in the nurses' job or work.

Ignorance. Basically, continued learning and self-directed personal growth is a very new concept in nursing. In the past, nurses did not keep up with new developments. In fact, years ago when nurses graduated, they were made to believe that they had finished learning and now were completed products. This concept is still quite prevalent. It is not as yet a practice by very many nurses to further their knowledge, enlarge their knowledge base, and be informed regarding current developments in nursing and related fields. Nurses do appreciate societal expectations that require change. They are also aware of inherent factors in institutional and professional development that make change almost inevitable, for example, computerization or the automation of activities that previously were done by hand. Yet, many nurses choose to live from day to day, not projecting future events or even preparing themselves for their inevitable occurrence.

Past experience. The effectiveness of change is most frequently interpreted in terms of one's own experience. If a situation demanding change is not too disimilar from one that has been part of a person's experience, that person is likely to draw on this experience and form an attitude in accordance with it. If the experience was positive, the person is more likely to view change as something desirable. Conversely, if the experience was negative, change will be rejected. In addition, experiences of a positive and gratifying nature tend to assist individuals in becoming more open and more accepting of new and different ideas. The opposite may be the case if negative experiences have been accumulated in one's life. As a commentator on change, it is often helpful to develop ideas for change based on past experience in similar or related matters. Because resistance to change is very much the result of previous negative experiences, it is helpful to analyze the two situations and to point out the differences in the new situation.

Lack of goal consensus. Resistance to change can also be attributed to a lack of goal consensus or a lack of harmony between those who would implement the change and those who would oppose it. In many institutions, notably in hospitals, the goals of the frontline practitioner are usually more patient oriented and thus more in keeping with practice principles. This in itself results in more change orientation. The goals of the administrative staff, on the other hand, are more in keeping with the immediate self-protective and self-perpetuating goal strategies of management does not advocate a change, the people on the lower echelon of the administrative ladder will resist it, largely as a result of suspicion and lack of confidence in anything that is advocated by management. Such suspicion is sometimes justified; when it is not, the change will suffer simply because its advocates are not enjoying credibility. Barriers to change are numerous and may include those in the social system and those in individuals. Some examples of barriers to change (adopted from Telfer, 1966) found in the nursing profession are: lack of time, disagreement on goals, inadequate finances to accomplish the necessary tasks, staff turnover, inadequate communication skills, inadequate supervision, lack of nurse interest and cooperation, inadequate top-level administrative support, nurse apathy, and inadequate means for communication.

Lack of felt need and insufficient economic resources. Resistance to change is related to a lack of felt need and insufficient economic resources to innovate. Nurses will resist accepting an innovation if they do not believe that they need the new information, program, equipment, or skill. Yet even if they "feel a need" or desire to adopt an innovation, they must also have what Zaltman, Duncan, and Holbek (1973:87) refer to as "the economic ability to utilize or to act upon the new knowledge." The nurse–change agent must not only present the proposed change to the target population but must also convince them that they need to adopt it. However, the nurse–change agent must determine in advance that the target population has the resources to adopt the new program, information, or skill. For example, previously we presented an example in which a group of nurses rejected a change in their work schedule (that is, from the traditional 8-hour day/7-day week to the 12-hour day/7 days on/7days off) because they had young families, which required that they not be away from the home for more than 8 hours each day. (In the Appendix, a case is presented in which the nurse–change agent actually overcame this problem.) Thus, even if the nurses preferred the new work schedule (indicated a felt need), their circumstances prohibited its adoption. Likewise, General Motors has convinced many people that they "need a Cadillac"; not many, however, can actually afford to purchase one.

One of the most difficult areas to convince nurses that they "need to change" is in regard to program curriculum. Many academic nurses refuse to consider the students' needs requiring a change in curriculum because they have a huge vested interest in the status quo.[2] For example, we hear academicians say, "If the curriculum is changed, I may lose my present position; with a new curriculum, I may have to teach more or I may have to teach another, less interesting course."

Passive resistance. Nurses frequently resist change by means of passive resistance. (Passive resistance is called passive aggression in abnormal psychology.) It refers to "a way of resisting the demands made by others with concealed inactive resistance such as procrastination, pouting, stubborness and inefficiency" (Fann and Goshen, 1977:35). Nurses pursue passive resistance because they perceive themselves as having an inadequate power base from which to control their work situations.

Nurses use passive resistance to resist change simply by not following the orders or directives of supervisors, administrators, or physicians. Moreover, they may not use an innovation properly or as completely as

---

2. To be sure, this attitude is shared by academicians in other professional schools besides nursing.

it should be used. Passive resistance was recently used by faculty at Western University, School of Nursing where the dean introduced a new evaluation form to her faculty without prior notice or faculty involvement. The faculty evaluation form was innovative in the sense that both the faculty members and their program chairperson were to be evaluated. Since the evaluation form was new, it was both lengthy and cumbersome. Faculty and program chairpersons were required to spend at least 40 minutes on each evaluation; this was particularly difficult for faculty members who taught in several programs and for those program chairpersons who had twenty or more faculty members.

The dean directed faculty and program chairpersons to return the evaluations within 1 week so that the results of the evaluation could be used by the promotions committee. Faculty and program chairpersons were displeased with the evaluation form. Mostly, they agreed that it failed to assess some crucial issues in teaching and research. However, they were powerless to reject the dean's directive to use the form. After 1 week, only 20% of the evaluations had been turned in, and after 2 weeks, the number rose to only 35%. Many faculty members told the dean's administrative assistant that they intended to turn in the evaluation but were too busy with their course work to comply. By the end of the semester, 30% of the evaluation forms had still not been returned. If the faculty had been involved in the selection of the evaluation instrument, adoption of the innovation may have been better.

SUMMARY

In this chapter, we presented some of the most relevant information to assist the nurse–change agent in stabilizing a change program, terminating the change relationship with the target population, and understanding the various reasons for and the nature of resistance to change.

Chapter 8

DETERMINING THE EFFECTS OF CHANGE

The nurse–change agent's task is not complete once a change has been effected. Not until the results of the change have been truly evaluated can the effectiveness of the work be established. By initiating an evaluation of the change program, the nurse–change agent determines whether or not the program works. Without evaluation, the true outcome of a change program cannot be ascertained. This is a major problem in health care settings in which change is often discontinued based on emotional response to it, rather than on objective data.

The principal method by which programs are evaluated is by comparing the results to prior expectations. If the results do not meet expectations, the program is considered unsuccessful. Through the evaluative process, the nurse–change agent can determine: (1) if the desired results were (or were not) achieved, (2) why the desired results were not achieved (if applicable), and (3) what changes can be made now to alter the change program to obtain the desired results. If additional and unexpected results occurred, the nurse–change agent will want to determine not only why they occurred but also what their consequences will be. Problems and procedures in evaluation will be discussed in this chapter in an effort to assist the nurse–change agent in planning for this important component of the change process.

NURSE–CHANGE AGENTS SHOULD ASSESS THE RESULTS OF THEIR EFFORTS

Because evaluation of change may yield traumatic results, most change agents do not want their efforts evaluated. In fact, according to Zaltman, Duncan, and Holbek (1973:99), they will "battle" vehemently to prevent an intrusion of this nature. Their apprehension for program evaluation is well founded: the criteria used in program evaluation may not be valid, thus distorting the outcomes. Change agents also contribute to this problem by not having developed their own evaluation protocols before implementing the change. Designing program evaluation at the time the change program is formulated has several benefits. According to Havelock and Havelock (1973:79), the benefits include: (1) forcing nurse–change agents "to plan and think clearly about what they want to achieve and how they can do it," (2) providing information as to whether the change program should be "continued, repeated, terminated or modi- fied," (3) providing continual feedback to the nurse–change agent so that "in-process program improvement" can occur, and (4) providing the nurse–change agent with personal reinforcement and feedback. Havelock and Havelock (1973) also contend that a change program's evaluation should actually begin before the change program is initiated to obtain optimal program results. In the early stages of the program's design, the nurse–change agent should attempt to evaluate (1) whether there is an actual need for the proposed change program and (2) whether the pro- posed change program is feasible (that is, can succeed).

Program evaluation is imperative if the effect of the change is to be meaningfully judged. Change program developers, sponsors, and change agents may not always find program evaluation necessary. They may choose not to conduct an evaluation of the change program because of the cost of such efforts and because of the time necessary to determine the results of it. Instead, face validity is commonly used to evaluate the ef- fectiveness of a change program. *Face validity* refers to whether or not the outcome of a change program *looks* or *appears* as if it has achieved its stated goals or supports the original intention of the program. What this means, then, is that the change agent declares the program a success (or failure) if it *appears* that it is a success (or failure). However, since a change program that appears successful may not actually be successful, this method cannot be considered program evaluation; thus an appro- priate means of evaluation must be designed.

The most common mechanism by which a nurse–change agent deter- mines the effectiveness of a change program is by assessing whether the program's goals were reached. For instance, did the nurses' work stop- page result in wage increases or did the nurses capitulate to the adminis- tration's pressure? Were the public health department's efforts to get public health nurses to increase their work loads successful or did the nurses maintain or reduce the number of patients they saw? Did the hos- pital's plan for decreasing nurse turnover eventuate in lower turnover? Did the nurse's efforts to improve the health status of her patients actually result in her patients' improving, remaining the same, or getting worse? Nurse–change agents ask questions such as these when they attempt to evaluate the success of their programs.

To evaluate a change program, the evaluator must have a clear understanding of the meaningful goals of the program. This statement assumes that the change program's goals are clearly conceptualized during the planning stage. If, however, the goals of the program are vague, the evaluator will be unable to determine if the program was successful. For example, a nurse practitioner in a rural family clinic was requested by her supervisor to initiate a weight loss club for clinic patients. The nurse practitioner stated the goal of this program as getting people to lose an average of 15 pounds during the 4 months of the program. A total of 20 people joined the program, and after 4 months of group counselling by the nurse practitioner, the group lost an average of 16 pounds. Was the program a success? The answer is difficult to ascertain.

The nurse practitioner and her supervisor were elated with the results. They believed that the program was highly successful and should not only be repeated at the clinic but extended to include other clinics. The administrator of the clinic, however, was not fully convinced that the program was successful. He had a nurse researcher from the university evaluate the nurse's data. The nurse researcher confirmed the nurse's finding about the 16-pound average weight loss. She decided, however, that not only should the patients have lost weight, but they should also have kept it off for a period after the program terminated. She interviewed 16 of the 20 patients 6 months after the program was over (four of them had moved or were otherwise unwilling to cooperate). She found that, on the average, the 16 patients had regained upwards of 85% of the weight they originally lost. She also found that although the patients had regained the weight they had lost, they were now much more cognizant of the nutritional value of their food and were very conscious of the foods they consumed. The nurse researcher reported that the change program was only partially successful: the patients had regained most of the weight they previously lost but were now on a much more nutritionally balanced diet.

The experience of the nurse practitioner shows that the goals of a change program should be clearly stated and well thought out before the program is initiated. The nurse practitioner's goals should have included patients not only losing weight during the program, but also not regaining it during a specified period after the program ended. Her goals should have included improvement in the patients' nutritional habits since nutrition was part of the program. This experience also clearly illustrates the problem inherent in using face validity as the criteria for success. For all intents and purposes, the program was a success. If the program had been evaluated, the nurse practitioner and her supervisor would have acclaimed the results without reservation.

Under most conditions, nurse–change agents will have to assume responsibility for evaluating the effectiveness of their own change programs. It is more appropriate if an objective person (that is, an outsider) conducts the evaluation, but our experience shows that if nurse–change agents do not evaluate their own program, no one will. However, when the nurse–change agents evaluate their own program, some persons may question the validity of the results since they validated them themselves. In other words, nurse–change agents have a vested interest in their program's successful outcome. In the case of the weight management program, it is clear that the nurse practitioner (change agent) had high hopes that her program would be successful and that the 20 people enrolled in it would each lose at least 15 pounds. She was optimistic about the program because she had organized, conducted, and developed its counselling module. She also wanted a successful outcome because it would reflect on the type of work she was doing for the clinic.

Critics of nurse–change agents evaluating their own change program might say that the nurses' high investment in the program would preclude them from conducting a critical evaluation of the program. They might also contest their evaluation on the grounds that they have neither the background nor the expertise in program evaluation. Both of these criticisms are reasonable. But given the other alternative, namely, no program evaluation, it is easy to see that the contribution the nurse–change agent can make is indeed valuable. Nurse–change agents are forced to evaluate their own change programs for three reasons: (1) they are likely to be the only person in the organization with sufficient time and motivation to conduct an evaluation, (2) they have a vested interest in determining whether or not the program works, and (3) they may be the organization's only employee who has the skills to evaluate a program or the time to learn how it should be done.

Unfortunately, most administrators are not concerned about the outcome of change programs that have only limited implications for the larger organization or that have no direct relevance, in their opinion, to the delivery of nursing care. Therefore, it is unlikely that the nursing administration will request evaluation of the following change programs: a program to get the nurses on a staff to stop smoking while on the unit, a program to help fellow nurses become more assertive, and a program to organize the parents of children in the hospital's children's unit to raise money for the unit. The change programs and others like them may, however, draw the attention of the nurse administrator if the results are par-

ticularly good (for example, the parents of children in the hospital, organized by the staff nurse, raised a large amount of money and promised
to raise an even larger sum) or extremely poor (for example, 80% of the
nurses who smoked threatened to resign or seek redress from the state
nurses' association of the Federal Labor Relations Board over the demand
of their supervisor that they not smoke on their unit even when they are
on their break or at lunch). Conversely, the director of nursing and the
hospital administrator will be greatly interested in change programs that
they view as having implications for the larger organization, for example,
the efforts of a head nurse that resulted in a dramatic decrease in the
streptococcus infection rate on her unit, the three nurses who succeeded
in getting one third of the nurses in the hospital to join their state nurses'
association, and the assistant director of nursing who discovered several
means for lowering staff turnover.

The more important the change program is to the successful operation
of the organization, the more likely the administration is to call for a
formal evaluation of the program's results. A hospital's administrator,
for example, will want to be certain that the findings of the assistant
hospital director concerning the nurse turnover rate are accurate. Implementation of a new recruiting program or an in-service socialization program without evaluation of their effectiveness is not acceptable. Implementation efforts that cost a considerable amount of money generally require some type of formal evaluation to ensure that the money is well
spent. Usually, face validity will serve as the basis for an organization to
decide if it wants to allocate funds for an evaluation.

Finally, a change agent should not draw conclusions from the results
or outcomes of a change program that are not justified. The nurse practitioner who developed and conducted the weight loss program felt sufficiently justified from her observations of an average 16-pound weight
loss per patient that she not only wanted to continue the program, but also
wanted it to be used in other nurse practitioner clinics. Obviously, the
nurse practitioner's exuberance exceeded the actual findings of her program. Her program did have positive results, but she drew conclusions
from it that went far beyond their general applicability. Notter (1974:
118) also cautions that researchers (and change agents) should not permit
their "personal experiences or opinions" to interfere with their objectivity
in drawing conclusions.

TIME NECESSARY TO EVALUATE THE EFFECTIVENESS OF A CHANGE PROGRAM

The time needed by the nurse–change agent to evaluate the effectiveness of a program varies from program to program depending on the

goals of the program. It should be pointed out at the outset, however, that change programs should optimally include an ongoing evaluation process. This allows the nurse–change agent to alter, continue, or increase efforts at the different stages to accomplish the desired results.

The goal(s) of the change program are the major factor determining how long after completion of the study the nurse–change agent must wait before evaluating the program's effectiveness. In some change programs, the goals can be achieved in a sufficiently short period so that the program can be evaluated immediately after its implementation. On the other hand, if it takes an extended period to fully realize the goals, the nurse–change agent may have to wait months or even years to evaluate the success of the program. Some examples will be helpful in illustrating this point.

The nurse practitioner who conducted the weight loss program decided that the outcome of her program could be evaluated immediately at the end of the 4-month program. The nurse researcher, on the other hand, concluded after studying the change program that program evaluation should wait until 6 months after completion of the program. The difference in length of time that the nurse–change agent and the nurse researcher believed to be necessary to wait before conducting the evaluation is directly related to their definition of the goals of the program. The nurse practitioner was concerned with weight loss. To the researcher, maintenance was as important a goal as was initial weight loss and, therefore, believed that it was appropriate to wait 6 months after the conclusion of the formal program before assessing the results of the program. As a result of the different lengths of time allowed to pass by the nurse-practitioner and the researcher before evaluating the program, one showed a large success and the other showed only a modest, partial success.[1]

At Western City Hospital, several nurses were sexually assaulted on their way from the parking lot to the hospital. Although the hospital's administration showed great concern for the safety of their employees, most of the women employees did not believe that enough was being done to ensure their safety and well-being. A small group of nurses decided to organize a protest against the administration for the purpose of ensuring their safety. The nurses met first with the hospital's chief of security and a police captain from the local police station to obtain some ideas about what could be done to reduce the danger in this area. Next, the nurses organized a series of meetings with female employees throughout

---

1. Weight management researchers would agree unanimously with the nurse researcher that a period of between 6 and 18 months must pass before a weight management program of this nature can be completely and appropriately evaluated.

the hospital to obtain their views about the situation. At these meetings, they also received some ideas on what the women could do themselves to increase their safety. Finally, the nurses met with the director of the hospital and the director of nursing to discuss the situation and to make suggestions for reducing the danger to female employees.

The group had decided before they met with the administration that they would not make "demands" because they feared that the idea of "demands" would incense the administration and increase their resistance to the group's suggestions. Rather, it was decided to present to the administration all the information obtained about the area, especially the fact, according to the police, that the area around the hospital had more incidents of attacks on women than any other area in the city. The group then presented a two-fold plan to dramatically reduce the danger to employees. The first part of the plan called for all female employees to walk in pairs or groups when they walked outside the hospital and always to carry a whistle. The second component of the plan requested that the hospital hire several additional security officers to cover the hospital grounds during the high-risk periods and to be available to accompany women to or from their automobiles if they could not find someone else with whom to walk. They also requested that the hospital petition the city to provide more (and better) street lighting and increased police protection. Finally, the group requested that the hospital develop plans to build its own off-street parking facility.

At first, the director of the hospital did not appear very sympathetic toward the nurses' request for assistance. However, when he learned that employees were also going to take an active hand in reducing their personal danger, he became more interested. He thought that the hospital could afford to hire several part-time security personnel and provide transportation where necessary. The director also agreed to present the off-street parking suggestion to the hospital's board of directors at their next meeting.

After the meeting, the four nurses who had organized the effort to make the area surrounding the hospital less dangerous to female employees and who represented the other female employees with the administration, were jubilant. One then asked, "Will these changes ensure our safety?" No one seemed to know. They decided that they should evaluate the results of these new procedures to determine the effectiveness of their plan. They agreed unanimously that a change without increased safety would not improve the situation.

The nurses met with different people throughout the hospital and developed an evaluation plan. They decided that one individual should consult with the administration over the status of the parking facility. Several others would work with security to maintain records of all criminal incidents reported. Finally a group of six women from the dietary, nursing, and housekeeping departments agreed to talk to women throughout the hospital to encourage them to report all unusual encounters to security. The nurses also agreed that the number of incidents would be examined at 3-month intervals for a period of 12 months. At the end of each period, they would decide how successful the plan was and decide if any changes in their plan had to be made. Clearly, in this example, the nurses recognized that any further action taken by the hospital would depend on an evaluation of the effectiveness of their present plan. The nurses also understood that it would take at least 3 months before an evaluation of the plan's effectiveness could be assessed.

RESULTS OF CHANGE PROGRAMS

Change does not necessarily mean improvement. If, for example, the organization of a nursing unit is changed in some way, it does not ensure that the quality of the care will improve or that the unit will be more efficient. In fact, there are many examples in which change has actually wrought a state worse than that which previously existed. Planned change, on the other hand, is change that is designed ostensibly to result in an improved state. Bennis, Benne, and Chin question, however, which changes are improvements and which are not. There is, they believe, a need for "some normative standards, some value criteria, by which changes can be judged good or bad, desirable or undesirable" (1976:96).

Most commonly, the normative standard or value criterion by which a change is evaluated as good or bad is determined by the change agent or by the group that is seeking to have some change imposed on another group (target population). Thus, the change agent may have one standard of success while the target population has another. For example, the administrator of a public health department wanted the nurses to attend to more patients per day than they presently did. He believed that the nurses were not using their time efficiently and could care for 20% more patients without sacrificing quality. To accomplish this change, he assigned his administrative assistant the task of motivating the nurses to increase patient visits. But the nurses (target population) did not agree with the change agent that an increase in the number of patient visits would not adversely affect the quality of the care they could provide. They asked the change agent to observe their schedules; as a result she realized the nurses were right.

The nurse–change agent's job is to implement a change and usually she sees herself purely as a technician. She may not consider a proposed change in terms of it's being good or bad or desirable or undesirable for one group or another. She usually is not put in the ethical quandary in which she is concerned about manipulating her clients or patients or "about the reposition of (her) own values upon those (she) is helping; about (her) temptations to use (her) influence to narrow and foreclose rather than to widen and release the free choices of (her) clients" (Bennis, Benne, and Chin, 1969:581).

The change agent typically pleads ignorance about the outcome of the change: "I don't know if increasing patient visits will or will not adversely affect the quality of care. If the nurses want to, they can lower the quality of care they provide and see even fewer patients. Only the evaluation of the results of the change can tell us if it is good or bad." In addition, the change agent may not care that the consequences of the change may be bad or undesirable for the target population. They frequently see themselves as devoid of ethical values.

To determine whether a change will be good or bad, the goals and possible consequences of the change must be examined before the change program is fully implemented. A change goal is "a state of affairs in the external environment towards which activities may be directed and which, if reached, terminates the sequence of activities (Horwitz, 1976: 280). But what is a goal for one group may not necessarily be a goal for another. The administrator of the public health department may have seen the increase in patient visits as a means of controlling costs. The number of patients may have been increasing at a much greater rate than the city's increase in the budgetary allocation to his department. The public health nurses did not view the administrator's goals of more patient visits as desirable because it interfered with their professional goals, such as quality of care, adequate salaries, and good working conditions.

A problem with using goal attainment as the major determinant of whether or not a change is good or bad is that once the goal is achieved, the change agent may be satisfied and not attempt to evaluate the effect of the change. It is possible that a change program's goals are achieved, and yet the results may be disastrous. In other words, the consequences of successful goal attainment may result in conditions worse than had existed prior to the change program's implementation. For instance, many of the public health nurses at City Public Health Clinic decided that they would rather quit their jobs than attempt to see even more patients than they presently did. They believed that they were already overworked and seeing more patients would not only reduce the quality of care further but open up increased possibility for malpractice claims. As a result of the health department's new policy, which require nurses to see more patients each day, 25% of the public health nurses resigned. Suddenly the department was in a crisis situation in which there were not only inadequate replacements but many patients with unmet health care needs. To provide short-term relief, the department agreed to compensate nurses who worked overtime. The department realized that eventually it would have to increase the hourly wages paid to nurses to attract more nurses to the department. Thus it developed that the solution was worse than the problem.

Frequently, the goal of a change program is to change the attitudes, knowledge, or skills of a target population. These types of outcomes deserve special mention because they must receive careful evaluation. For instance, a head nurse at one nursing home was very concerned about the prejudice expressed by some of her staff toward minority patients. She decided to initiate a program to reduce their prejudice (that is, change their attitudes). Before she began, however, she had the staff fill out an attitudinal scale that measured prejudice. She decided that her program would be a success if she found a significant change in her staff's scores on the scale from before to after they had been in her program.

In Western Hospital, the director of continuing education devised a program to show the nursing staff how to use a new intravenous (IV) system. To determine the success of the program, she worked with the staff of the company that sold the hospital the new system and they developed an examination to measure the nurses' knowledge in using the new system. They also developed a checklist evaluation instrument that the nurses' supervisors could use to determine the nurses' skill in using the new system.

As previously stated, the nurse–change agent is most likely to evaluate a change program as successful if the program reaches its goals. To this end, then, the goals of change programs must be concrete, realistic, and reachable. When goals are vague, nurse–change agents may not have a clear picture of what they should attempt to achieve in the program.

REPORTING THE RESULTS

According to Havelock and Havelock (1973:82-83), a thorough change program design will include a statement of (1) how the results of the evaluation are to be utilized, (2) possible audience(s) to which the results should be reported, (3) the mode for transmitting the results (that is, written report), and (4) some indication of how the audience(s) might use the results of the evaluation.

The reports of a change program can be used in several ways. The most common one is to justify the action of a group. For example, a state nurses' association used the results of its evaluation of a strike to support its contention that the strike would help the nurses achieve their desired goals. Similarly, the director of a public health department reported to the public health nurses employed by his department that there had not been a marked decline in the quality of nursing care even though nurses were now required to make more patient visits per day.

Another use of the results of a change program evaluation is "to suggest modifications in the program—to shift the composition of inputs, perhaps to reemphasize some objections and de-emphasize others" (Cain and Hollister, 1972:137). For instance, the evaluation plan proposed by the nurses at Western City Hospital to increase their safe passage to and from their automobiles would indicate whether the plan had to be modified. It would show whether there was a need for additional police and security personnel or whether the plan, as developed, was viable. The change program at Status Hospital (Chapter 6) offers another example. There, one of the nursing units was found to be highly ineffective. The hospital's administration decided to reorganize the unit in an effort to increase its effectiveness. All reorganization efforts failed, however. When the change agent evaluated her efforts, she found that the unit had traditionally given higher priority to service than to cost containment, which was the modus operandi of the new management. The idea of reorganizing the unit was finally shelved in favor of the hospital's employing a clinical psychologist to assist employees in their efforts to better deal with patients who were extremely ill. This turned out to be the right approach to this problem.

The results of a change program evaluation might also suggest that the program itself should be eliminated. For example, the public health nurses at City Public Health Clinic went on strike when they were told that they would have to increase their work load because no new nurses could be employed as a result of the passage of Proposition 13. Discussions held with striking nurses and their representatives showed that they would not accept the unilateral decision of the health department. Ultimately, the health department acquiesced and agreed to reduce both the number of clinics it operated and the number of hours they were opened instead of insisting that nurses see more patients.

The results of an evaluation are useful to various groups depending on their involvement in the change program. The following is based on Havelock and Havelock's (1973:82) listing:

1. Persons involved in developing the program who can use the data to modify or redesign the present or future programs.

2. The target population that can use the information to help work through the feelings it might have about the program.
3. Program sponsors who will be able to determine if their resources were used appropriately and effectively and if they should sponsor similar programs in the future.
4. Researchers, students, and change agents who have an interest in the change process.

It is customary to convey evaluative results of a change program in the form of a report. The extent and the complexity of the report depend on (1) the sophistication of the readership, (2) previous agreements regarding the nature of the report, (3) demands and policies by the employing and/or funding agency, and (4) the manner in which the report is intended to reinforce the need and the efficaciousness of the change. Usually the report is released in two versions: one, which is brief, resembles a summary; it is mainly distributed to the target population and to individuals tangential to it; the other, longer, more detailed, and more sophisticated version is distributed to the change's sponsors and to students and researchers of change. Like all written statements, this report will also represent a permanent document for all to see. This fact must be remembered when, in the period of change completion, the desire to finish and be done with the project may persuade the change agent to take less care with the report than was the case with the change process.

Sharing the report with wider audiences through publication should always be considered. Nurses need to read about each others' innovative attempts and their results. Nurse–change agents benefit from publishing the report of an instituted change because it helps them to perfect writing and communication skills.

Case studies, found in Appendix A, provide descriptions of the entire process of implementing change and will assist the reader in an attempt to integrate all component parts of the change process as contained in this book.

SUMMARY

In this chapter we illustrated, by using various examples, the importance of program evaluation in assessing nursing change. It was pointed out that unless nurse–change agents evaluate their change programs, no one else will do it appropriately. Face validity is the most prevalent form of program evaluation; if it looks successful then it is successful. But this most simplistic form of evaluation also has serious shortcomings. Timing of the evaluation is also important to obtain a true assessment of the program's success. We also showed that the results of a change program may (or may not) mean improvement, depending on the group evaluating the results. To one group, the change may be highly positive and a definite improvement, while to another group, the opposite is true. Finally, the necessity of reporting the results of a change program and the nature of the report were discussed.

APPENDIX

The following four case studies report the efforts of successful and unsuccessful nurse–change agents. The events described took place over varying lengths of time and illustrate some of the armentaria constituting the strategies and tactics used by nurse–change agents in implementing change. These detailed case studies describe six distinctive change steps or parts: (1) background of the nurse–change agent, (2) nurse–change agent's initial contact with the target population or by the target population, (3) definition of the problem, (4) change plan and action, (5) evaluation of the change, and (6) disengagement of the nurse–change agent. However, in some instances one of these change steps may be excluded because of the nature of the change.

Because all nurses and nursing students are prospective change agents, these case studies are designed to assist the prospective nurse–change agent in both implementing a change and understanding the dynamics of the change process. Earlier we stated, however briefly, that not all change is desirable, and thus, efforts to negate or prevent change efforts may be positive. When nurses believe that it is within their best interests to thwart a change process, they too, will benefit from these case studies because they clearly illustrate the full change process.

List of cases
Case 1: Changing the IV administration system in a hospital
Case 2: Reorganizing a school of nursing
Case 3: Changing "on duty" shifts to a different schedule
Case 4: Nurses on strike

Case 1 ■ CHANGING THE IV ADMINISTRATION SYSTEM IN A HOSPITAL
Background of nurse–change agent
Bonnie Casey is a 33-year-old registered nurse. Twelve years ago she received her associate degree in nursing and began working as a staff nurse at Good Samaritan Hospital. Although she was working full-time, Bonnie still managed, not

without considerable personal and family sacrifice, to finish her baccalaureate degree.

Bonnie is married and the mother of two daughters. During the 12 years she has worked at Good Samaritan, Bonnie was out of work for only about a year—6 months after each child was born. Bonnie loves her work and sees it as a career. Her husband, a school teacher, understands her love for her work and is very supportive of her. Besides, Bonnie's income, which is almost $18,000, is greater than her husband's.

Bonnie was first promoted to head nurse when she completed her baccalaureate degree; she was promoted to night supervisor 2 years later; and 2 years ago, when she finished her master's degree, she was promoted to assistant director of nursing service. Bonnie no longer provides patient care; however, her first love is patient care and she continues to press for high quality of care provided to patients.

Contact with target population

Good Samaritan Hospital, like many other large medical centers in the United States and abroad, serves as a teaching center for nursing students, medical students, and residents. It wasn't long after Bonnie came to work at Good Samaritan that she recognized the existence of a potentially serious problem in patient care: the inserting of and caring for IVs. Medical students and residents were required to start all IVs; staff nurses were then to maintain them. Since senior medical students and residents had always been responsible for starting IVs at this hospital, no one questioned their role.

Soon after Bonnie was promoted to assistant director of nursing, several nurses mentioned to her informally that a significant number of patients on their units were getting infections from their IVs. They said that the medical students and the residents were using the best IV needles (catheter or steel), and the nurses were checking and changing the dressing carefully enough; yet, infections occurred.

At a monthly meeting of the administrative staff of nursing service, Bonnie brought the "problem" to the attention of the group. She asked if other units were experiencing problems with IV infection. To her amazement, half the head nurses said they frequently had problems of this nature. Following a rather lengthy discussion in which various reasons for and solutions to the "problem" were suggested, the director of nursing requested that Bonnie determine the extent of the "problem."

Definition of the problem

Bonnie did not know how to determine if IV infections were significant. She knew that increased attention was being paid toward the elimination of iatrogenic diseases (diseases caused by physicians and their activities). She decided to go to the medical library and have a computer search (MEDLINE) made to identify articles and books that might help her in her task. She used IV infection and iatrogenic disease as the key words on which the computer could scan for relevant resources. Unfortunately, this effort only generated a few relevant articles, one of which discussed how one hospital had successfully introduced an IV therapy team.

Next, Bonnie decided to review all the material she could find on IVs. She

IV INFECTION RECORD CHART

Patient No.	Date infection noticed	Type of IV needle	Period IV in since last changed	Period (total) patient been on IVs
1.				
2.				
3.				
4.				
5.				

even called several manufacturers and requested information on their products. She then called a meeting of all head nurses. She told them that the only way to determine the extent of IV infections was if records were kept on each unit. Accordingly, she provided each head nurse with a chart to record required information for a 2-week period beginning the first of the month. (See above.) She carefully reviewed the chart with the nurses. Bonnie also alerted the director of nursing to the survey and sent an explanatory memo to the director of the hospital.

During the 2 weeks in which the head nurses were charting the existence of IV infections, Bonnie visited all the units to answer questions, review the IV chart, and examine infections identified by the head nurses. The results of this survey showed that of the 3400 patients who were receiving IVs during the 2-week period, there were approximately 387 instances of infection, an 11.4% infection rate. Neither Bonnie nor anyone else she discussed this with knew if the rate was high, average, or low; all agreed, nonetheless, that the rate seemed to be high, especially if any changes could be made to reduce the infection rate. Bonnie presented her findings to the director of nursing at the next monthly administrative staff meeting.

The director of nursing agreed with Bonnie's conclusion (and the consensus of the administrative staff at the meeting) that a problem existed in the starting, care, and maintenance of the IV needles. She appointed Bonnie to head a committee to (1) identify what IV system changes might be made and (2) assess the cost of the various alternatives. She requested that Bonnie complete the report within 4 weeks.

Change plan and action

Bonnie gathered together a committee that included two head nurses, one physician, one resident, and one pharmacist. The physician and resident were appointed to the committee by Dr. Stone, the hospital's medical director, with whom Bonnie met to discuss the IV therapy problem. Dr. Stone was initially defensive about the role of medical students and residents in causing IV infections. However, Bonnie assured him that the director of nursing did not seek to embarrass the medical staff but only to seek a method for improving IV service. When

Bonnie told Dr. Stone that the committee was going to investigate the effectiveness of a full-time IV therapy team, he seemed pleased. Apparently, he was not unwilling to relinquish control of IV administration in the hospital because he said, "The students and residents really have more important things to do than starting IVs anyway."

Bonnie felt very good about how her meeting with the hospital's medical director had gone. She knew that changing the IV system would be extremely difficult without his support since (1) he might have a vested interest in the status quo and (2) he was a sufficiently powerful person at the hospital that he could block a change in how IVs were started and cared for. Bonnie had one concern, however: had she misled Dr. Stone into thinking that an alternative to medical students and residents starting IVs would be found. She knew that was only one of several possible changes.

At the first meeting of the ad hoc committee to study IV therapy infection, Bonnie told the committee members that the committee needed to do the following: (1) contact hospitals in the region to determine the IV therapy system they used, and (2) assess the cost versus the benefit of those systems that appeared most acceptable.

The committee found two ways in which IV therapy was administered at different hospitals in the area: (1) by medical students and residents who started the IV therapy, while registered nurses checked, cleaned, and maintained them and (2) by an IV therapy team.[1] Several variations on how the IV therapy team functioned were also identified. In some hospitals, the IV therapy team started all IVs, and the staff nurses checked and maintained them. In other hospitals, the IV therapy team not only started all IVs but checked and maintained them on a daily basis. In a few hospitals, the IV therapy team started, checked, and maintained all IVs but was not called on to "trouble shoot" when a problem with flow or pain arose. The committee also observed that a wide variety of IV therapy systems (that is, different tubing, IV containers, and motors) were used by the hospitals.

It appeared to the committee members that the introduction of a specially trained IV therapy team at Good Samaritan Hospital would resolve the injection problem. Only in those hospitals in which the IV therapy team started all IVs, checked and changed dressings daily, restarted new IVs, and was available to the nursing and medical staff 24 hours a day for "trouble shooting" was the effort of the IV therapy team acclaimed. In most of the other hospitals that did not fully utilize the skills of trained IV therapists, there was some doubt about their effectiveness. This concern was especially prevalent in hospitals in which the IV therapy team had to depend on the nursing staff to check the IV, change the dressings daily, and resolve IV flow and pain problems. The committee concluded that they would endorse the concept of the IV therapy team in their report to the director of nursing.

Next, the committee tried to evaluate the cost of an IV therapy team. Considering the hospital's bed capacity (600 beds), the committee had to decide: (1) the optimum number of IV therapy team members for three shifts, 7 days per week and (2) the salary of team members and the team leader. Based on the size of IV therapy teams at other hospitals and the fact that Good Samaritan was a tertiary medical care center (that is, a hospital which received most of its pa-

---

1. In this state, IV therapy team members had to be specially trained RNs.

tients through referral from other hospitals), the committee decided that a seven-member team plus one team leader was necessary. This would be sufficient to have three team members on duty on the day shift, 5 days per week, and at least one member on duty on all other shifts, including weekends. Usually, there would be two team members on duty on the 3-to-11 shift during the week. The committee also determined that registered nurse IV therapy team members could be started off at $6.00 per hour with the team leader receiving $8.00. The committee estimated the yearly expenses of an IV therapy team at $100,000, excluding training and benefits.

Bonnie wrote the committee's report and submitted it to the director of nursing. After the director read and evaluated the committee's report, she met with the committee. The director commended the committee for its hard work. She said that she was in full concurrence with the report, but the cost of implementation was substantially more than she had envisioned, especially in light of the hospital presently incurring no direct costs for IV therapy. But, she did note, that the cost to the hospital of an average of more than 300 IV therapy infections per 2-week period was also a substantial sum. The director told the committee that she would meet with the hospital's director to discuss the results of the study.

During the following 2 weeks, Bonnie was anxious about the hospital's decision. She knew that the $100,000 for the IV team was realistic; she also knew that the hospital did not spend money unless the board of directors thought the expenditure was necessary. Finally, Bonnie knew that without a major overhaul in the hospital's IV therapy system, the number of IV therapy infections would continue. Bonnie also felt powerless. She knew that her study was correct in promoting the IV therapy team approach as necessary at Good Samaritan Hospital. But she couldn't do anything more than she had already done to promote the idea. Others were to make the decisions. Bonnie was not used to this lack of control.

In two weeks, the director of the hospital told the director of nursing that the board of directors of the hospital had authorized the creation of a division of IV therapy within the department of nursing. The director of the hospital said that he was very pleased with the board's decision. He said, however, that he wanted the department of nursing to assess the effectiveness of the new IV therapy team once it had been implemented. Even the hospital's medical director was pleased with the decision. He wrote a memo to Bonnie thanking her for her initiative and effort in development of the IV therapy team for the hospital. Bonnie was very pleased.

The change strategy used in this effort was that a committee was to investigate the different methods used by hospitals to administer and maintain IV therapy and to recommend to the director of nursing the system or systems that appeared best for Good Samaritan Hospital. The change tactics used by Bonnie were:

1. She formed a committee of nurses, physicians, and a pharmacist.
2. She met with the hospital's medical director to inform him of the committee and to request that he appoint a physician, a resident, and a pharmacist to it.
3. She arranged for the committee to meet with IV therapy specialists at hospitals in the region that used different administration and maintenance approaches.

4. She helped the committee collate all the data it collected and then draw a conclusion.
5. She wrote a report supporting the committee's decision.
6. She presented the report to the director of nursing.

Assessing effectiveness

With the assistance of a sociologist from the university with which the hospital was affiliated, Bonnie conceptualized an evaluation plan for the IV therapy team that called for a before-and-after methodology. By including the head of the IV therapy team, Bonnie expected to gain her expertise and her full cooperation. The tactic was successful on both counts. The extent of the IV therapy problems would be assessed 1 month prior to the IV therapy team becoming operational and then for 1 month after the team had been functioning for 1 month. Bonnie wrote up the methodology indicating that the head nurses would collect the data on special data sheets, and she would spot check their work. She also indicated the types of comparisons she expected to make regarding the time periods. Bonnie then presented the evaluation plan to the director of the hospital and the director of nursing. They thought the plan was good. Specifically, the plan was as follows:

1. The head nurses on all units collected data on all IV therapy infections/complications for 1 month prior to the introduction of the IV therapy team. The IV therapy team did not become operational for several months after the plan was approved. All head nurses were given an hour of training to familiarize them with the different categories of problems.
2. Bonnie checked on the charting of the IV therapy infections/complications on a daily basis.
3. One month after the IV therapy team had been operational, the head nurses again collected data on IV therapy infections/complications.
4. Bonnie again checked on the accuracy of the charting.
5. Bonnie, the head nurse of the IV therapy team, and the sociologist then compared the two periods. They compared periods by total number of complications and by type of complications and infection only.

Bonnie was delighted to find out from her evaluation that the introduction of the IV therapy team dropped the incident of both IV therapy complications and infections significantly. In fact, for infections alone, there was a decrease of over 75% from the before to the after period. Bonnie speculated that as the IV therapy team gained more experience, the incident rate would drop even further. The results of the evaluation validated the hospital's expenditure for an IV therapy team. It also came to Bonnie's attention that as a result of the evaluation, staff nurses on the units became aware of the expertise of the IV therapists and did not feel uncomfortable about calling for them when they had problems with IV flow.

Bonnie compiled the results of the IV therapy team evaluation and presented it to the director of nursing, who then turned it over to the director of the hospital. Both of them congratulated Bonnie on an excellent study. The director of the hospital was pleased that the decision was made to create an IV therapy team.

Disengagement of the nurse–change agent

Following the evaluation, it was easy for Bonnie to "disengage" from the IV therapy study; the director of nursing asked her to examine another problem in nursing service. In addition, she had her regular duties in staff development that she had neglected to some extent while working on the IV therapy program. However, once a month Bonnie made a special effort to have lunch with the leader of the IV therapy team to discuss how it was working out. She also put IV therapy on the agenda for the monthly administrative staff meetings. Otherwise, Bonnie rarely got involved with IV therapy.

Case 2 ■ REORGANIZING A SCHOOL OF NURSING'S ADMINISTRATIVE STRUCTURE
Background of nurse–change agent and initial contact with target population

Cindy Safdie, R.N., M.S., Ph.D. has been Dean at the School of Nursing at Private University for the past 2 years. She is 47 years of age. She received her doctorate in sociology 5 years ago and considers herself an expert on the process of social change. Prior to accepting the position of Dean at Private University, Dean Safdie was associate dean of the school of nursing at a large state university. Dean Safdie is well known in nursing and travels out of town to make speeches and consult on the average of one day every week. She describes her first 2 years at Private University as successful, rewarding, and very challenging. Despite her many successes, she believes strongly that more improvements are still needed to further the development of the school of nursing.

Definition of the problem

Private University, School of Nursing has 50 full-time and 40 part-time faculty members. These 90 faculty members are responsible for a student body of approximately 500 students—450 undergraduates and 50 graduates. Like most other schools of nursing, the administrative or management structure of the school consists of a dean, an associate dean, and department heads. In all, there are five departments at Private University, School of Nursing: (1) public health, (2) medical-surgical, (3) psychiatric, (4) geriatric, and (5) maternal and child health. All faculty are members of one department or another. Department chairpersons have a considerable amount of authority—they have control over departmental budgets and faculty. Department chairpersons negotiate their budget and faculty size (that is, increase or decrease in number of positions) with the dean.

Although Dean Safdie has final administrative responsibility for the school of nursing, departmental chairpersons are also powerful. The dean makes school policy, and the chairpersons are expected to carry them out in their respective departments. But chairpersons can, and occassionally do, act contrary to Dean Safdie's decisions and interests. Usually, conflictual actions by chairpersons are not obvious or blatant; they tend to be subtle actions (that is, passive resistance) negating a decision of the dean. All department chairpersons are tenured; however, they serve in their administrative capacity purely at the discretion of the dean. In this case, all the department chairpersons, except one, had been department heads prior to Cindy's arrival as dean at Private University.

Almost from the beginning of Cindy's tenure as dean, the chairpersons have been resistant to cooperate fully with her. The chairpersons had been enthusiastic about Cindy's selection as dean, but none wanted to relinquish any of the power they had developed during the tenure of the previous dean, who was considered to be weak. The most serious challenge to the chairperson's power came when

Cindy sought to use faculty from one department to work in another. Frequently, the school would lose faculty from one department and be unable to replace them immediately. Usually, this adversely affected the student-faculty ratio. To remedy this difficulty, Dean Safdie once tried to negotiate using faculty from the department of medical-surgical nursing in the department of maternal and child health nursing. The chairperson of the medical-surgical department, from which the dean wanted to "borrow" faculty, vigorously resisted the move.

Dean Safdie also observed problems with the department administrative scheme when it came to assigning nonclinical faculty members. Inasmuch as her school of nursing had an integrated curriculum, it was difficult for Cindy to assign physiologists, experimental psychologists, anatomists, medical sociologists, and the like. These faculty members taught students in all undergraduate (and even graduate) departments, as did most clinical faculty members. Cindy studied this problem over a long period. She spoke to many academicians about the issues, but no one seemed able to provide her with a viable alternative. Cindy was also caught in another predicament: she was a product of the department administrative system herself and had generally thought it was useful.

At the monthly meeting of the deans of Private University, Dean Safdie was told by the Dean of the School of Engineering about a new organizational scheme he had heard about. The scheme eliminated departments by creation of a grid system of programs and divisions. Everyone belongs to a division of their choice; people may elect to join more than one division, but they can only vote for a chairperson in one division. Divisions are professional interest areas. In nursing, they would include medical-surgical, psychiatric, research, gerontology, and so forth. Faculty members belong to as many programs as the dean needs them to teach. Therefore, a faculty member may possibly teach in the human development, behavioral science, and physical science programs. Each semester, faculty members may find that the programs in which they are to teach have been changed. Programs are directed by individuals appointed by the dean, who makes sure that the program runs smoothly. Dean Safdie was so enthusiastic about the grid that she immediately created one for the school (Table A-1).

Planning action steps

Dean Safdie described the grid system to her associate dean. She explained that the grid system would (1) increase the school's flexibility to meet its changing teaching needs, (2) increase the dean's administrative power, (3) eliminate the school's need for highly paid department chairpersons, (4) increase faculty representation on the dean's cabinet, and (5) provide faculty with an opportunity to select professional interest areas (division) they wished to join. The associate dean was equally excited about the prospects of the grid system for the school of nursing. Cindy and her associate dean then constructed the strategy they would use in changing the school of nursing's management structure. It included the following:
   1. Develop a detailed written proposal to be presented to the university's president
   2. Present the plan to the faculty
   3. Meet with department chairpersons
   4. Place everyone in their appropriate programs and have them identify the division or divisions they wished to join
Cindy chose the strategy of not informing the chairpersons in advance of the

Table A-1. Grid system for private university

Programs	Divisions					
	Med/Surg nursing	Psychiatric nursing	Public health nursing	Maternal and child nursing	Pediatric	Research
Human development						
Physical assessment						
Physical science						
Behavior science						
Basic skills						

change (assuming the change was approved by the president of the university) because she did not want them to have a chance to develop resistance to it among their faculty members before she had an opportunity to present it to them.

Before devising the necessary tactics for actually implementing the change in management structure, Dean Safdie developed a detailed proposal on the new structure. She then shared her proposal with several deans at other schools of nursing. In each case, the response was cautious enthusiasm. The deans believed that the idea was excellent; however, they thought that the department chairpersons would not react very positively to the change.

Cindy made an appointment with the president of the university to discuss her proposal. She submitted the draft of the proposal to him several days in advance of their meeting so that he could read the proposal. The president showed considerable interest in the proposal when he met with Cindy. He said that elimination of departments was unusual, but he was willing to consider it for the school of nursing if it was warranted. Cindy reiterated the point she made in the proposal that professional schools have different needs than nonprofessional ones (for example, Arts and Sciences). She also noted how the new system would save the school a considerable amount of money because all faculty could be used to their fullest. The president asked Cindy about the future role of the school's department chairpersons. Cindy said that some of them would become program directors and others would lose their administrative responsibilities, their secretaries, and other privileges. Cindy indicated that she did not think the department chairpersons would readily accept the change, but she thought that the change was in the best interests of the school.

The president said he would approve the change, but he cautioned Cindy to be as diplomatic as possible in dealing with the faculty. He said that many faculty members would probably feel insecure about such a major management overhaul. He also said that chairpersons should not lose the incentive salary they received as department chairperson until their contract had expired. Having the approval of the president, Cindy and her associate dean devised the following tactics for implementing the change:

1. A special faculty meeting would be called to present the management structure change to the faculty. A copy of the new management scheme would be given to each faculty member. Cindy would explain how the new scheme would work. The provost of the university would be invited to the meeting to represent the university and to give legitimacy to the management structure change.

2. The faculty would be asked to immediately select a divisional affiliation. The associate dean would then meet with the members of each division to answer any questions and to supervise the election of one person from each division to the dean's cabinet.

3. Dean Safdie would meet individually with all the department chairpersons to explain the change and how it would affect them.

4. Persons selected by the dean as program chairpersons would be notified immediately and they would meet with Cindy to discuss their role. They would be instructed to hold a meeting with their faculty members to discuss their responsibilities and assignments. These persons would also be informed that they would be given 1 month's salary in the summer for taking on the responsibility of program chairperson.

5. Faculty members would be informed of their program affiliation(s) and told that their respective program chairperson(s) would contact them to discuss their assignments.

Cindy then put the strategy and tactics into effect. The faculty meeting lasted for over 4 hours because many faculty members, especially the deposed department chairpersons, reacted very negatively to the management structure change. Many faculty members who had always been members of a department indicated considerable apprehension about the change. They were particularly concerned with who their new program chairperson might be and what their new responsibilities would be. Almost all the faculty members believed that they should have had some input into the decision to change the school's management structure. Cindy assured them, however, that the management structure of the school existed at the pleasure of the dean.

Assessment of effects

Dean Safdie was certain that the new management structure would benefit the school, especially in long-range terms. She knew that there would be more flexibility in how the faculty could be used that would ultimately result in great budgetary savings.

Approximately half the faculty considered the change as completely unacceptable. This group, led by the dissident department chairpersons, thought they could overturn Cindy's decision if they could place enough pressure on her from faculty and alumni. Accordingly, they called a meeting for interested faculty and alumni. They requested that the executive director of the state nurses' association conduct the meeting. Three groups came to the meeting: dissidents, faculty members who favored the change and who tended to be personal friends of Cindy and/or the associate dean, and a group of new faculty and alumni who did not understand the situation sufficiently well to make a decision. Interestingly, the meeting was called when Cindy was away on a consulting trip. Although the executive director of the state nurses' association tried valiantly to get the opposing groups to discuss the change, her efforts were in vain. The meeting turned into a gigantic shouting match. After several hours, the deposed department chairpersons said they were going to seek legal advice and take their case to the president of the university.

During the next 4 weeks, the faculty and students were paralyzed. The president held numerous meetings; the deposed department chairpersons handed out position papers and held extemporaneous public discussions; and faculty members discussed the situation in class. Although the dean sought to reassure the faculty that the change was in their best interests, the fact that the management structure had changed caused great anxiety. At the end of the 4 weeks, the president again met with the faculty to tell them that he upheld Dean Safdie's decision and, in fact, applauded her innovation. The deposed department chairpersons submitted their resignations immediately. The only exceptions were two chairpersons whose husbands' jobs prevented them from moving.

Only after the president of the university announced his unequivocal support for the new management structure of the school of nursing and the deposed chairpersons had submitted their resignations did normalcy return to the school of nursing. However, even though Cindy Safdie had won in her effort to change the management structure, she believed that the university had not supported her sufficiently. She decided to look for another position and immediately found a prestigious position at another private university school of nursing in the midwest. After a short but intensive search for a new dean, the associate dean was appointed to the deanship of Private University, School of Nursing.

Several years after the new management structure had been in effect, the new dean reports complete satisfaction with it. She says that there have been no problems from faculty members, and the school has been able to save a considerable amount of money through full utilization of its faculty. Prospective faculty members report some concern with the management structure, but their fears are quickly allayed when they talk to current faculty members about it.

Disengagement of the nurse–change agent

Even with the resignation of Cindy, disengagement by the nurse–change agent was not complete. Since the associate dean had been a significant part of the "change team" and had stayed, it might be contended that the nurse–change agent never relinquished control of the change plan. Even today, the division-program grid management structure remains in effect at Private University, School of Nursing, and the dean remains in complete control of its evolution to the extent that all suggested alterations in it (for example, that the research division be given different status than the other divisions so that all faculty interested in research might belong to it) require clearance from her.

Case 3 ■ CHANGING "ON DUTY" SHIFTS TO A DIFFERENT SCHEDULE
Background of nurse–change agent and initial contact with target population

Heidi Miller has almost always been considered a rebel. She chose nursing over the objections of friends and relatives, because she believed that nursing offered her an opportunity to work with people and to provide them with care. Heidi is 23 years of age; she received her A.D. degree from a community college and then went on to complete her baccalaureate degree in nursing. Even in this respect, she was different. Most of the students in her class did not think it was necessary to get their B.S.N. because the salary differential was not that substantial and most of the hospitals in the area promoted nurses with associate degrees almost as quickly as nurses with baccalaureate degrees to supervisory positions. But Heidi had other ideas; she wanted to be sure that she could go on to graduate school. Heidi's experience in college was somewhat stormy. Her parents had socialized her to ask "why" whenever something did not make sense to her. In addition, she was always interested in new (and hopefully better) ways of doing things, including nursing care. She read many nursing journals including the *American Journal of Nursing* and *Nursing Outlook.* She scanned the *Journal of Nursing Research* and *Nursing 77-79.* Accordingly, she occasionally irritated her instructors by forcing them to go into more depth about a topic or practice than they had intended to so they could answer her probing questions. Her questions included "Why do we do this instead of that?" or "Isn't this practice no longer considered as effective as another one?" These questions also forced more than one instructor to give her an angry stare.

Heidi did very well in school; she graduated with a 3.89 (out of a possible 4.00). She had no difficulty in obtaining a staff nurse position at what she considered to be the best hospital in her city: Pacific General Hospital. She liked the hospital because it was a major hospital and offered her an opportunity to rotate through many services before she had to choose a single one. After rotating through all the hospital's services, Heidi chose medical-surgical nursing. She was very excited with her choice because the nurses seemed professional, they provided what she thought was very good patient care, and she thought she could learn a lot about nursing from them.

Definition of the problem

Heidi read in a nursing journal article about the successful response of a nursing staff to a hospital's decision to change its "on-duty work shifts." A small, private hospital changed its "on duty" shifts from 8-hour days, 5 days a week to 12-hour days, 7 days a week, with the next 7 days off. The number of staff members was exactly the same, except they worked on four shifts: A, B, C, and D. When, for example, the A shift worked from 8 A.M. to 8 P.M., shift B worked from 8 P.M. to 8 A.M., and shifts C and D were off. This schedule continues for an entire week, after which shifts C and D return to work.

The article reported very high worker satisfaction. Staff members worked hard for a week, but then they could devote all their time and attention to family, friends, projects, themselves, and so forth. Many of the nurses believed that this schedule afforded them an optimal work situation; they could provide for their patients for an entire 12-hour day and they could take a vacation every other week. In other words, the staff nurses worked only 25 weeks a year (84 hours per week) because they were off every other week and they had 2 weeks for vacation.

Heidi was intrigued with the idea of the 12-hour, 7-day, 1 week on and 1 week off "on duty" schedule. On the one hand, it allowed for greater continuity of care since the one nurse could care for the patients during most of the time they were awake. On the other hand, the nurse would be off every other week.

Heidi had no idea how she should go about getting the director of the hospital and the director of nursing to accept this innovative "on duty" work schedule.

Change plan and action

Heidi knew that she had to devise a plan of action (a change strategy) with specific tactics to implement this "on duty" schedule. After reading several books about change and talking to several professors from her alma mater, Heidi devised the following change strategy and change tactics.

Change strategy

1. Review the literature about the 84-hour "on duty" workweek.
2. Develop a proposal telling how this "on duty" schedule could be implemented at Pacific General Hospital.
3. Present the proposal to the hospital's administration.
4. Survey the staff's interest in the new "on duty" work schedule.
5. Implement the plan.
6. Determine whether the new "on duty" work schedule is meeting expectations.

To carry out this plan or strategy successfully, Heidi devised the first series of tactics that would determine whether or not the hospital would try out this "on duty" schedule.

Change tactics

1. Go to hospital library and consult with librarian about relevant literature.
2. Send a letter to the hospital with the 84-hour "on duty" workweek request-

ing information such as how female staff members with young children were enticed to try out the new schedule and how the hospital dealt with staff members who refused to make the change.

3. Discuss informally the 84-hour "on duty" work schedule with supervisors and colleagues.
4. Draw up an informal proposal to present to her supervisor and the director of nursing.
5. Make a formal proposal to the director of the hospital incorporating suggestions from the director of nursing.

The hospital library, although not nearly as complete as the libraries Heidi was used to, had most of the important nursing journals, plus an *Index Medicus*. Heidi reviewed the *Index Medicus* for any heading that might provide references on nurse "on duty" work schedules. She found several citations that appeared relevant. Next, she asked the librarian for ideas on how to complete her literature review. The librarian mentioned *Index Medicus* and a Medlar Search. The librarian said that the hospital had access to a computerized medical library search that could review the titles of thousands of articles and books for ones that might be relevant to Heidi's needs. Heidi and the librarian selected some key words that the computer could use to identify relevant articles and books. The librarian told Heidi that the Medlar Search would take a week to complete.

Next, Heidi wrote a letter to the authors of the article that reported the success of the 84-hour, "on duty" workweek. She told them that she was interested in trying to implement a similar "on duty" work schedule at Pacific Hospital and any assistance they could give would be greatly appreciated. She also asked them specifically about the nurses with small children and about persons who resisted the change.

During the following week, Heidi discussed the 84-hour week with most of her friends at the hospital. She said that she read about the idea and thought it really sounded good. She asked for their opinions about it. Most of her friends were both positive and negative toward the idea. Heidi got the impression that the biggest obstacle to the change was inertia: these nurses had always worked 40-hour weeks and they were used to it. Some of the nurses wondered what they would do during the week they were off; others were unsure about how easily their families would adjust to their working 12-hour shifts. Most thought the idea had exciting prospects and suggested to Heidi that she bring it to the attention of the administration.

Heidi made a point to have lunch with her supervisor. She explained the new "on duty" schedule to her and asked for her thoughts about it. The supervisor was cautiously optimistic about the plan. She said that she believed the plan would not only require more personnel, but Pacific Hospital would have additional difficulty recruiting nurses, since the "on duty" work schedule was so unusual.

Undaunted, Heidi continued her efforts to gain as much information as possible about the advantages and disadvantages of the 84-hour "on duty" workweek. She even contacted several instructors from her school of nursing. None of these persons were helpful, however, since they were unfamiliar with the 84-hour work schedule. The Medlar Search was only marginally helpful to Heidi. It provided her with several leads (for example, articles that superficially discussed the new "on duty" work schedule), but none of the articles provided her with more information than she already had.

After several weeks, Heidi received a letter from one of the authors of the article that described the 84-hour "on duty" work schedule. The author wrote that the hospital at first gave staff an option to work a 40- or 84-hour week. Those people who wanted to work the 84-hour week were grouped on the same units. Initially, 45% of the nurses favoring the change increased to 70% and continues to increase. New nursing staff applicants did not appear to be deterred from applying at the hospital. The hospital had the most trouble with mothers who had preschool children; this group is least likely to adapt readily to the new "on duty" work schedule.

With the information Heidi had collected plus her own ideas, she drafted a proposal for an 84-hour "on duty" work schedule at Pacific Hospital. In the proposal, Heidi gave considerable attention to the advantages of this "on duty" schedule for improved patient care and staff morale. She also made the point that to facilitate this work schedule, the hospital needed to provide day (and night) care for children of nursing staff on duty. Heidi gave the draft to her supervisor and asked her for any suggestions before discussing the proposal with the director of nursing. Heidi's supervisor thought the proposal was well developed. Nonetheless, she said that she was not convinced of the benefits of the new work schedule. She said she would speak to the director of nursing and set up an appointment for Heidi to talk with her.

A week after Heidi spoke to her supervisor, she met with the director of nursing. The director told her that she was impressed with her proposal. However, she felt that getting the staff to change to the new "on duty" work schedule would be a difficult task. Heidi said she would like to determine the staff's interest in making the switch. To this end, she proposed developing a questionnaire. Heidi also proposed that the director of nursing send her to visit the hospital in which the "on duty" work schedule had been successfully implemented. The director of nursing said she would support both efforts, but she wanted to review the completed questionnaire.

Heidi immediately called the author of the article with whom she had corresponded and told her that she wanted to visit her hospital. The author said it was a good idea, and after clearing the visit with her director of nursing, she set up a visit day for Heidi. Heidi's plan in making the visit was as follows: (1) discuss in depth the strategy and tactics used by the nurse–change agent(s) to get staff members to change over to the 84-hour "on duty" work schedule, (2) discuss with staff members who had changed and who had not changed the reasons for their particular behaviors, and (3) discuss with the director of nursing whether or not the anticipated benefits of the change had been realized.

Heidi's visit was very successful. She came away even more convinced that the 84-hour "on duty" work week was beneficial to patients, staff, and hospital. The average patient remains hospitalized for about 3½ days, and during this time he relates to one nurse almost exclusively since the nurse is on duty from 8 A.M. to 8 P.M. In addition, the nurses who made the switch really enjoyed their weeks off, and as far as the director of nursing could discern, staff morale was up and turnover was down. Heidi also had received some ideas for the questionnaire she was to prepare.

When Heidi returned to Pacific Hospital, she wrote a review of her trip and sent it to her supervisor and to the director of nursing. She believed that it was politically important to include the supervisor in the project since she had been so supportive during the plan's formative period and would be an important ally in supporting the project. With all the information gathered Heidi began to construct a questionnaire to survey the nursing staff's interest in switching to the 84-hour "on duty" work schedule. She had contacted several former nursing instructors who agreed to review the questionnaire.

The questionnaire had 25 questions. She introduced it with a complete but brief description of the 84-hour "on duty" work schedule. This description included a notation that hospitals that used this schedule found patient satisfaction to be higher because continuity of care was greater. Moreover, hospitals usually established a child care center, day and night, for those parents who required this service. She wrote that the purpose of the survey was to determine nursing staff's interest in working on this new schedule. She also stated that the results of the survey were not binding but constituted a mechanism by which nursing administration could determine the staff's attitude toward the new schedule. After she drafted the questionnaire, she requested that a few close colleagues review it and make suggestions for its improvement. Heidi discussed the suggestions with her friends and incorporated several of them into the questionnaire. Next, Heidi sent copies of the questionnaire to her former instructors. She asked that they send the questionnaire back to her within a week's time. When the questionnaire was returned by her instructors, she was elated to find that the only changes made were in wording. One of the instructors suggested that Heidi include several questions requesting information about the respondent's age, family status (that is, married, single, divorced, or widowed), number and ages of dependents, and work unit. The instructor explained that the inclusion of these data would assist Heidi in making sense of the survey results. This instructor also said that a statement about the anonymity of the questionnaire should be included to increase participation.

Heidi made the suggested changes and additions and gave a copy to her supervisor. The supervisor read it carefully because, as she explained to Heidi, she felt a part of the study. Her comments were complimentary, and she told Heidi to send a copy to the director of nursing. Approximately 1 week after the director of nursing received the questionnaire, she met with Heidi. Like Heidi's supervisor, the director was impressed with the questionnaire. She said she would clear the survey with the director of the hospital. The director of nursing assured Heidi that this was only a formality; now she needed to decide how the questionnaires were to be distributed and collected. Heidi told the director of nursing that she estimated that the survey would take no more than 10 minutes to complete, and she wondered if she could administer them to the nursing staff when they changed shifts and had patient review. With some assistance from friends, she said she could survey the entire nursing staff within a short period. The director concurred but said than when the questionnaires were handed out, the staff must be told that they did not have to fill them out if they did not want to do so. Heidi agreed. A few days later, Heidi received word from the director of nursing that the director of the hospital had agreed to the survey.

Within 5 days, all the nurses in the hospital had been surveyed; only 10% refused to complete the questionnaire. It took Heidi a little more than 2 weeks to analyze the results of the survey since she had to do this during her free time.

The results were positive; more than 60% of the nurses indicated that they not only liked the 84-hour "on duty" work schedule idea, but they were willing to try it out. Heidi was happy with the finding that nurses with young children were not more likely to resist the change idea than were nurses without young children. Apparently, nurses with young children saw the hospital's offer of day care as the optimal way to care for their children without expense. As one nurse wrote, "during breaks and off weeks, I can be with my daughter, and this is more time than I presently have with her." Heidi compiled the results of her survey and discussed them with her supervisor, who was equally impressed. The supervisor told Heidi that she would make an appointment to discuss the survey's findings with the director of nursing.

Heidi was so optimistic about the chances of being able to actually implement the new "on duty" work schedule that she decided to develop the change strategy and tactics necessary to implement the change just in case the director of nursing gave her approval to the plan. If she prepared a plan before the meeting, Heidi reasoned, then she could present it to the director of nursing at that time and save the need for an additional meeting.

The following is the change strategy Heidi developed to implement the proposed 84-hour "on duty" work schedule. She would select a small number of units (with about 30% of the staff) in the hospital to be converted fully to the new "on duty" work schedule, and she would give nurses on these units and elsewhere in the hospital, if necessary, an opportunity to work the new "on duty" schedule. After the new "on duty" work schedule had been tried on these units for 6 months, she would attempt to gradually increase the number of units using the new "on duty" schedule. To implement the change strategy, Heidi devised the following change tactics:

1. Identify two medical-surgical units and one pediatric unit in the hospital with a combined staff of about 30% of the total staff to be converted to the new "on duty" schedule.
2. Advertise to all staff which units are to be converted and indicate that staff members who do not wish to change over can be switched to another pediatric or medical-surgical unit. Announce that openings on the units with the new "on duty" schedule will be filled on a "first come, first served" basis.
3. Open day/night care centers for children of nurses working the new "on duty" work schedule. Send notices to all staff members about the day/night care center and indicate that the size of the facility's staff can only accommodate children of parents on the 84-hour "on duty" shift.
4. Develop an orientation for all the nurses electing to work the new "on duty" schedule.
5. Set up and conduct orientation classes for nurses on the new "on duty" schedule.
6. Divide the staff into A, B, C, and D shifts. The B and D shifts will be smaller since these persons work the night shift. If there is an insufficient number of nurses for the night shift staff members will have to rotate through the night shift.
7. Schedule discussion sessions with each group as it completes its first, second, and third 84-hour "on duty" work schedule. During these sessions, questions can be asked and problems can be resolved.
8. Develop an evaluation plan to be implemented after the nurses have been working the new schedule for 3, 6, and 9 months. Included in the

evaluation should be patient satisfaction, nurse morale, and job satisfaction.

Heidi felt satisfied with her change strategy and change tactics. She thought she had considered most, if not all, of the important points. The use of the child care center was perhaps the weakest tactic. She theorized that since the hospital wanted to get nurses into the 84-hour "on duty" work schedule, the child care center should be offered as an amenity to them only. Nurses working the 40-hour week would have to take care of their own baby sitting problems. She believed that if the hospital did not establish this policy, there would be less incentive for the nurses to change.

Two agonizingly long weeks later, Heidi and her supervisor met with the director of nursing and the director of the hospital, who had been invited by the director. The director of the hospital immediately took charge of the meeting. He stated that he was impressed with Heidi's professionalism as a change agent. He thought she had developed an excellent questionnaire and analyzed the results of the survey correctly. He said that he had no experience with the 84-hour "on duty" work schedule, but he was intrigued by it, especially if it could reduce staff turnover and increase patient satisfaction through greater continuity of care. In an effort to familiarize himself with this "on duty" work schedule, he had called a few hospitals with similar work schedules and found the directors to be highly satisfied with them.

Heidi was amazed at the reception she received. She never thought of herself as a change agent and now the director of the hospital was praising the work she had done. Heidi was very happy, indeed.

The director of nursing then said that the board of directors of Pacific Hospital had agreed for nursing service to try a pilot project with the new work schedule. She wanted Heidi to implement a plan as soon as she could. Heidi said that she had anticipated a positive reaction from the hospital's management and had already developed a change strategy with change tactics. With that, she distributed the materials. During the following 3 hours, the director of the hospital, the director of nursing, Heidi, and her supervisor discussed and evaluated each tactic she proposed for implementing the new 84-hour "on duty" work schedule.

Whether the hospital could legitimately exclude nurses working the 40-hour week from the child care center was the major area of discussion. The director of the hospital recognized the "carrot" effect of the center but was dubious about using it as a weapon to induce nurses to switch to the new schedule. Heidi's supervisor then made a suggestion: why not open it to all nurses but give priority to those working the 84-hour "on duty" schedule. If utilization increases to the point where the service became too expensive, the nurses could be charged a fee for its use; however, the nurses working the 84-hour week could receive incentive pay for working the longer shift and this would reduce the cost of the day care to them. The supervisor's suggestion appealed to everyone. The director of the hospital told Heidi that she had his support, financial and otherwise, to begin implementing the new work schedule, which she did immediately.

With the help of the director of nursing, Heidi and her supervisor identified two medical-surgical units and one pediatric unit that would have their shifts changed. The supervisor located a room in the hospital that was painted and prepared as a child care center with beds, furniture, and toys. She then instructed the personnel department to hire four full-time and two part-time staff persons to run the center. In the meantime, the director of nursing sent notices to the staff members working on the three affected units and on all the other units in the hospital describing the change and announcing that the new "on duty" work schedule would be operational the first of the following month. The notice also asked for volunteers to work the new "on duty" work schedule as well as announcing that the new child care center was opening soon. Interested staff members were told to send a note to the director of nursing; the phone numbers of the director of nursing and Heidi were provided for persons who needed further information and/or questions answered.

Response to the call for volunteers was outstanding. Over 50% of the 200 nursing staff members (110) sent notes to the director of nursing that they wished to work the new work schedule. Since 35 of the 60 nurses working on the three units changing to the new "on duty" schedule volunteered to work the new schedule, it was necessary to select only 25 nurses from other units.

Heidi was elated with the results; the response of the staff was greater than she had hoped for. The high response rate also allowed for selection of staff that Heidi, her supervisor, and the director of nursing thought would work out best. Moreover, the response made it possible for at least two additional units to be quickly converted as soon as the change was justified as a result of the evaluation. With 110 volunteers, Heidi had no trouble selecting two night and two day teams.

During the 3-week period prior to beginning the new "on duty" schedule, the director of nursing and Heidi met frequently with the nurses selected to work on the three units. They told them that the units would function the same way as those with 8-hour "on duty" work schedules; however, the staff on the new schedule would have greater opportunity to be involved with their patients (at least during the day shift) because they would be with them all day long. Heidi told the group that the 12-hour shift might cause some personal problems and they should immediately see their supervisor or her for assistance in working these out. Heidi also told the nurses that she would be conducting an evaluation of the effectiveness of the new 84-hour "on duty" work schedule. To accomplish this task, she needed the complete cooperation of the staff. An evaluation was necessary because this "on duty" schedule was new and untested. Therefore, it was necessary to assess whether or not it was more effective than the traditional "on duty" schedule. By the time the new work schedule was to be put into effect, Heidi, her supervisor, and the director of nursing had the child care center in operation, the cafeteria prepared to meet the new eating needs of the staff on the three units, notified personnel of the payroll changes of the nurses on the new schedule, and developed some measures for evaluating the effectiveness of the change.

On the first of the month, shifts A and B began their 84-hour "on duty" workweek; shifts C and D were used throughout the hospital for only 30 hours. At the end of the week, shifts C and D began their 84-hour "on duty" work schedule, and shifts A and B took the week off.

Each week for the next month, Heidi met with the staff of each shift as it completed its week's shift. She discussed their morale, tiredness, response of patients, and the whole 84-hour "on duty" work schedule concept. She was able to report to her supervisor and the director of nursing that staff morale was very high; the staff was tired at the end of its shift, but the longer they worked the new schedule the better able they were to pace themselves; patients seemed satisfied with their nurses being present during the entire day and for most, if not all, of the period they were hospitalized; and finally, staff liked the new schedule. Another indication of staff acceptance was the constant flow of messages from nursing and non-nursing staff members requesting transferral to the new schedule. After 6 months and a positive evaluation, the hospital began expanding its 84-hour "on duty" work schedule to other units.

Evaluation of the change plan

While the hospital was preparing to change the three units to the new "on duty" work schedule, Heidi began developing her evaluation plan. She went to the library and located several books on program evaluation as well as several studies of hospitalized patient satisfaction. Heidi also located a research study assessing hospital staff nurse satisfaction. After reading these, she went to see two of her former instructors to get some ideas for an effective evaluation plan. Her efforts resulted in the following:

1. Development of a patient satisfaction questionnaire.
2. Development of a job satisfaction questionnaire for staff members.
3. Develop a form for collecting information from nurses who resigned from the new work schedule.
4. Devise a plan to monitor patient satisfaction before and after introduction of the new work schedule and on units with the new "on duty" work schedule and the old "on duty" work schedule (40 hours per week) but during the same period.

Before putting the evaluation plan into effect, Heidi presented the plan with accompanying questionnaires and termination form to her supervisor and the director of nursing. The three of them discussed the plan, questionnaire, and form; after some changes they agreed that the evaluation plan was ready for implementation.

During the last few weeks preceding the change in the three units to the new "on duty" work schedule, Heidi, in addition to orienting the nurses to the new work schedule, administered the evaluation questionnaires to patients and staff members. The staff satisfaction questionnaire was administered before and after the new "on duty" work schedule went into effect; it was also administered to a group of nurses who were on the old "on duty" work schedule 2 months after the new schedule was introduced.

An assistant director of nursing was assigned by the director of nursing to conduct all termination interviews with nurses who elected to leave a unit with the new "on duty" work schedule. It is interesting to note that in the first 6 months that the new schedule was in operation, none of the nurses on the units resigned or changed units. Elsewhere in Pacific Hospital, the nurse turnover rate averaged 30%.

Heidi expected high patient satisfaction as a result of her review of the literature. Her expectations were met as patient satisfaction was 80% on units before they were changed to the new schedule and 93% after the change. Whereas 93% of the patients on the units with the change in working schedule were satisfied with their care, only 82% of patients on other units surveyed at the same time were satisfied. The differences were significant. Furthermore, staff satisfaction was found to be significantly higher on the units with the 84-hour "on duty" work schedule.

Heidi was thoroughly delighted with the results of the evaluation. She was positively reinforced by her initial interest in the new "on duty" schedule. The hospital changed an additional three units and, 1 year later, was getting ready to change another three units and to extend the "on duty" schedule to nonnursing personnel.

Disengagement of the nurse–change agent

The director of nursing kept Heidi involved in the change of units to the 84-hour "on duty" work schedule until 80% of the nursing staff at Pacific Hospital was working the new schedule. At that point, the director of nursing told Heidi that she was extremely pleased with the change; however, the change was sufficiently internalized that the hospital did not need a special change agent running it. To show her appreciation for Heidi's excellent work, she offered Heidi a position as assistant director of nursing. After considerable thought, Heidi chose to delay accepting the position until she had another year of "seasoning" as a nurse. She believed that she could be a much better nurse administrator if she knew more about nursing.

Case 4 ■ NURSES ON STRIKE
Background of nurse–change agent

Melanie Martin is a 28-year-old graduate nurse who has practiced for 4 years. Prior to entering nursing school, Melanie was first a secretary and then a real estate agent. She went to Baptist Hospital School of Nursing in the city where she was born and raised. After graduation, she selected the obstetric unit in Baptist Hospital, a 600-bed, general hospital. Like many of her classmates, Melanie chose Baptist Hospital because she felt very much at "home" there. She knew many of the doctors, nurses, hospital administrators, and other staff members.

Contact with the target population and definition of the problem

Baptist Hospital is 15 years old. When it was built, it was the largest hospital in South City. Since that time, very few additional rooms have been added even though the population of the area had increased by 45%. Baptist Hospital, like most other hospitals, admitted patients to specific units according to the patient's diagnosis. Thus, ophthalmology patients went to the ophthalmology unit, obstetric patients to the obstetric-gynecologic unit, and surgical patients to the unit that performed the specific type of surgery. Although the demand for beds increased, the bed occupancy rate in the hospital only reached 80%. However, the hospital found that it was refusing patients even though it was not at full occupancy. To reverse this situation and thereby increase the occupancy rate of the hospital, the administration decided to have "open admissions," that is, patients would be admitted to the hospital whether or not a bed was available on the appropriate unit. However, the hospital would attempt to move patients to the appropriate unit as soon as a bed was available.

The nursing staff was both worried and upset over the hospital administration's decision to "open admissions." Most of the nurses felt inadequate in caring for a wide variety of patients, especially those nurses who had been caring for specific patients over a long period. In other words, nurses who had been working exclusively on the ophthalmological surgery unit for a long period felt unsure of themselves in treating and caring for obstetric patients.

The nurses at Baptist Hospital, like those at other hospitals, developed their own patient care plans (referred to as individualized care plans). Each individualized care plan was developed for the nurse's specific patient and, thus, was individualized. Most experienced nurses had little trouble developing an appropriate individualized patient care plan within their clinical specialty experience. The introduction of "open admissions" ended many nurses' dependency on experience in developing individualized patient care plans. How could a nurse develop a care plan for an obstetric patient when she had not cared for an obstetric patient in 6 years? The hospital's director of nursing told the nurses that they would have to use library resources to develop their care plans if they were unfamiliar with a particular problem. The nurses asked the director of nursing, without any response, how they could use the library when they had many patients to care for besides having patients with a condition with which they were unfamiliar?

Melanie, like most of her friends and co-workers, was very apprehensive about the hospital's switch to "open admissions." Although, it was only 4 years since she had graduated from nursing school, where she had rotated through most of the major hospital services, she really had forgotten much about caring for patients others than those with obstetric-gynecologic problems. She knew that she would not be able to develop a complete patient care plan for patients who did not have obstetric-gynecologic problems.

Soon after "open admissions" was initiated at Baptist Hospital, Melanie began to receive an abundance of calls from nurses on other floors with gynecologic patients. In each case, they wanted to know what should be included on their patient's care plan. Melanie found herself in the same situation when she had to care for a male patient who had undergone abdominal surgery. She immediately called a nurse friend on a medical-surgical unit who would be familiar with this type of patient. Her friend was very helpful, and Melanie believed that she was able to give her patient adequate care. The whole procedure of having to call another nurse to find out how to plan the care for a patient bothered Melanie. Not only did the process waste her time but also that of the "consulted" nurse.

Melanie thought of an idea by which the quality of care could be maintained even if a nurse had to care for a patient whose care requirements were not familiar to her. Her idea was for the hospital to encourage its nurses to develop standardized patient care plans that could be used throughout the hospital. Specifically, she envisioned the nurses in each specialty developing patient care plans for their patients. These care plans would be developed in such a way as to include normative variations between patients. By allowing for normative variations, the care plans would direct the nurse to different activities depending, for instance, on symptoms and severity of condition.

Change plan and action

Melanie thought her idea was good. But before she shared it with anyone, she wanted to make sure that the idea would actually work. She went to the medical library and looked through the *Index Medicus* under the general heading of nursing for articles about patient care plans. To her amazement, she found several in the best nursing journals. She got two of the journals and immediately found that there were already several available sets of so-called standardized nursing care plans. These could be purchased and used. The idea for these standardized care plans was the same as Melanie's—to improve nursing care delivered to patients. However, the authors wrote that some nurses, even if they were familiar with the nursing problems of their patients, did not develop adequate nursing care plans. The availability of standardized care plans that the nurse could augment (that is, personalized to meet the particular needs of the patient) would help to ensure an optimal level of nursing care.

Melanie made copies of the articles that she believed best made a case for using standardized patient care plans. Now, however, she was stymied. "What do I do next?" she asked herself. She decided to use the hospital's suggestion box as her first point of attack. She wrote a short but complete narrative about the problems nurses were having with open admissions and suggested standardized patient care plans as a viable solution. She cited the articles she found and indicated a willingness to help implement standardized care plans in the hospital.

After waiting 3 weeks, Melanie became very disillusioned with the hospital's suggestion program. She did not receive notification from the hospital that her suggestion had been received, let alone considered. Her first inclination was to forget the whole thing; if the hospital could not even acknowledge receipt of her suggestion, why should she waste her time trying to improve the quality of nursing care, increase nurse efficiency, and improve nurse morale. After 2 more weeks of depression, a good portion of which resulted from the kidding she received from friends who knew her suggestion had not been acknowledged, Melanie decided that patient care was really the issue, not the hospital. She was interested in standardizing patient care plans because patients would benefit from them.

But Melanie was still unsure how to introduce a change into Baptist Hospital, especially one as major as standardized care plans. If administration did not listen to staff suggestions, how receptive would they be to change? One of Melanie's friends suggested that she find out what happened to her suggestion before she tried some other approach or before she gave up on the idea. Melanie called the office of the administrator of the hospital and asked one of his assistants about her suggestion. The first person she spoke to told her he did not know anything about the suggestion plan, but perhaps someone else in the office did. But no one did. The first assistant hospital director told Melanie that as far as he could determine the hospital had stopped the program because there rarely was a suggestion worth evaluating. "Well, where is the suggestion I put in the suggestion box on R-17," Melanie asked? "Probably still in the box," replied the assistant hospital director.

Melanie was angry, confused, and amused—a suggestion plan that was inoperative and her suggestion was still in an unused suggestion box. She told the assistant hospital director that she had an important suggestion to make to improve the quality of patient care, but the suggestion was in an unopened box. She told him she wanted her suggestion back. The assistant director said he was sorry about the confusion over the suggestion box, and he would return the suggestion to her personally. That same afternoon, the assistant director returned Melanie's suggestion to her. He again apologized; he said that he had taken the liberty of reading the suggestion and was interested in it. He also said that he would make copies of the suggestion and distribute it to the director of nursing and the director of the hospital. In a few days, there would be a staff meeting and it would be discussed there.

A few days later, Melanie received a note from the director of nursing. She acknowledge Melanie's suggestion and wrote that she had created a task force to look into standardized patient care plans. Melanie was glad to be acknowledged but also disheartened by not being included on the task force. Rightly or wrongly, she felt let down and abused. If her idea was worthy of a "task force," why wasn't she included on it? How could she be a change agent if the "powers that be" would not give her any authority to help make change? The whole situation bothered her.

One month after Melanie received the note from the director of nursing, the feature article in the hospital's newsletter announced that Baptist Hospital was going to use standardized patient care plans in situations in which the staff was unsure of the optimal way to care for a patient. Standardized care plans had been purchased and were to be made available throughout the hospital.

Melanie was thrilled that her suggestion had been accepted, but at the same time skeptical as to whether the standardized care plans purchased from an outside firm would be sufficiently applicable to the needs of the patients at Baptist Hospital. It was Melanie's idea for Baptist Hospital's nurses to create their own standardized care plan.

Within the week, the head nurse on each unit introduced the standardized care plans to their staff. Large, loose-leaf notebooks were placed at the nurse's station for use by the nurses. The head nurses told the staff that if they had any difficulty developing a care plan for their patients, they should consult the standardized care plans.

It soon became obvious to Melanie and most of the staff that the standardized care plans frequently were too general to help them sufficiently with certain types of patients. In this case, the nurse would have to call one of the nurses on the appropriate unit for advice and instructions. Usually, the nurse would write these instructions down on the back of the care plan so that they could be used by other nurses if they had a similar case.

After working with the new standardized care plans for 6 months, Melanie observed that the ones on her unit were almost entirely rewritten. There were arrows directing the user to the back for variations in the care plan and many directions were scratched out. Melanie thought it would be valuable if a group of nurses would go through all the standardized care plans and rewrite and update them to make them more applicable. Melanie decided to go directly to the director of nursing with her suggestion. She wanted very much to be on this committee, and she felt discussing the situation with the director would increase her prospects.

Melanie was able to get an appointment with the director of nursing for the following week. She took a set of the standardized nursing care plans with her to illustrate her point. The director quickly reviewed the standardized care plans as Melanie made her suggestion. After a while the director told her that her suggestion was interesting, but she was not convinced that changing the care plans would improve the quality of care that nurses would give. "Besides," she said, "the care plans are already augmented, and why should the hospital waste money changing them?" Melanie said that whereas her unit had worked very conscientiously on their standardized care plans, other units had not. Therefore, this would cause considerable divergency in the quality of nursing care. But as persuasive as Melanie was and as aggressive as she was in making her point, the director of nursing could not be swayed. Melanie left her office feeling very frustrated.

Melanie decided that she would rework the standardized care plans on her own unit. If other units wanted copies, they could come and get them. She did not feel very appreciated at Baptist Hospital; the patients on the unit where she worked would nonetheless receive good care.

It is obvious that Melanie never was able to develop a change strategy with change tactics so that the standardized care plans could be implemented in Baptist Hospital. The director of nursing assumed control of the idea for change and developed her own change strategy and tactics. But, interestingly enough, Melanie's determination and drive to provide optimum nursing care spurred her to continue her efforts to make the standardized care plans as good as possible.

Assessing effectiveness

Melanie had no way of assessing the effectiveness of the standardized care plans. As far as she knew, the director of nursing did not attempt to determine if they were more effective than individualized nursing care plans. But Melanie did know that the standardized care plans helped her and her colleagues; when she itegrated the additional ideas of the staff into the care plans that the hospital had purchased, they helped even more. Finally, many head nurses, hearing how Melanie had made the care plans more appropriate to Baptist Hospital patients, made copies of the ones on her unit.

Disengagement of the nurse–change agent

In one sense, there was no need for Melanie to disengage from the change population: she was never allowed to fully effect a change. However, she was very much a force, informal to be sure, in getting standardized care plans into Baptist Hospital. Melanie only remained at Baptist Hospital for another year; she left for a "better" job at a hospital in the same area.

BIBLIOGRAPHY

Adams, D.: The monkey and the fish, cultural pitfalls of an educational advisor, Int. Dev. Rev. **2:**22-24, 1960.

Ajzen, I., and Fishbein, M.: Attitudes and normative beliefs as factors influencing behavioral intentions, J. Pers. Soc. Psychol. **21:**1-9, 1972.

Allen, F. R.: Sociocultural dynamics, New York, 1971, The Macmillan Co.

Appelbaum, R. P.: Theories of social change, Chicago, 1970, Markham Publishing Co.

Asch, S. E.: Opinions and social pressure, Sci. Am. **217:**31-35, 1955.

Aspree, E.: The process of change, Supervisor Nurse **6:**15-24, 1975.

Bailey, J. T., and Claus, K. E.: Decision making in nursing: tools for change, St. Louis, 1975, The C. V. Mosby Co.

Barnett, H. G.: Innovation: the basis of cultural change, New York, 1953, McGraw-Hill Book Co.

Bartlett, A. C., and Kayser, T. A., editors: Changing organizational behavior, Englewood Cliffs, N.J. 1973, Prentice-Hall, Inc.

Bartlett, A. C., and Kayser, T. A.: Organizational change: a trial synthesis. In Bartlett, A. C., and Kayser, T. A., editors: Changing organizational behavior, Englewood Cliffs, N.J. 1973, Prentice-Hall, Inc.

Benne, K. D., Bradford, L. P., Gibb, J. R., and Lippitt, R. O., editors: The laboratory method of changing and learning, Palo Alto, Calif., 1975, Science and Behavior Books.

Bennis, W. G.: Changing organizations, McGregor Memorial Lectures, Cambridge, Mass., 1966, The M.I.T. Press.

Bennis, W. G., Benne, K. D., and Chin, R.: The planning of change, ed. 3, New York, 1976, Holt, Rinehart and Winston, Inc.

Bennis, W. G., Berlew, D. E., Shein, E. H., and Steele, F, I.: Interpersonal dynamics ed. 3, Hamewood, Ill., 1973, Dorsey Press.

Bentley, P.: Health care agencies and professionals: a changing relationship, New York, 1977, National League for Nursing.

Berger, B.: Societies in change, New York, 1971, Basic Books.

Bertran, A.: Social organization, Philadelphia, 1972, F. A. Davis Co.

Bevona, C. M.: The nursing cap. In Miller, M. H., and Flynn, B., editors: Current perspectives in nursing: social issues and trends, vol. 2, St. Louis, 1979, The C. V. Mosby Co.

Blum, H. L.: Planning for health: development and applications of social change theory, New York, 1974, Human Sciences Press.

Bohr, R. H., et al.: Employee protest and social change in the health care organization, Am. J. Pub. Health **61:**2229-2235, 1971.

Bowman, R. A., and Culpepper, R. C.: Power: R_x for change, Am. J. Nurs. **74:**1053, 1974.

Brooten, D. A., Hayman, L. L., and Naylor, M. D.: Leadership for change: a guide for the frustrated nurse, Philadelphia, 1978, J. B. Lippincott Co.

Brown, L. R.: Seeds of change: the green revolution and development in the 1970s, New York, 1970, Praeger Publishers, Inc.

Bruhn, J. G.: Planning for social change: dilemmas for health planning, Am. J. Public Health **63:**602-606, 1973.

Bryk, J.: Learning performance in the defensive driving course and the self-instruction program, research report, New York, Nov., 1973, National Safety Council Research Dept.

Buckley, W.: Sociology and modern systems theory, Englewood Cliffs, N.J., 1967, Prentice-Hall, Inc.

Cain, G. G., and Hollister, R. G.: The methodology of evaluating social action programs. In Rossi, P. H., and Williams, W., editors: Evaluating social programs, New York, 1972, Seminar Press.

Campbell, A., and Convers, P. E.: The human meaning of social change, New York, 1972, Russell Sage Foundation.

Change, conflict, continuing education, competency, Supervisor Nurse **10:**26-27, 1979.

Christman, L.: Change is in order, editorial, J. Nurs. Admin. **1:**9, 1971.

Christman, L.: Dammit—do it strategy for change, Hosp. Topics, **52**(7):67, 1974.

Christman, L.: Knowledge, change and nursing care, Am. J. Nurs. **66:**2627-2629, 1966.

Cochran, T. C.: Towards a useful model for social change. In Taylor, G. R., and Ellsworth, L. F., editors: Approaches to American economic history, Charlottesville, Va., 1971, University of Virginia Press.

Coe, R. M., editor: Planned change in the hospital, New York, 1979, Praeger Publishers, Inc.

Coleman, J. S.: Conflicting theories of social change, Am. Behav. Sci. **14:**633, 1971.

Copp, L. A.: Inservice education copes with resistance to change, J. Cont. Ed. Nurs. **6**(2):19-27, 1975.

Dalton, G. W.: Influence and organizational change. In Bartlett, A. C., and Kayser, T. A., editors: Changing organizational behavior, Englewood Cliffs, N.J. 1973, Prentice-Hall, Inc.

Day, H.: Change can be planned and effected, Supervisor Nurse **5:**147-149, 1974.

Deal, J.: The timing of change, Supervisor Nurse **8:**73-79, 1977.

Etzioni, A., and Etzioni, E., editors: Social change: sources, patterns and consequences, ed. 2, New York, 1973, Basic Books, Inc., Publishers.

Fann, W. E., and Goshen, E. E.: The language of mental health, ed. 2, St. Louis, 1977, The C. V. Mosby Co.

Ford, L. C., and Silver, H. K.: The expanded role of the nurse in child care, Nurs. Outlook, Sept., 1967.

Garant, C. A.: The process of effecting change in nursing, Nurs. Forum **17**(2):153-167, 1978.

Gerlach, L. P., and Hine, V. H.: Lifeway leap: the dynamics of change in America, Minneapolis, 1973, University of Minnesota Press.

Gerlach, L. P., and Hine, V. H.: People, power, change: movements of social transformation, Indianapolis, 1970, The Bobbs-Merrill Co., Inc.

Gibson, C.: The concept of change, Maine Nurse **4:**13-16, 1973.

Girouard, S.: The role of the clinical specialist as change agent: an experiment in preoperative teaching, Int. J. Nurs. Stud. **15:** 57-65, 1978.

Glenn, R. N., et al.: Assessing the potential of change in institutions, Psychiatr. Q. **49:** 322-330, 1977.

Gordon, M.: The clinical specialist as change agent. In Riehl, J. P., and McVay, J. W., editors: The clinical nurse specialist, New York, 1973, Appleton-Century-Crofts.

Green, L. W.: Change-process models in health education, Public Health Rev. **5:** 5-33, 1976.

Gross, N., Giacquinta, J., and Berstein, M.: Implementing organizational innovation: a sociological analysis of planned change, New York, 1971, Basic Books, Inc., Publishers.

Grossman, L.: The change agent, New York, 1974, AMACON.

Hage, J., and Aiken, M.: Social change in complex organizations, New York, 1970, Random House, Inc.

Havelock, R. G.: The change agent's guide to innovation in education, Englewood Cliffs, N.J. 1973, Educational Technology Publications, Inc.

Havelock, R. G.: Planning for innovation, Ann Arbor, 1971, Center for Research on Utilization of Scientific Knowledge, University of Michigan.

Havelock, R. G., and Havelock, M. C.: Training for change agents, Ann Arbor, 1973, Institute for Social Research, University of Michigan.

Heneman, H. G.: Collective bargaining, a major instrument for change, Am. J. Nurs. **68:**1039-2042, 1968.

Herder, F.: The psychology of interpersonal relations, New York, 1958, John Wiley & Sons, Inc.

Hollander, E. P.: Principles and methods of social psychology, ed. 3, New York, 1976, Oxford University Press.

Hollander, E. P., and Hunt, R. G., editors:

Current perspectives in social psychology, ed. 4, London, 1976, University Press.

Homans, G. C.: The human group, New York, 1950, Harcourt Brace Jovanovich, Inc.

Hornstein, H. A., et al., editors: Social intervention: a behavioral science approach, New York, 1971, The Free Press.

Horwitz, M.: The conceptual status of group dynamics. In Bennis, W. G., Benne, K. D., and Chin, R., editors: The planning of change, ed. 3, New York, 1976, Holt, Rhinehart and Winston, Inc.

Jones, M.: Nurses can change the social systems of hospitals, Am. J. Nurs. **78:**1012-1014, 1978.

Kasulis, J.: Cognitive structure, segmented analyses and communication effectiveness, unpublished Ph.D. thesis, Evanston, Ill., 1975, Northwestern University.

Kelman, H., and Warwick, D. P.: Bridging micro and macro approaches to social change: a social-psychological perspective. In Zaltman, G., editor: Processes and phenomena of social change, New York, 1973, John Wiley & Sons, Inc.

King, B. T., and McGinnies, E.: Attitudes, conflict, and social change, New York, 1972, Academic Press, Inc.

Knable, J., and Petre, G.: Resistance to role implementation, Supervisor Nurse **10:**31-34, 1979.

Koss, E.: Health in regionville, New York, 1954, Columbia University Press.

Kothandapani, U.: Validation of feeling, belief, and intention to act as three components of attitude and their contribution to prediction of contraceptive behavior, J. Pers. Soc. Psychol. **19:**321-333, 1971.

Kramer, M.: Reality shock: why nurses leave nursing, St. Louis, 1974, The C. V. Mosby Co.

Larsen, L.: Reflections of change in nursing, Kansas Nurse **12:**2-3, 1972.

Lassey, W. R.: Leadership and social change, Iowa City, Iowa 1971, University Associates.

Lauer, R. H.: Perspectives on social change, ed. 2, Boston, 1977, Allyn & Bacon, Inc.

Lawrence, P.: How to deal with resistance to change, Harv. Busi. Rev. **47:**4-8, 1969.

Lee, I.: Cope with resistance to change, Nursing 73 **3:**6-7, 1973.

Lee, K. H.: Social marketing strategies in nutrition education, unpublished Ph.D. dissertation, Evanston, Ill., 1975, Northwestern University.

Levenstein, A.: Effective change requires change agent, J. Nurs. Admin. **9:**12-15, 1979.

Levenstein, A.: Problem solving techniques for managing change, Hosp. Top. **52:**42, 1974.

Levine, M. E.: The four conservation principles of nursing, Nurs. Forum **6:**45-59, 1967.

Lewis, E. P., editor: Changing patterns of nursing practice, New York, 1971 American Journal of Nursing.

Lippitt, G.: Visualizing change: model building and the change process, Fairfax, Va., 1973, NTL Learning Resources Corp.

Lippitt, R., Watson, J., and Westley, B.: The dynamics of planned change, New York, 1958, Harcourt, Brace Jovanovich, Inc.

Loewenberg, F., and Dolgoff, R., editors: The practice of social intervention: roles, goals and strategies, Itasca, Ill., 1972, F. E. Peacock Publishers, Inc.

Lundborg, L. B.: Future without shock, New York, 1974, W. W. Norton & Co., Inc.

Marriner, A.: Conflict theory, Supervisor Nurse **10:**12-16, 1979.

Marriner, A.: Current perspectives in nursing management, vol. 1, St. Louis, 1979, The C. V. Mosby Co.

Mauksch, I., and Rogers, M. E.: Nursing is coming of age through the practitioner movement, pro: I. Mauksch, con: M. E. Rogers, Am. J. Nurs. **75:**1834-1843, 1975.

McFarland, G. K.: Implementing change in a nursing service, personal communication, 1978.

Merton, R. K.: Social theory and structure, New York, 1956, The Free Press.

Middlebrook, P. A.: Social psychology and modern life, New York, 1974, Alfred A. Knopf, Inc.

Miller, M. H.: Academic inbreeding in nursing, Nurs. Outlook **25:**172-177, 1977.

Miller, M. H.: Changes in self-perception of nurse practitioner: stress, assertiveness, and sex role ideology. In Miller, M. H., and Flynn, B. C., editors: Current perspectives in nursing: social issues and trends, vol. 1, St. Louis, 1977, The C. V. Mosby Co.

Miller, M. H.: Nurses' right to strike, J. Nurs. Admin. **5:**35, 1975.

Miller, M. H.: Special interest groups of the ANA: an analysis. In Miller, M. H., and Flynn, B. C., editors: Current perspectives in nursing: social issues and trends, vol. 1, St. Louis, 1977, The C. V. Mosby Co.

Miller, M. H., and Dodson, L.: Toward a theory of professional work stoppage: the case of nursing. In Miller, M. H., and Flynn, B. C., editors: Current perspectives in nursing: social issues and trends, vol. 1, St. Louis, 1977, The C. V. Mosby Co.

Miller, M. H., and Flynn, B. C.: The American Nurses' Association: to join or not to join. In Miller, M. H., and Flynn, B. C., editors: Current perspectives in nursing: social issues and trends, vol. 1, St. Louis, 1977, The C. V. Mosby Co.

Miller, P. W.: Open minds to old ideas: new look at reorganization, Nurs. Admin. Q. **3:** 77-84, 1979.

Millman, H. H., editor: Nursing personnel and the changing health care system, Cambridge, Mass., 1978, Ballinger Publishing Co.

Milo, N.: Health care organizations and innovation, J. Health Soc. Behav. **12:**167-173, 1971.

Morrow, J. T., et al.: Developing strategies to effect change (#52-1537), New York, 1974, NLN Publ. Div. Community Planning 1-29.

The Nations Health: Washington, D.C., **9:** 1, 1979,

Nehls, D., et al.: Planned change: a guest for nursing autonomy, J. Nurs. Admin. **4:**23-27, 1974.

Notter, L. E.: Essentials of nursing research, New York, 1974, Springer Publishing Co., Inc.

Okediji, F. O.: Overcoming social and cultural resistances, Int. J. Health Ed. **15:** 3-10, 1972.

Olsen, A.: Change takes time, Nursing Admin. Q. **1:**51-59, 1977.

Olsen, M. E.: The process of social organization: power in social systems, New York, 1978, Holt, Rinehart and Winston, Inc.

Osgood, C. E., and Tannebaum, P. H.: The principle of congruity in the prediction of attitude change, Psychol. Rev. **62:**42-55, 1955.

Parsons, T.: A functional theory of change. In Etzioni, E., and Etzioni, A., editors: Social change, New York, 1964, Basic Books, Inc.

Pierce, S. F., et al.: Changing practice: by choice rather than chance, J. Nurs. Admin. **6:**33-39, 1976.

Pierik, M. M.: Experiment to effect change, Supervisor Nurse **2:**69-75, 1971.

Porter, K. W.: Change for patients' sake (Milwaukee, Ws., St. Mary's Hospital) J. Nurs. Admin. **3:**37-42, 1973.

Poulin, M. A.: Nursing service: change or managerial obsolescence, J. Nurs. Admin. **9:**40-43, 1974.

Presidential address: Tenth annual American Nurses' Association convention, Am. J. Nurs. **7:**799, 1907.

Reinkemeyer, A. M.: Nursing's need: commitment to an ideology of change, Nurs. Forum **9:**340-355, 1970.

Robertson, T.: Innovative behavior and communication, New York, 1971, Holt, Rinehart and Winston, Inc.

Robinson, R.: Toward a conceptualization of leadership for change, Adult Educ. J. **20:** 131, 1970.

Rodgers, J.: The clinical specialist as a change agent, J. Psychiatr. Nurs. **12:**5-9, 1974.

Rodgers, J.: Theoretical considerations involved in the process of change, Nurs. Forum **13:**160-174, 1973.

Rogers, E. M.: Change agents, clients and change. In Zaltman, G., Kotter, P., and Kaufman, I., editors: Creating social change, New York, 1972, Holt, Rinehart and Winston, Inc.

Rogers, E. M.: Social structure and social change, Am. Behav. Sci. **14:**767-782, 1971.

Rogers, E. M., and Bhomuk, D. K.: Homophily-heterophily: relational concepts for communication research, Public Opinion Q. **34:**523-538, 1971.

Rogers, E. M., and Shoemaker, E. F.: Communication of innovations: a cross cultural approach, New York, 1971, The Free Press.

Rogers, E. M., and Svenning, L.: Modernization among peasants: the impact of communication, New York, 1969, Holt, Rinehart and Winston, Inc.

Rokeach, M.: Beliefs, attitudes, and values, San Francisco, 1968, Jossey-Bass, Inc., Publishers.

Rose, M. A.: Organization in the hospital:

some strategies for nurses, Nurs. Admin. Q. **3:**89-93, 1979.

Rosenstock, I. M.: Why people use health services, Milbank Mem. Fund. Q. **44:**94-127, 1966.

Rothman, J., Erlich, J., and Teresa, J.: Promoting innovation and change in organizations and communities, New York, 1976, John Wiley & Sons, Inc.

Schaller, L. E.: The change agent, New York, 1972, Abingdon Press.

Schwier, M. E., and Gardella, F. A.: Identifying the need for change in nursing service, Nurs. Outlook **18:**56-62, 1970.

Scurrah, M., Shani, M., and Zipfel, C.: Influence of internal and external change agents in a simulated educational organization, Admin. Sci. Q. **16:**113-121, 1971.

Shetland, M. L.: Changing needs and changing roles, Occup. Health Nurse. **20:**17-19, 1972.

Silver, H. K., and Ford, L. C.: The pediatric nurse practitioner of Colorado, Am. J. Nurs. **67:**1443-1444, 1967.

Silver, H. K., Ford, L. C., and Stearly, S. G.: A program to increase health care for children: the pediatric program, Pediatr. Nurs. Currents **14**(4):1-2, 1967.

Simeon, S. R.: Educators as change agents in the institution of nursing, J. Contin. Educ. Nurs. **6:**7-12, 1975.

Smith, A. D.: The concept of social change, London, 1973, Routledge and Kegan Paul Press.

Smith, I. A.: Personal and professional objectives for change, Occup. Health Nurs. **25:**18-20, 1977.

Smoyak, S.: The confrontation process, Am. J. Nurs. **74:**1632, 1974.

Spalding, W. B.: The dynamics of planned change, New York, 1958, Harcourt, Brace Jovanovich, Inc.

Stein, L.: The doctor-nurse game, Am. J. Nurs. **68:**101-105, 1968.

Stevens, B.: Effecting change, J. Nurs. Admin. **10:**23-26, 1975.

Stevens, B. J.: Management of continuity and change in nursing, J. Nurs. Admin. **7:** 26, 1977.

Sullivan, M. E.: Processes of change in an expanded role in nursing in a mental health setting, J. Psychiatr. Nurs. **15**(2):18-24, 1977.

Sutton, J. M.: Nursing: change and how change has been effected, Alumni Mag. **74:** 13-18, 1977.

Swanson, G. E.: Social change, Glenview, Ill., 1971, Scott, Foresman and Co.

Taker, J., Saunders, B., and Etlaro, S., editors: New roles and changing relationship—new directions in the nursing profession, University Park, Pa., 1974, College of Human Development, The Pennsylvania State University Press.

Taylor, J.: Introducing social innovation, J. Appl. Behav. Sci. **6:**69-77, 1977.

Telfer, R. G.: The dynamics of change, The Clearing House **41:**131-135, 1966.

Thompson, L. F., Miller, M. H., and Bigler, H. F.: Sociology: nurses and their patients in modern society, ed. 9, St. Louis, 1975, The C. V. Mosby Co.

Thomstad, B., Cunningham, N., and Kaplan, B.: Changing the rules of the doctor-nurse game, Nurs. Outlook **23:**442-427, 1975.

Tobin, H. M., and Wise, P. S.: The process of staff development: components for change, St. Louis, 1979, The C. V. Mosby Co.

Toffler, A.: Future shock, New York, 1970, Random House, Inc.

Watson, G.: Resistance to change, Am. Behav. Sci. **14:**745-746, 1971.

Watzlawick, P., Weakland, J., and Fisch, R.: Change: principles of problem formation and problem resolution, New York, 1974, W. W. Norton & Co., Inc.

Weed, L.: Medical records, medical education and patient care, Cleveland, 1969, Case Western Reserve University Press.

Welch, L. B., editor: the nurse as change agent, Nurs. Clin. North Am. **14:**305-383, 1979.

Western Interstate Commission for Higher Education: Models for culture diversity in nursing: a process for change, final report, Boulder, Co., July, 1978, WICHE.

Whisler, T. L.: Information technology and organizational change, Belmont, Calif. 1970, Wadsworth Publishing Co., Inc.

Zaltman, G., editor: Processes and phenomena of social change, New York, 1973, John Wiley & Sons, Inc.

Zaltman, G., and Duncan, R.: Strategies for planned change, New York, 1977, John Wiley & Sons, Inc.

Zaltman, G., and Schwartz, R., editors: Perspectives on social change, New York, 1973, John Wiley & Sons, Inc.

Zaltman, G., Duncan, R., and Holbek, J.: Innovations and organizations, New York, 1973, John Wiley & Sons, Inc.

Zaltman, G., Kotter, P., and Kaufman, I.: Creating social change, New York, 1972, Holt, Rinehart and Winston, Inc.

Zander, A.: Resistance to change: its analyses and prevention. In Bennis, W. G., et al., editors: The planning of change, New York, 1966, Holt, Rinehart and Winston, Inc.

Zimmerman, B. M.: Changes of the second order, Nurs. Outlook **27:**199-201, 1979.

Zollschan, G. K., and Hirsch, W.: Social change: explorations, diagnoses, and conjectures, New York, 1976, John Wiley & Sons, Inc.

INDEX